News Media and Power in Russia

The end of communist rule in the Soviet Union brought with it a brave new world of media and commerce. Formerly state-owned enterprises were transformed, often through private ownership, and new corporations sprang up overnight to take advantage of the new atmosphere of freedom.

Until now, most research on media and news production in Russia has focused on the scope of government control and comparisons with the communist era. However, extra-governmental controls and the challenges of operating in a newly capitalist environment have been just as important – if not more important – in the formation of the new media climate. *News Media and Power in Russia* fills this gap, examining the various agents who "make" the news, and discussing the fierce struggle among the various agents of power involved, including news producers themselves. Drawing on existing theories and scholarship, the book provides a wealth of detail on the actual daily practices of news production in Russia, arguing that power relations in newsmaking are not just external intrusions into the pure process of the reflection of reality, but that the interaction of variously motivated agents is an intrinsic part of the news production process. Original research is combined with compelling first-hand accounts of news production and dissemination to provide an incisive look at the issues and power structures Russian journalists face on a daily basis.

The book will be useful for scholars and students of media studies and Russian politics, and essential for those wishing to have a deeper understanding of the post-Soviet media world in Russia.

Olessia Koltsova is currently an associate professor in mass communication in the Department of Sociology of the Higher School of Economics, St Petersburg. During the last nine years she has been researching Russian news production and post-Soviet media transformation.

BASEES/Routledge series on Russian and East European studies
Series editor:
Richard Sakwa, Department of Politics and International Relations, University of Kent

Editorial Committee:

George Blazyca, Centre for Contemporary European Studies, University of Paisley

Terry Cox, Department of Government, University of Strathclyde

Rosalind Marsh, Department of European Studies and Modern Languages, University of Bath

David Moon, Department of History, University of Strathclyde

Hilary Pilkington, Centre for Russian and East European Studies, University of Birmingham

Stephen White, Department of Politics, University of Glasgow

This series is published on behalf of BASEES (the British Association for Slavonic and East European Studies). The series comprises original, high-quality, research-level work by both new and established scholars on all aspects of Russian, Soviet, post-Soviet and East European Studies in humanities and social science subjects.

News Media and Power
in Russia

Olessia Koltsova

Routledge
Taylor & Francis Group

LONDON AND NEW YORK

First published 2006
by Routledge
2 Park Square, Milton Park, Abingdon, Oxon OX14 4RN

Simultaneously published in the USA and Canada
by Routledge
270 Madison Ave, New York, NY 10016

Routledge is an imprint of the Taylor & Francis Group, an informa business

© 2006 Olessia Koltsova

Typeset in Times by Wearset Ltd, Boldon, Tyne and Wear
Printed and bound in Great Britain by MPG Books Ltd, Bodmin

British Library Cataloguing in Publication Data
A catalogue record for this book is available from the British Library

Library of Congress Cataloging in Publication Data
A catalog record for this book has been requested

ISBN10: 0-415-34515-4 (hbk)
ISBN10: 0-203-53697-5 (ebk)

ISBN13: 9-780-415-34515-6 (hbk)
ISBN13: 9-780-203-53697-1 (ebk)

Contents

Tables

Preface

The initial goal of this study was to shed some light on the way news is really made. By the word "really" I meant something that I as a former journalist had considered obvious and that sharply contradicted the beliefs of non-media people who were driven by early post-Soviet euphoria. "Really" meant that news is overwhelmingly a product of strategic interactions of individuals and groups with different interests – interests that make people want to shape the final product in a certain way. Thus, situations usually thought of as a "biased reflection of reality" had another meaning for me: the "bias" seemed not only an inevitable evil, it was just a constituent of news making. If nobody had any "egoistic" interest in news production, it would not appear at all. And an expectation – then widespread – that all actors, including politicians, advertisers, news sources and journalists themselves, would act in accordance with the public interest, looked quite naive.

Before I began gathering material to illustrate this vision, it had seemed not very difficult to embrace all possible kinds of influence, all impulses of power that a news item is subject to. The only thing that one needed to do was to go to the heart of the production network – the journalistic newsroom. I assumed that, by observing journalistic work and talking to my former colleagues, I would be able to pull out the full chain of power interactions preceding and leading to the emergence of news. However, reality disproved my belief.

It soon turned out that rank-and-file journalists usually communicate only with two groups of agents: media executives and sources of information. This meant that all other influences are mediated for journalists by one or both of these groups and reporters seldom know what stands behind the actions of their counterparts. Thus the initial sources of power could not be traced. Nor could it be discovered what motivations these hidden agents had, what actions they committed, and how they interacted with each other. Journalists themselves rarely found it important or interesting; to them, the most significant influence was the structure of their labor: professional routines, technical limitations and restrictions of format. Indeed, this is exactly the impression one receives on entering the newsroom. But this is only the tip of the iceberg.

To find out who else participates in the game and how it is done, I had to broaden the scope of my research tremendously. I turned to "the other side" – people outside media organizations – asking them about their strategies for dealing with the media. But as soon as I touched on questions of power, stretching out beyond the sphere of the legitimate, obtaining data became very difficult. It took a lot of time to find respondents and to get their trust. Therefore I had to use many secondary sources – in fact, almost any I came across. This posed the problem of reliability and the difficulty of analysing heterogeneous data, but it seemed the only way to reach my goal.

Looking for solutions in academic literature, I indeed found much had been written on related matters. In fact, some topics, such as journalistic professional routines, were thoroughly studied; but studies on questions of power in the media looked more spotty and disconnected. Studies of post-communist media were very much about structures and very little about real people's actions. Finally, I adopted an approach to my subject that may be called dynamic: my major unit of analysis is an action; given my topic – a typical action of power understood as the imposition of an actor's will on others (practice of power). This helped me to catalogue the stories I came across and classify them into groups; a typology of actors, their resources and practices emerged from this activity. It constitutes the body of this book.

My understanding of the role of social science led me to aim the book at a relatively wide audience. Though it contains parts interesting only for academics (e.g. Chapter 1), empirical chapters may attract social science and journalism students, media professionals, NGO activists, policymakers etc.

Chapter 1 contains an analysis of relevant academic literature, description of the theoretical approach, key notions, and a note on method and sources. All other chapters are empirical. Chapter 2, which together with Chapter 1 forms the auxiliary Part I of the book, introduces the reader to the historical context of the Russian media. Part II is the core of the book, providing evidence for the major categories of the theoretical model addressed in Chapter 1. Chapters 3–7 deal with power practices of external agents, from the "strongest" to the "weakest." They include: so-called state agents (Chapter 3), sources of legitimate and illegitimate violence (Chapter 4), media owners (Chapter 5), advertisers (Chapter 6), and sources of information (Chapter 7). Chapter 8 is devoted to internal influences and speaks about rank-and-file journalists. Finally, Chapter 9 is a piece about those who stand at the border between the internal world of media organizations and their external environments: media top managers. This chapter relates their practices with those addressed in the previous chapters, and explains why audience is considered a pseudo-agent in this study.

Part III contains four special studies. Complementing the seven empirical chapters addressing national media, Chapter 10 looks at the local level of media life and outlines a typology of regional media-political configurations. The cases described in Chapters 11 and 12 are to some extent similar: they tell the stories of the rise and fall of two TV channels. The first, however, deals with "centralization" of TV, that is transferring the broadcasting resources of a national channel located outside Moscow to the capital. It also illustrates the struggle of various power agents "within" the state. The second is the well-known story of *NTV*. It illustrates the use of TV by various groups for their purposes, reconsolidation of the state and its struggle with its external competitors for power. Chapter 13 is devoted to the role of media in the Chechen war.

Acknowledgments

For writing this book I owe thanks to many people and organizations.

The first organization to support me was the Centre for Independent Sociological Research at St. Petersburg which gave a grant for the participant observation at the editorial office of a newspaper in 1997. Then studying at the PhD program of the European University at St. Petersburg allowed me to go on with my research for three years. The Moscow Scientific Public Fund, with support from the Open Society Institute, supported my observation at TV newsrooms. Finally, the Research Support Scheme of the Open Society Institute (grant 684/2000) funded my study of "external agents of power" and work on the text of this book.

In the course of these years I also had two opportunities to study media theory abroad, which was of central significance for my research. This became possible thanks to the Centre of International Mobility of Finland which funded my travel to the university of Tampere, and the Research Scholarship Exchange Program of USIA with ACTR/ACCELS which supported my trip to the Duke university, NC, USA.

My warmest thanks I owe to Victor Voronkov, the director of the Centre of Independent Social Research, who became my first teacher of social science and did it purely on voluntary basis. A key role in my professional socialization was also played by my academic supervisor Professor Vadim Volkov (Higher School of Economics, St. Petersburg). I am grateful as well to my second supervisor, Boris Firsov (European University at St. Petersburg), who guided me through the final stages of the work on my thesis which became a part of this book.

In the sphere of media studies I owe special thanks to Professors Kaarle Nordentreng (Tampere University, Finland), Ellen Mickiewicz (Duke University, USA), Colin Sparks (Westminster University, UK), and above all John Downing (University of Texas at Austin, USA). They all gave me academic advice on my research, and John Downing repeatedly wrote detailed comments on my first article in English, which is also used in this text. I am also thankful to Professor Elena Vartanova (Moscow State University), Dr. Dmitry Gavra (St. Petersburg State University), Dr. Andrey Alexeev (RAS Sociological Institute, St. Petersburg), Dr. Vladimir

Gelman (European University at St. Petersburg) and Georgy Derdirov (St. Petersburg University of Economics and Finance).

I would also like to express my special thanks to my anonymous respondents whom I cannot name here, and to my family who put up with my devotion to this work for all these years.

I am grateful to Sage Publications Ltd. for permission to reproduce extracts from my article "News production in contemporary Russia: practices of power," published in *European Journal of Communication*, Vol. 16(3): 315–35, copyright Sage Publications, 2001.

Part I

Theories, methods and historical context

1 Catching the wind

Theoretical approach to the study

To say "media production" or "practices of power" is to imply some regularities in these processes. But what regularities may be observed in a society that is experiencing an intensive social change? In a society where everything is fluid and unpredictable and escapes both academic analysis and everyday experience of participants? Is it possible to study such a society? As an insider who has tried to do it, I would answer yes, to some extent. And, what is more important, it is very worthwhile: it is not often that history gives us a chance to create an account of a rapidly changing social reality – a reality in which institutions emerge before our eyes, revealing their roots in society and unmasking the most covert patterns of social organization. Moreover, I believe that these patterns are not specific to Russia; my guess is that they are typical of some other or may be even all media systems, with the only difference that Russia is a more convenient place to reveal them. If this assumption is right, Russian experience may tell us something about the phenomenon of news production in general.

Post-socialist[1] media: conceptual problems

There is little novelty in regarding power as constitutive of any media production. Understanding power as action or practice is not new either. Thus, "practices of power in Russian news production" – the subject I intend to examine here – may seem just a new name for a well-studied phenomenon. However, the distance between the emergence of ideas and their application in particular empirical studies turns out to be a long one. Although the issue of media control both before and after the collapse of the Soviet Union has generated a large body of literature, until very recently it usually had a single focus. What mostly attracted the attention of scholars from the "West"[2] is the question of the development of press freedom (or, as one of my Western colleagues has put it more succinctly, "does Russian government still pressure the media?").

This question is important, but the way my colleague asked it indicates several common, albeit gradually vanishing, Western clichés about the post-socialist media (often borrowed by "Eastern" scholars who tend to ascribe to Western research a higher symbolic status). First, in many cases these media are (implicitly) examined through the prism of traditional normative discourse of press freedom, although other approaches have been successfully used in studies of both Western and "Third World" media. In fact, the latter have been investigated more thoroughly than those of the former Soviet block. Second, applied to post-socialist media, "freedom" usually means freedom from government control, though there exist other ways of conceptualizing freedom and power, as we shall see illustrated in some detail later in this chapter.

Third, such statements as the one about the Russian government "still pressurizing the media," betray the existence of a common though usually silent assumption that Western governments have ceased to do so. Colin Sparks (Sparks and Reading 1998) is one of those scholars who also points out the existence of similar assumptions. He reproaches his colleagues for permanent, explicit and implicit comparisons of fully manipulated "Communist" media with an idealized system of Western "free" media, that itself has hardly ever existed in reality.

However, in non-comparative perspective many Western scholars often criticize domestic media. For example, while straightforward pressure and open conflict are not widely known in the West, Herman and Chomsky's famous study (1988) has made the existence of external influence apparent. This has given the scholars grounds to conclude that explicit exercise of power by the US government must be substituted by mechanisms of domination. Thus a wide range of power relations in Western news production has been studied with a variety of approaches drawing a polyphonic picture of the multiform social influences experienced by media professionals.

Strangely enough, when it comes to post-socialist media, the scope of academic inquiry has been predominantly narrowed to normative theories of democracy, often merged with the theory of modernization. Though the latter may not be used explicitly, it enters the analysis of non-Western media in a more concealed way. Modernization theory implies that all societies move, or should move, along the same trajectory: from inferior (pre-modern, pre-capitalist, authoritarian) to superior (modern, capitalist, democratic). So, with or without reference to the notion of modernization, the role of post-socialist media is usually evaluated according to their ability to promote this unitary course of development – this applies, for example, to the most complete account of Russian TV production and control over it by Ellen Mickiewicz (1997). Sometimes media are even expected to *want* to become independent from normatively undesirable forms of control (political, economic) and to subject themselves to normatively approved forms (legal, control by public opinion). Other scenarios of development are considered deviation. It is this normative orientation that leads to the situation in which even general overviews of the develop-

ment of post-socialist media often become built up around the topic of liberation from government control (*The Media after Communism* 1994;
Broadcasting after Communism 1995).

The main problem with this approach is that it tends to substitute
descriptive or explanatory concepts with prescriptive categories which
weakens analysis of *any* society – either "Eastern" or "Western." In early
1990s it led to "developmentalist" and "transitional" hopes for rapid post-
socialist Westernization that never materialized. Some scholars have tried
to avoid this gap. Thus, Slavko Splichal, in his study of Eastern European
media (1994), makes his normative approach explicit and carefully
divorces its prescriptive and descriptive elements. This leads him to conclude, among other things, that desirable democratic change cannot be
expected if a society does not possess social actors willing and able to
bring about this change. Since media professionals themselves have not
demonstrated such qualities, the change may only come if some other
actors mobilize themselves for it.

A further step in understanding why the long-expected change did not
happen, and what was really going on in post-socialist countries in the
1990s, is to acknowledge that the authoritarianism-democracy axis is not
the only one along which societies can change. Thus, one of the most
important dimensions of change in post-Soviet Russia was movement from
the old institutional structure to its decline and later to new institutionalization. This included disintegration and further consolidation of the State
and broader processes of dispersal and monopolization of power.

Some media scholars have come close to consideration of these questions. Ivan Zassoursky's book on Russian media (1999), although still
more narrative than analytical, described a whole series of various battles
in which media have been objects, subjects, and instruments. As a Russian
media insider, Zassoursky is completely free of any illusions concerning
journalists' willingness to bring about democratic changes.

Two works of the same period have been profoundly critical of existing
approaches as well (Downing 1996; Sparks and Reading 1998). John
Downing convincingly demonstrates the irrelevance of the concepts of
public sphere and civil society for any description of post-socialist societies
and shows the limitations of political economy. Instead, he characterizes
the situation in the Russian media as a "competitive pluralism of power"
(Downing 1996: 145).

Colin Sparks – whose critical approach has been already mentioned –
similarly notes that the struggle between different power centers may
explain the development of post-socialist media much better than any
normative approach. Sparks is the first to list some of these powers for
Eastern Europe. He describes four types of agents: politicians, businessmen, media organizations' top managers and employees (Sparks and
Reading 1998: 137). Both books, though they contain well justified criticism of the previous studies and suggestions for further research, do not

put them into practice, at least on Russian material. Sparks studies Eastern Europe only; a chapter on post-Soviet media in Russia in Downing's book is based on secondary sources.

At the same time, their attention to agency is a new trend in studies of post-socialist media; until recently, besides being normative, such studies have mostly been concentrated on macro-institutional analysis. Both "Western" and "Eastern" scholars have investigated questions of media ownership, legislation, formal state control and technological innovation/ backwardness (e.g. Lange 1997; Kandybina and Simonov 1999). All these important issues have little to say about periods when institutions are weak or even nearly dissolved, which is exactly the case of Russia in the 1990s.

Power in media studies: gaps and bridges

A third obstacle to theorizing post-socialist media, along with dominance of the normativist and institutional approaches, is that the different relevant areas of inquiry have been largely disconnected (this is pointed out by many scholars, e.g. Davis *et al.* 1998: 77–9). Though, for example, Downing bridges the theoretical gap between general political science, concepts of transition and media studies, much empirical evidence from Russia still needs to be introduced into the analysis. At the same time, scholars engaged in Russian, Slavic and East-European studies, along with "native Eastern" scholars, demonstrate the deepest knowledge of diverse empirical material, but they have often been reluctant to apply mass communication theories to this material.

Mainstream media theories, on the other hand, have been developed with material from the stable Western, mostly Anglo-American world (studies sensitive to local contexts do exist but form a minority). Within the mainstream, relevance for my work is found in a number of relatively autonomous areas of inquiry that address various aspects of power, influence and control experienced by media.

Studies of news production have generally taken the form of ethnographic description (e.g. Tuchman 1978). In Russia, there was only one study of this kind; it was carried out at the editorial office of the most official Soviet newspaper *Pravda* in 1987, at the peak of *perestroika*, and was made by a Western scholar (Roxburgh 1987). Ethnographic studies have mostly addressed the dependence of media making on routines inherent to the profession of journalism, while extra-media power relations have been studied by a different set of scholars. Here, to repeat, power (control) has usually been associated with (authoritarian) governments or, for Western media, more readily with big business (e.g. Tunstall and Palmer 1991). Still other scholars have studied power relations between journalists and their sources (Ericson *et al.* 1989), while others have addressed the power of ideology (Glasgow University Media Group 1976). Here a unit of analysis was usually an individual. Various approaches from sociology of knowledge, as well as economic and conflict theories were used, depending on what facet of the phenomenon was stressed – conflict or exchange. Political communication scholars were at the same time studying the media strategies of politicians and the role of journalists in the relations with and between the former (e.g. Paletz 1987; Mancini 1993).

Not much dialogue seems to have occurred among any of the mentioned areas, while to my mind they cry out for integration – at least if one intends to get a full picture of media production and its exposure to a whole range of social influences. The latter might include local political context (e.g. post-socialist transformation) among others.

Some integrative efforts, however, have been made. One of the early attempts was Curry and Dassin's *Press Control around the World* (1982) that gathered articles with different approaches to power and influence in the sphere of media. In general, the political-economic trend in the book has turned out to be dominant, but such texts as the constructivist and ethnographical piece by Gaye Tuchman have also found a place there. The concluding article by Jane Curry briefly lists various kinds of influence on media – from the most structural, such as literacy rates, to those produced consciously by agents. Besides traditional ownership and legislation, the list includes privileges/discrimination in funding, advertisements, licensing, access to information; confiscation of printed issues, personnel control (in particular, dismissals and co-optation), fines, arrests and, finally, direct threats to health and life. Curry assumes – and I tend to share this vision – that these practices can be encountered in different countries and in different combinations, but their very range is limited.

The idea of collecting and systematizing various influences on media was developed by a number of other scholars as well. Thus, Dimmick and Coit (1982) discern seven levels of influence: supra-national, society, media industry, supra-organizational, community, intra-organizational, and individual. Shoemaker and Reese (1996) offer a similar, though more elaborated "hierarchical model" scaling power influences from "micro" to "macro" social patterns. Their model is visualized as a set of concentric circles, with individual influences in the center, followed by media routines, media organization influences, extra-media influences, and, the outer circle, ideology, embracing all the other circles. Again, this scheme is meant to apply only to American media, but the major problem with it is that the scholars integrated very different empirical data from various studies and thus approached their subject in a very broad and somewhat abstract way. Using this model for concrete empirical research would be a little problematic. It puts together very different definitions of influence (personal/structural, intended/unintended) and thus provides no single unit of observation, although it shows some alternatives among which one may choose.

Since for reasons elaborated further below I chose to look at influence in terms of agents and their conscious actions, of special relevance are studies developing classifications of such agents. George Gerbner (1969), for instance, discerned a number of "power roles": clients, competitors, authorities, experts, other institutions, and audience. Although he regarded these roles as patterns of institutional pressure, some of them, such as clients or experts, can be easily reconceptualized as willful actors committing deliberate actions. Joseph Turow (1992), picking up the term "power roles," develops a narrower classification conceptualized predominantly in economic terms. His unit of analysis is a media organization that interacts with its environment on the basis of available resources and takes the role of either a service producer or a client. Its counterparts are other types of organizations, or "power roles" whose classification is borrowed uncritically from "in vivo categories"[3] used within the media industry itself.

Analyzing media production as an industry is Turow's explicit goal; consequently, he applies a standard classification of social actors that can be met in many other industries as well. This makes mass media comparable with other spheres of economic activity, but deprives them of their specificity. Looking from an "industrial" angle, Turow also gives priority to those actors who are better seen from this position: various satellite businesses surrounding media organizations deserve detailed classification, while those who stand "outside" the industry are termed, for example, just "authorities" though the latter may be also divided into many subgroups. This asymmetry is complemented with broadly uncritical vision of actors' typical activities. In some cases those activities that are usually declared by the actors themselves are listed as their actual functions, e.g. it is said that a typical practice of the authorities is to regulate and arbitrate between others. In other cases actors are ascribed those typical activities which have been widely accepted as real by (republican) public opinion: thus, trade unions are first of all seen as a source of boycotts and other disruptions. Despite my critical attitude to Turow's typology of power roles, my own classification of power agents is built up not without its influence (see the following three sections).

A dynamic approach to power in media

Power

As I tried to show above, the question of power, and its companion terms of influence and control, have received significant attention both in the studies of post-socialist media and in general mass communication theory. Yet not much reflection on the concept seems to have taken place; at least I failed to find any that could help me interpret media phenomena that I observed.

Outside media studies the concept of power has always aroused heated discussions, mainly because the term itself is extremely vague and allows a legion of interpretations. It may be understood as property, resource, potential, relationship or action; as personal or structural effect; as intended or unintended impact etc. Thus power is difficult to divorce not only from control or influence, but also from force, coercion, manipulation, authority, domination, hegemony, limitation, restraint – the list may be continued.

When studied empirically, power – like some other broad concepts – acquires another unwanted feature. Taken without further specification, it embraces all heterogeneous terms mentioned above and tends to promote messy accounts and conclusions. When using a precisely defined notion, one immediately finds out that, what can be differentiated analytically, empirically merges into an indivisible amalgam. Hence, following the precise definition of power, one risks getting the picture much reduced; otherwise, one makes more and more additions and, finally, runs into an infinite broadening of the initial concept. Therefore, I think, what can be defined is a preferred notion that will be focused on, but the text to be meaningful must include related phenomena.

To develop a wholly new theory of power in media is, probably, too ambitious a goal for this book, so I shall limit myself to elaborating a concept applicable to my data and to positioning it among other concepts. For the latter purpose, it will be enough to rely on a compendious classification of approaches to power offered by Mark Philp (1996: 657–61).

He distinguishes four groups of such approaches. The first deals with ability to bring or actual bringing of both intended and unintended change into the environment of the object of power, irrespective of its (non-) compliance with the object's interests. This broad vision of power, in fact, equates it to any causality and is represented by the Foucauldian tradition. The second view considers only those changes which in the absence of power would not be undertaken by its object, although the change itself may still be both intended or unintended, personal or structural. This group of theories includes most Marxian approaches, with their notions of domination and hegemony. The third approach describes power as a conscious action of an agent who brings change out of his/her motivations, but not necessarily against the resistance of the object of power. This view is the closest to various game theories. Finally, the last view narrows power to an agent's conscious actions committed against the will of the object of power.

Although initially my search for an appropriate concept of power was inspired by the works of Michel Foucault, the vision finally adopted in this study is clearly closer to the third group of approaches. I focus my research on human actions that intend to change the final object – a media product – in accordance with agent's interests as they are understood by the agent him/herself. Philp criticizes this approach for its inability to give a non-reductionist account of structures and institutions (Philp 1996: 659). Partly

I agree, but for a number of reasons addressed in some detail later in this chapter I concentrate my analysis on agents and their practices. The latter term, by which I denote manifestations of power, is borrowed from Michel Foucault (power as "something that is rather exercised than possessed" – Foucault 1977: 26). However, I use the word in a simpler and more concrete way – to mean typical actions of successful imposition of an agent's will. This definition has much in common with that of Max Weber (1968: 53) but, while he defines power as ability to conduct one's will, I look at the action itself. Ability, as something not observable, is not addressed and is reduced to its manifestations in various power resources. Next, restricting power to successful impositions of will, I, in fact, often consider unsuccessful actions as well, since they constitute an important part of the game. Next, I pay much attention to *re*-actions, that is, to how power is assimilated, accepted or resisted; this focus is borrowed from Foucault's follower and critic Michel de Certeau (1984). It presupposes blurring the boundary between subjects and objects of power and regarding all of them as agents with their resources. Although these resources may be distributed very unevenly, all participants of the situation are thus understood as capable of action.

Another idea I owe to Foucault is the postulation of the productive character of power: by imposing their will, subjects of power may not only restrict, but open new possibilities to its objects. The simplest example in the sphere of media production is exchange of subsidies for favorable coverage (advertisement, propaganda). Although the subsidizer sets limits to some clusters of media content, s/he, on the other hand, offers a media organization the possibility to endure and, therefore, to produce various content not related to the subsidizer's interests. Many subtler examples may be given. A source of journalistic information (let us take the case of an "honest" source) restricts the data given away to those which s/he finds newsworthy; at the same time s/he helps the journalist by arranging social reality which otherwise might be meaningless or could require unreasonable time for interpretation.

Narrowed to its restrictive component, power nearly equates to control – the term that, in fact, has been most frequently used in studies of power in media, mostly with negative connotations. At the same time, what is meant by this term often stretches beyond restriction and suppression. For instance, elements of media control listed by Curry (Curry and Dassin 1982: 265) embrace subsidies and cooptation; Sparks' "agents of control" (Sparks and Reading 1998: 137) include media professionals – the last to be suspected of solely restrictive actions towards their products. Control in such cases is a slightly misleading word. Thus, I have chosen the term *power* not only to distance it from the negative connotations of *control*, but also as an explicitly broader concept. Control, influence and other adjacent notions are used as synonyms.

The duality of restrictive and productive facets of power determines two major forms of imposition of an agent's will. I have conventionally called them negative and positive practices of power, loosely correlating them with notions of negative and positive sanctions, as used in theories of social control. By negative practices of power I mean actions in which the media production process is altered by direct agent's actions, while resistance of others is physically suppressed (e.g. withdrawal of journalists from places of events, or of sources' voices from the air), or change is made via actions of others, threatened with negative sanctions. By positive practices I mean direct alteration of media production process where no resistance of others occurs (such as making media product by a source), or change of media products through actions of others when their obedience is reached through implementation of positive sanctions. Thus, while sanction-based influences in social control theories presuppose some predictability and existence of rules, negative and positive actions are broader notions and include non-rule-governed decisions. This rough distinction of the negative and the positive is developed in a more detailed classification of power practices two sections below.

Actors and institutions

Elaborating the approach outlined above in reference to (post-Soviet) media, I would like to begin with some further explanations about actors and institutions. Actors, or agents in this study, are reduced to individuals and groups or teams, while institutions are denied the quality of agency. If institutions were regarded as agents of power and, at the same time, power was understood as a purposive action that imposes one's will on others, then, inevitably, institutions must have been ascribed both purposes and ability to act. This seems misleading. For example, when media as an institution are ascribed a goal to mirror reality, there emerges a concept of bias – as if media as a social actor has deviated from its initial purpose, and as if an unbiased reflection can really exist (which, to my mind, is totally disproved by the evidence I have encountered). If it were so, news would almost entirely consist of routine actions, such as someone brushing her teeth, driving to work and having lunch. I can hardly imagine a person who would consider such events news, unless under some very exceptional circumstances. On the contrary, news is usually viewed both by producers and consumers as a change against the general background of stability and routine, a meaningful deviation from it. Criteria of meaningfulness may vary, and deviations may be marked both as positive and negative, but a newscast is not a model of reality, but a collection of cases of such deviations. Moreover, news is more valued both by producers and consumers, the more it deviates from the background. Even if we agreed that, for public good, society needs some other understanding of news, I doubt that, in actual news production, the "deviational" vision of news would cease to exist. Thus, to my mind, less focus on institutions and more attention to actual agents, their opinions and actions, may lead to better understanding of media production in general.

At the same time, my study has a special reason to reject institutions or organizations as main units of analysis. In a society undergoing trans-formation especially, but to some extent elsewhere as well, the interests of individuals do not completely coincide with those of organizations – by "interests of organizations" I understand just conditions that allow the latter to be successful. Thus, in a long struggle for the *Peterburg – 5 Kanal* (see Chapter 11) its personnel cannot be identified with the company: since the "interest" of the channel was in its economic effectiveness, and the personnel were acting against it. The interest of each employee was to keep her job, while preserving the huge staff was justified by ambitions to broadcast for the national audience (this had a direct impact on content as well). Moreover, personnel could not be named as an actor either, since it split into trade unions that were fighting each other.

Generally, no single institution or profession may be regarded as the only producer of media content as a whole or even of a separate news item. On the one hand, the institution of mass media is not internally monolithic, and while each news item is a collective product, some groups within the institution may be sometimes or always excluded from produc-tion of a particular piece or genre. On the other hand, the range of people taking part in media production transcends the institution of mass media: it includes owners and sponsors of media organizations, representatives of the State, sources of information etc. A TV story or a newspaper article is a product of their complex interaction.

Their role in media production differs: direct and indirect, "mild" and "hard," stretching from general recommendations to editing to merely "making stories." For instance, in Russia making news stories – or pieces masked as news stories – "outside" media organizations by such groups as PR agencies is not exceptional. Such stories are then inserted into news-casts and newspaper layouts along with "genuine" news. Thus there is no clear boundary between what can be called internal and external influ-ences (by the latter I mean any influence whose agent is located outside a media organization and outside the community of media professionals). Such a boundary is maintained precisely because the journalistic commun-ity is regarded as the only *legitimate* agent of media production, while all other influences are normatively undesirable and, therefore, external. Consequently, maintaining this distance plays to the positive image of both sides and that is why it is carefully preserved, but I would refrain from taking this situation uncritically.

Of course, the boundary between media organizations/communities and their environment exists to the extent to which it is constructed by the participants of the process, and in this sense it is a social fact. Furthermore, though internal and external agents are both necessary for media produc-tion – and that is what unites them – at the same time there is an important

difference between them. Those inside the community of media professionals have a specific resource: a privileged access to production in its
primary sense, that is to merely shooting, writing and editing. Though each
message results from interactions of multiple actors, it is media insiders
who fuse them together in their actions, while all the rest have to act
through media people. That is, media people mediate all other's actions:
outsiders seldom "interact" with the final product directly. As all the rest,
media professionals aim at maximizing their influence, but they are the
key link in this chain (or network).

Another facet of this situation is that resources of power are not
monopolized by any of the participants: either by journalists themselves,
or official media owners, or their hidden backers, or advertisers, or State,
or audience. This means that influences in this field are not uni-directional.
Michel Foucault formulated this idea more broadly: "there is not any
binary and global opposition between the dominant and the
dominated.... Neither a ruling caste, nor groups controlling state appara-
tuses, nor people making the most important economic decisions, – none
of them controls the whole network of power that functions in the
society..." (Foucault 1996: 194–5). Thus journalists must not be seen
either as omnipotent manipulators or as totally manipulated servants.

Moreover, I would refrain from concluding that media production is
shared by a number of institutions – at least, such a division is not the
whole story. To a great extent newsmaking is determined by actions of
individuals who choose to unite into teams across institutional boundaries.
This is especially true for societies and periods where/when institutions
have been weakened, as in the case I deal with, but not solely to them.
Polsby made a similar observation in a very different context, describing
US society as "fragmented into congeries of small special-interest groups
with incompletely overlapping memberships, widely different power bases,
and a multitude of techniques for exercising influence on decisions salient
to them" (cited from Philp 1996: 658). Although not intended to describe
anything close to Russian news production in the 1990s, this vision is in
fact very similar to Downing's competitive pluralism of power. The only
difference is, probably, that in Russia fighting groups have not necessarily
been small. Of course, this view should not be taken to the extreme: a
society where institutions have completely ceased to exist is hard to
imagine. But such an approach helps to highlight those aspects of news
production (in Russia) that usually get less attention.

Practices, motivations, and resources

Actions that result in media products are not a chaotic number of accidents: some types of actions are persistently repeating – this is what I call
practices. The concept of practices has both its advantages and weak
points. Aimed at finding easily observable units of social reality, the

concept, on the one hand, is helpful in struggling with normativism: it describes how people really act, and not how it is required by prescriptive rules (such as laws or moral imperatives). On the other hand, mere observation of human actions tells us much of *how* people act and little of *why* and *what* they do it *for*. Answering the *how*-question is central for revealing techniques, methods and strategies, but not enough for their meaningful interpretation. First of all, it is insufficient for deciding whether the observed action falls into the object of study. Thus, in my case I have defined the main unit of analysis as a story identified at least by some of its participants or observers as an attempt to impose someone's will. This means that in order to classify an action as a practice of power – my object of study – one has to make a judgment on the motivations of its participants, that is, to answer the questions *why* and *what for*. I have not found any solution other than relying on what participants or observers declare about the presence or absence of power in a particular situation, and then finding similar stories.

Having discovered a few most typical reasons why various agents would want to determine form or content of a media product, I conventionally divided them into two groups:

1   Agents' values and beliefs: ideals of objectivity, of press freedom, of journalistic social responsibility, enlightenment, self-expression.
2   Agents' interests:

    a   obtaining direct income from media as a form of business;
    b   obtaining indirect benefits from dissemination of certain information (advertising-propaganda motivation). It may be publicity for a good or a service of a business unit, self-advertising of a popular singer or politician, promotion of a certain idea that can provoke an action favorable for an agent (e.g. stock tender, adoption of a law or mass protests).

In Russia, as my research has shown, the advertising-propaganda motivation is dominant. Generally, while income is possible through any kind of business, advertising-propaganda activity is possible only through media, unless the target audience is narrow and localized. This is the specific feature of media as a resource: they are an instrument for forming opinions leading to intended consequences, and the latter may be then converted into various forms of capital, including income again. In Russia the commercial potential of media is weak for a number of reasons, among which the relatively low purchasing power of audiences has, probably, been the main one. Simultaneously, advertising-propaganda resource has been for other various reasons in big demand; first of all it has been vital in privatization and the further redistribution of former state property. That is why the corresponding set of motivations has dominated the actions of many power agents.

Motivation leads to emergence of action, but its form depends on resources the agent possesses. Analytically, resources most important for media production easily fall into three categories (Koltsova 2001a: 320):

1   access to open violence;
2   economic resource (monetary capital and other property);
3   informational capital (information – raw material of which news is made; possibilities to manipulate it, and access to it).

Access to open violence produces open conflicts or direct obedience, economic capital provokes exchange relations, and information leads to what may be called "information management," a specific activity of creation of meanings and promotion of favorable interpretations (I would call it manipulation, had I not wanted to avoid the negative connotation of the latter term). However, the coherence of this analytical scheme is subverted by the necessity to consider two other kinds of resources, that cannot be ignored if we want to get a meaningful picture of media production.

4   The first – or, rather, the fourth – resource is access to creation (and enforcement) of prescriptive rules. On the one hand, rule-imposition is just one of the possibilities opened up by possession of other resources, since compliance to the rules is reached either by force, or through exchange relations, or by information management (e.g. domination). On the other hand, application of all other resources is usually regulated by some rules. Those who can create such rules and effectively enforce them have an advantage, and often they possess a whole range of different resources. The picture gets even more complicated when rules are created by one set of actors (e.g. parliamentarians) and enforced by another (e.g. police). The latter in this case may use the rules in very unforeseen ways, still the former do not completely lose the ability to carry out intended influences. In short, access to rule-making is such a complex and important matter that it makes great sense to analyze it as a separate type of resource.

5   Similar qualities are demonstrated by something that I have earlier called privileged access to media production. Again, analytically it may be reduced to the first three types, but since it is absolutely central for understanding the dynamic of media production, it would be better to single it out. It basically means that our society is structured so that not everybody can at any given moment start producing and disseminating symbolic goods, such as news stories. There are a lot of barriers to this possibility, and those who have overcome them can use their advantage strategically. Consequently, most other individuals find it more reasonable to negotiate with or pressurize those possessing the advantage than to try to get it themselves.

Types of agents and team formation

The suggested typology may exhaust basic types of resources, but the range of agents can hardly be reduced to those five types. In reality, agents may possess more than one resource (empirical overlapping of analytically distinct "power roles," and uneven distribution of them among real agents was noted by Gerbner back in 1969). In addition, different agents may form alliances with holders of other resources, which produces an endless range of practices. However, the number of the most usual combinations of resources is not infinite; these combinations correspond to nine types of agents that I could discern during my research. They are listed in Table 1.1 with the numbers of resources they possess, in accordance with the numeration of resources introduced above (1–5).

Of these types, state agents, as they are defined in this research, are the most contentious concept, since the phenomenon it tries to describe is very complex. Of all Russian social institutions, the State is the one that experienced the most dramatic decomposition during the 1990s. Functions usually monopolized by the State (e.g. legitimate violence) were exercised by various competing groups, while the State itself considerably reduced both the range and the quantity of its usual activities. Still, formal boundaries of the State and its parts (e.g. police, governors' administrations, courts etc.) never disappeared, but people employed in these areas adopted new practices (for more details see Chapters 2–4). Thus, while the State's existence was questionable, people who acted on its behalf played a very important role in the life of Russian society in general and in media production in particular. To describe this situation, I have defined state agents as individuals who occupy positions in state structures that give them one or more resources 1 through 4, including legitimate violence.

Table 1.1 Agents and their resources

Agents	*Resources*
Agents of external influence (those located outside media organizations and community of media professionals)	
State agents	1–4
Other (illegitimate) sources of violence	1
Owners	2, 4
Advertisers	2
Sources of journalistic information	3
"Representatives" of audience (polling organizations)	3
Audience – pseudo-agent, does not have its own strategies (see text)	–
Agents of internal influence (media insiders)	
Media top managers	4, 5
Rank-and-file journalists	5

Along with the term *state agents*, the concept of *the State* in its usual sociological meaning is also used throughout the text.

Other sources of violence are conventionally termed illegitimate (though this distinction has only a very limited application for Russia of the 1990s – see Chapter 4). Owners and advertisers form a group of economic agents. All listed agents act – though with varying frequency – as sources of information: individuals who mediate social reality for journalists. The latter are divided into two types: rank-and-file reporters who to some extent control the format of news and the choice of sources, and media top managers who mediate all other external influences for reporters.

The audience is called a pseudo-agent for a number of reasons. It is true that the appeal to the audience's interest is widely used by all players to legitimize their activity, but this does not mean that the audience is a real player. Neither viewers nor readers have direct influence on media producers; most often they do not communicate with journalists. Rather, it is their image that participates in the game. And an image is something that can be defined and redefined more easily than a relationship with a real actor. As one of the interviewed reporters put it, "Audience is a myth that a journalist invents for himself. But if there is no such myth, one just starts working for his colleagues" (Interview 5) (a similar conclusion can be found in Shoemaker and Reese 1996: 96). Even when measured through ratings, audience has a status in decision-makers' minds which is closer to that of values, rules and habits than to actual individuals. Besides, the audience does not have its own strategies of action. On the contrary, people from polling organizations (who may claim to represent audience) do have their strategies, but their goals are very different from the interests of audience members. Finally, in Russia exclusion of audience from the game is especially noticeable, and this will be the matter of special consideration in Chapter 9.

Media people are also active agents; they not only react to the actions of external agents, resisting or obeying, but also initiate different kinds of interactions, including power relations: impose their will on their external partners, on each other and on the final media product. Like others, they use a whole range of techniques, from direct and indirect exchange to threats. And here it is important to acknowledge that their interests are not more (though not less) bound by values than those of all the rest. In other words, if journalists think of freedom of press, they do so no more often than state agents think of fair laws or advertisers think of honest business.

As I hope to have shown in this brief overview, Gerbner's observation about unequal distribution of resources among different types of agents seems very applicable to Russia. The picture is even more complicated since different agents may unite into temporary or permanent alliances. The former are no doubt more typical of the fluid Russian society of the

1990s; nearly all agents were changing strategic partners so rapidly that shifts could be hardly traced even by those who were much closer to the "scene of battle" than I. However, relatively permanent groups were also visible – even when some members quit them, and others joined, the general structure remained. When a leading actors(s) managed to unite agents with different resources and effectively coordinate their interaction, such groups grew into huge and internally complex entities, composed of individuals from different social institutions. Since different institutions tend to produce different kinds of resources, if one seeks to combine resources, it makes sense to look for partners in a multitude of institutions. That is why I have termed such teams "cross-institutional groups" (CIGs).

In the 1990s such groups were usually centered around an individual, or a limited number of individuals who possessed the biggest resource of any nature – state, economic etc. But to be successful, any such group had to assure a certain set of resources. First, it had to provide an economic basis by purchasing or getting informal control over a business unit, preferably the one in which state agents had a special interest (e.g. oil, electricity). Then, it had also to include state agents themselves, preferably those having access to distribution of material public resources. Few such groups could exist without "security" departments or partners who enforced fulfillment of contracts and rules and played the role of intelligence service (for more details see Chapter 4). Finally, the most advanced CIGs established, obtained or otherwise included media organizations as providing them with advertising-propaganda resource.

Ignoring the illegal or semi-legal character of many of the listed activities, one can easily notice that growing CIGs acquired many qualities making them resemble regular corporations and the State itself. In fact, in the situation of "State deficit," these groups became proto-state structures competing for resources. Cutting across traditional institutions, they often became more consolidated than the former, while splits between CIGs were sometimes deeper than boundaries between ordinary institutions. Very little separated CIGs from informal institutionalization when the State began returning to the stage, thus marking the end of the studied period. CIGs' practices in relation to news production, that in the course of their development became built into multi-step strategies and entire campaigns, will be the matter of the following chapters.

Summary

In this chapter I have tried to show the difficulties of studying power relations in media in general, and in post-socialist media in particular. I have tried to outline an approach that to my mind may help to overcome these difficulties. The key notion of this approach is practice of power understood as typical action of imposition of the agent's will. It allows making sense of news production in a rapidly changing society, where the concept of social institution is of limited use. It also lets us catch different degrees of regularity and routinization, bringing into analysis interactions without rules, and ad hoc decisions. Regarding media products as resulting from interactions of multiple agents with different purposes also promotes a more realistic vision of newsmaking than suggested by more normatively oriented approaches.

Note on sources and methods

Data collected for this book may be divided into two groups:

1   Field notes and interviews made during observations inside media organizations. They provide description of practices of media insiders and their vision of the process of newsmaking.
2   Interviews with external power agents and experts, and secondary sources. They contain data about strategies of actors trying to influence news production from the outside. Case studies are also based mostly on secondary sources.

Observations include:

1   Participant observation at the editorial office of a daily newspaper in one of the big Russian cities "Starograd" (January–July 1997). It can be called a reconnaissance that provided general knowledge of media production in Russia. Here the observed newspaper will be nicknamed "*Vesti Starograda.*"
2   Observations in the St. Petersburg affiliates of two national TV channels, one private and one state owned (*PTV*, Autumn 1998, and *STV*, Autumn 1999 respectively). These observations allowed me to see differences and similarities between different kinds of media. Here a more rigorous research plan was followed, only certain patterns were observed and documented, and journalists were interviewed so as to include different groups – from rank-and-file reporters to anchors and editors.
3   Two series of visits to a private and a state-owned TV station in St. Petersburg (1998). Together these three sets of data produce a full and detailed ("thick") description of the practices of rank-and-file news producers in St. Petersburg and give some insights into strategies of media top managers.
4   A short observation at a newsroom of a national TV station (Moscow, January 2001). This observation helped to extrapolate earlier conclusions beyond St. Petersburg and "Starograd" and allowed the collection of some data specific to national media that could not be obtained at the local level.

During the same period of time there were taken eighty interviews of varying length – from fifteen minutes to 1.5 hours. Some of them turned out to be hollow or irrelevant; a number of interviews were not recorded at the respondents' request. The most informative interviews, as well as those representing a new type of respondent, were transcribed entirely and annotated in the margins; these commentaries were later transformed into analytical categories. An example of an annotated transcript of an interview fragment is presented at the end of the book. Other interviews were outlined and/or transcribed partially; all recorded interviews were preserved on tapes and referred to when necessary.

Of 80 interviewees approximately one half are media professionals: interns, freelance and full-time journalists; reporters, columnists and anchors; editors and administrators. Of special importance are three media top managers who in general are extremely difficult to reach. Agents of this type possess the fullest picture of the studied phenomenon, and their point of view was of great value. The other half of the interviewees are agents of external influence and experts. These interviews cover all types of agents discussed in this chapter, except the owners, the most closed group. Their absence in the panel is regrettable, but it does not seem to damage the general concept of the study. The relevant information was to a great extent available from people who surround owners, such as media managers, public relations professionals, experts in electoral campaigns, media analysts, and representatives of journalistic NGOs. The list of interviews cited can be found at the end of the book.

Among secondary sources one of the most important is the "Monitoring" archive of the Glasnost Defense Foundation (paper-published databases 1996, 1997; Web-published databases 1998, 1999, 2000).[4] It collects cases of conflicts related to mass media throughout Russia that are reported by volunteers and presented as one-paragraph stories. The number of cases varies annually from several hundred to a few thousand.

Other secondary sources were particularly important for the four special studies (Part III). Thus, the story of St. Petersburg television was based on a special collection of about forty newspaper publications and on numerous personal contacts with TV people. The Chechnya story relied much on the Internet materials (as a source that is the least controlled by anti-separatist agents of power). *NTV* story was just a "non-stop TV serial," carefully watched with notes, and checked against Internet publications and expert interviews.

The validity of the data was ensured by the repetitiveness of cases, and by location of the same story in several sources. It is also important that respondents represented groups with competing interests; this often allowed seeing different facets of the same phenomenon. I gave special attention to checking the results by showing parts of them to respondents and experts. Three respondents from St. Petersburg read one of my articles and gave their comments; three respondents and three experts from Moscow did the same.

The analysis of such heterogeneous material presented a special difficulty. What united all the collected data was that they constituted a body of narratives. This suggested the choice of the main unit for further analysis: a story representing a practice of power. Such stories were carefully searched for and marked in the texts, the emerging typology being repeatedly amended. The analysis was over when no new types could be traced.

2 Russian media system
Historical background

Soviet media system

The development of the Russian mass media system in the 1990s may be better understood by first looking at the heritage that passed to it from its Soviet predecessors. This chapter gives a general description of the Soviet media system and outlines the major stages of its later transformation. Since my book deals with power practices, I consider here only this aspect of media functioning. However, it should be kept in mind that Soviet and Russian media history has not only been about power, control, and domination: it has also been much about entertainment, popular culture and everyday activity. The fact that I do not address all this here should not obscure the existence of these facets of reality.

Returning to the power dimension, I will begin with a word that can metaphorically describe the essence of Soviet society: "corporation." Indeed, a well consolidated institution of Party-State was the only owner, employer, distributor and decision-maker, while the people played roles of subordinate employees. Media were just one of the departments of this corporation performing the prescribed functions. Of course, the system did not always work smoothly – in fact, it finally collapsed because of inner contradictions – but then no real corporation ever functions without problems.

As in other corporations, nearly all open relations in the Soviet Union were mediated by superiors, taking the form of subordination, coordination or bargaining, while relations aside from superiors could exist only in a hidden form. For example, the well-known phenomenon of *samizdat* (self-publishing) – a practice of book copying and dissemination initiated by individuals – was illegal and persecuted and, therefore, had limited circulation and influence. All other actions of protest were private and individual, and their success could be only temporary or local (Interviews 1, 7, 9, 11).

Another effect of such societal organization on the media was their independence of advertisers and audiences. Absence of market, with its private property and competition, made advertisement redundant for producers of goods and services. Its mode of existence resembled that of propaganda: campaigns specially planned by the state and put outside the realm of the market. Nor did fully subsidized media need commercials. Their connections with their declared audiences, though they existed, took peculiar, non-market forms (see below in this chapter). The real audiences were still the state-corporate top managers: it is on their opinion that the subsistence of media organizations and their personnel depended.

Conventionally, the late 1960s may be considered the time when the Soviet media system took the form in which it survived until the collapse of the USSR. It was then that the voice of the Soviet political elite really penetrated into every home transmitted by a well coordinated media army, with television being its "general." Even under Stalin (late 1920s–1953) media, although closely censored, had not been as pervasive. Partly that was due to the absence of television, and because Stalin obviously preferred the print press to radio (Hopkins 1970, Goryaeva 2000): it was the pre-war decade that brought the USSR a multilevel system of newspapers and magazines addressing all possible social groups. In a country with a relatively low literacy rate such a policy might seem strange, but Stalin's reorganization of radio sheds some light on this strangeness: in the late 1920s live broadcasting was substituted with reading pre-edited texts through a wire radio network (Goryaeva 2000). This was an early display of the Soviet elite's inclination to privilege control of media production over control of reception. In this situation any broadcasting was taken rather as a headache than as an advantage.

There is not enough evidence to claim that Stalin tried to slow down development of television. Anyway, Soviet TV owes its albeit late start to Stalin's successor, Nikita Khrushchev (1953–64), who ascribed it an important role in the country's cultural development and general modernization. Very soon television presented an even bigger difficulty than had radio: to control both sound and picture appeared harder than to control just the audio signal. At that time the only alternative to live broadcasting was rather expensive film. However, in the late 1960s a number of events took place that permitted the political elite to solve this problem.

In 1967 the *Orbita* satellite system was launched, giving the possibility of covering the whole territory of the USSR by Moscow-controlled broadcasting and thus creating the first national TV channel (the future *Channel 1*) that offered the same programming throughout the country. Although at first terrestrial transmitters were too few to carry the signal to all settlements, it was a step forward compared to the previous period of disconnected local TV studios. By the end of the 1960s television covered about a half (Hopkins 1970: 250), and by the mid 1970s – two-thirds of the population (Ovsepian 1999: 165).

The main program of *Channel 1* was the nightly newscast "Vremya" (Time) that first went on air in 1968. The significance of "Vremya" for Soviet national identity and culture is hard to overestimate: every evening at 9 o'clock the whole nation gathered at the screen for a family supper to figure out what the new statement of the authorities would bring to their lives. By the same time recording on magnetic tape had become common. This allowed the preliminary censorship of all materials (Gleizer 1989: 99–102). "Vremya" was an exception, but still its texts were thoroughly edited prior to air and no improvization was possible.

National TV, wire radio and the system of print press together comprised a consistent and smoothly working hierarchical structure. It was controlled, on the one hand, on the basis of the official Soviet doctrine about mass media and, on the other, through the institution of centralized censorship.

Soviet official doctrine of mass media

The Soviet political elite openly proclaimed that propaganda for the policy of "the Party and the government" and upbringing of "decent citizens of the Soviet society" was the most significant task of Soviet journalists. Even the Soviet term for mass media – "means of mass information and propaganda" – reflected this idea. The word "propaganda" became omitted in official discourse only in the early 1990s. The Soviet policy towards mass media originates from Lenin's thesis that newspapers must be a "collective propagandist, agitator and organizer" (Lenin 1979: 11). Thus one of the most effective steps of the political elite in its strategy concerning mass media was the legitimization and normalization of their instrumental function. Media were openly expected to support the Soviet regime. This, first, made demonstration of "independence" and "objectivity," obligatory for Western news producers, unnecessary. Second, it allowed freedom of speech to be redefined as freedom from capital and from offstage political influence, as open partisanship (Lenin 1975: 49–50). Therefore, the freedom of Western, hostile media could easily be declared false (Siebert *et al.* 1998: 156). In this situation journalists lost one of their major resources: the possibility of appeal to democratic values, as they were understood in the West.

This, however, does not mean that this doctrine was wholly internalized by journalists. Wilbur Schramm's claim that this was so in his classical work *Four Theories of the Press* was based on materials of the Stalin period (Siebert *et al.* 1988). Later studies (Hopkins 1970: 150–2), as well as my interviews 7, 9, 10, 11, show that journalists agreed with the part of the official thesis defining them as a *means* of agitation and propaganda, and often did not see it as evil. At the same time they rejected the claims of the officially declared *goals* to serve the public interest: journalists considered them a screen for the true interests of the ruling groups. It may be concluded that, at least in the late Soviet period, the mass media policy of the Soviet political elite was regarded as external and illegitimate interference.

Centralized system of control

Official ideas about media were supported with a well balanced and centralized system of enforcement. Although not written in any laws, this system had stable and relatively clear rules of the game, which referred to all aspects of media activities. For instance, media formats were controlled from the outside, and some genres had priority over others. Representatives of the Party were members of so called "artistic boards," which were to approve feature films and other non-news TV production. At the same time, this is not to imply that the system was ideally effective: some things depended on editors' and censors' personal qualities. Occasionally censors helped "unorthodox" writers (Hopkins 1970: 148) or editors stood up for more informal style of media products (Interview 7).

The heart of the control system was state censorship, embodied in *Glavlit*, the Chief Board of Literature and Publishing established in 1922. After Stalin's death it was renamed the Chief Board for Providing Security of State Secrets in the Press, but the Russian abbreviation *Glavlit* continued to be used in conversational speech. Officially *Glavlit* was responsible to the Soviet of Ministers, but in practice it was mostly subordinate to the Communist Party bodies and open to other influences. *Glavlit* had a staff of censors, officially called "editors" (since the term "censor" was not compatible with any freedom of speech, even a "true party freedom"). Editors supervised all institutions dealing with production and dissemination of symbolic goods: mass media, publishing houses, libraries, etc. Rank-and-file censors worked on the basis of closed instruction lists marked "Secret" or "Limited circulation only" (Interview 13, similar facts are confirmed in general in Hopkins 1970). There were two groups of instructions: those which referred to state secrets, and those related to ideology. The first group included instructions issued by various state ministries and government departments. This list could contain bans on showing pictures of bridges, or aerial photographs of cities, mentioning names of military industrial enterprises, or publishing statistics on drug addiction or on military conscription, etc. The list of bans in the ideological sphere (to mention people out of favor, unpleasant events, books, works of art) was composed by the Party bodies. The censors had no right or authority to show the instructions to journalists, but they held "preventive" meetings and gave oral advice. When *Glavlit* instructions became outdated, they were to be sent back to Moscow or carefully torn into small pieces (Interview 13). Censors were given the right to make decisions on all regular problems, but they often consulted the respective authorities. De facto their decisions were final, and could not be appealed against to higher organizations.

Party bodies also controlled media aside from *Glavlit*. Every local committee of the Communist Party contained a Propaganda department, which included sectors responsible for different media, as well as a Culture department which controlled radio and TV production as to due artistic level. Though the departments had official status, they gave only oral instructions (Interview 9) – which perhaps, together with tearing up papers, was a common practice in covering up tracks. Nevertheless, there existed quite clear unwritten rules prescribing the correspondence between the ranks of party bosses and the ranks of editors. If an editor did not follow instructions given by a higher rank party boss, s/he faced telling consequences (Interview 15): one of the most powerful means of enforcing the Party's decisions was personnel management. Party bodies appointed all media executives, and all of them were obliged to be Party members. Sometimes they were recruited from within media organizations and were elected to the corresponding Party committees after appointment. But in many cases they were chosen from among Party functionaries, who were quite ignorant of journalism, and for whom such appointments were just an interim step in their Party career. Techniques of recruitment also included ideological education at journalism departments of universities, severe job competition, and institution of "tutors" for young journalists at their workplaces. All this ensured selection of the most politically loyal people.

Other agents of influence on media production – ministries, enterprises, law-enforcement bodies – in other words, anybody who had any power resources, could also act in addition to *Glavlit*. But what is important is that they always acted via the party authorities: it was to them that all phone calls were addressed, and it was they who decided whether to take these calls into consideration (Interview 1).

Another essential feature of the controlling system was that top party functionaries managed to supply mass media with a relatively coordinated and agreed image of events, situations and themselves. Of course, intra-elite struggle did exist but, until *perestroika*, it did not shake the foundations of the system. "Anna Soroka," a newspaper journalist from Starograd, recollected:

> It also happened like this: the city [Party] committee gave an instruction to publish a critical article about the director of a particular factory; he had become too impudent, they said. So you were permitted to criticize this way. And then they fired him, but it looked as if it was not their own initiative, but the initiative of the journalists. That's how they used [us].
>
> (Field notes 1: 06.05.1997)

Thus it should be taken into account that a substantial part of criticism of which the Soviet journalists were so proud was initiated by the system itself. This phenomenon was indeed very similar to what later became known as "information wars": a type of struggle between power agents in which media are the main resource and weapon. Yet it was not the case that journalists never initiated any resistance to various outside pressures –

either for normative reasons or out of their own interests. Some of their tactics will be addressed below.

Paradoxes of the Soviet system

One of the paradoxes in the Soviet system was the combination of an extremely formal and thorough control over media production with little attention to control of media perception by the audience (Mickiewicz 1997: 28). This situation seems to have two main causes: belief of the political elite in the direct and hypnotic power of mass media and the economic independence of media from their audiences. Some feedback did exist but took a specific form. Most letters to editorial boards contained complaints and requests to help: in this way common people tried to solve their personal problems, such as getting a new flat. Such letters were sent to the respective authorities, and in some cases the further development of events was monitored by media. In these cases necessary measures were taken, and officials held responsible could be punished. Participation in solving the problems of common people is a subject of special pride for Soviet journalists (Interview 16 and informal talks).

Still, correspondence of this sort did not give any information on audience response to mass media products. Twice in Soviet history media professionals initiated studies of their audiences; both initiatives were in the end discontinued by the authorities. The first attempt was made during NEP (New Economic Policy) – a brief period in 1920s marked by the relative freedom given to private entrepreneurship. These studies had much in common with regular marketing surveys (Volkov 1998: 330–6). Discussions on techniques of control over people's minds were shut down together with NEP itself. They were reborn during the "Khrushchev thaw" in the 1960s, when the first sociological surveys on media consumption disproved the thesis about the omnipotence of electronic media.

This time the research did not cease completely after Khrushchev's dismissal, but it did meet constant obstacles. Thus, the classical work by Boris Grushin (Grushin and Onikov 1980), completed in 1974, was considered so dangerous that it was published only six years after completion, and then only partially (Wolfe 1997: 307). But other research works carried out in different Russian towns revealed similarly "dangerous" trends. One of the first complex audience surveys in the country was supervised by Boris Firsov, then director of Leningrad TV. It showed that the local audience preferred sports and entertainment programs, giving medium ratings to news, while political and educational programs were the most unpopular (Firsov 1969: 70, 159). Based on this research, Firsov's programming policy was too liberal, and he finally lost his director's position (Interviews 7, 9). The first practical steps to consider and use audience preferences were not undertaken by state leaders until 1985 (forced newspaper subscription is hardly worth mentioning).

It is not surprising, then, that a system which controls media production more than perception gives priority to preliminary censorship over restriction of access to information. Of course, such control also existed: classified enterprises, monopoly of Moscow media for international information, etc. Yet very often facts were widely known, but could not be published; this resulted in a sharp contradiction between media-constructed reality and people's everyday experience.

All this gave rise to skepticism towards official rules and towards mass media already before *perestroika*. It led to various practices of resistance or to "misuse" of rules, both by audience and by journalists. Being sure that official rhetoric on mass media was hypocritical and could not bring about any public good anyway, some journalists followed the rules exclusively for their career development. The institution of mass media provided a good channel of upward mobility for those who "worked in the right way." Others tried escapism, looking for less strictly controlled niches, e.g. small circulation newspapers, writing on "morality topics," etc.

More rare than adaptation strategies, practices of resistance were far from shaking the established system. Journalists could use "readers' letters" as an argument for their reformist suggestions; another resource might be support by well-known "men of art" whose opinion could not be ignored because of their popularity. Still others sought support using contradictions between different members of the political elite.

As for rank-and-file censors, with them the rules of the game were never debated, being fixed for both parties. As TV editor "Voronets" testified, the only chance for a journalist was to persuade the censor that the discussed media product did not contradict these rules, but nothing could be done after the censor's negative resolution:

> [I]f a censor said no, then it's final. Then – you are welcome to search, dig around, find necessary materials, go to a chief censor, try to convince him that his subordinate is wrong – you were allowed to do all that if you could actually discover anything. But you would either be worn out ... you had to have a sort of instinct to understand that you'd better not do this or that. The main thing was not to kick against the pricks, because to do that was useless.
>
> (Interview 9, July 1998)

It was in the pre-*perestroika* period when struggle with an external enemy (in the person of the power elite) became an integral part of professional identity for many journalists. This heroic image was to flourish in the coming years of transformation.

Transformation

Perestroika: decay of the old system

The Russian word *perestroika* means rebuilding and reorganization; usually the boundaries of this period are considered to coincide with the years of Mikhail Gorbachev's rule (1985–91). Gorbachev belonged to that faction of the political elite who believed that the Soviet system, being obviously less effective than its Western competitors, needed some amendments. An important part of the *perestroika* policy was the doctrine of *glasnost*. Glasnost, meaning openness and publicness, is derived from the word *glas* (voice), and thus also implies voicing something that had previously been silenced. When declared officially, glasnost immediately intensified journalistic practices of resistance against the "external enemy," and very quickly the situation went out of control.

At first secondary ideological bans were lifted. Because of the obvious discrepancy between media-constructed images and everyday life *glasnost* first appeared in mass media as verbalizing things that everybody knew but could not say publicly (Konstantinov 1998). Even in the early stages of *glasnost* not all such statements were approved by the authorities. Activities in defiance of bans extended, and different methods were used.

On TV the first and most essential of such methods was live broadcasting. In 1986 a youth program "12 etazh" (The 12th storey) allowed indignant statements of high-school students addressed to educational officials to be broadcast. Later Eduard Sagalaev, the host of the program, was very surprised that none of the officials responsible for TV phoned him after the broadcast. As he assumed afterwards, each official was sure that the program had been approved by another (Mickiewicz 1997: 68). Throughout the country, journalists regarded such cases as precedents, and started making them a common practice. To restore a particular ideological taboo after that became more and more difficult. The years 1987–8 saw the press flooded with revelatory publications about Stalin's regime. In 1989 media raised one of the last topics which had remained untouched: Lenin. The first unorthodox mentioning of the leader, though it might seem quite innocent to an outsider, produced a scandal: a Russian celebrity publicly proposed to bury Lenin's remains. This statement would have never appeared on air, but TV journalists tricked the censors using Russia's division into different time zones. Usually party officials previewed program versions broadcast to the Far East, after which densely populated European Russia, including Moscow and Leningrad, received censored programs. This time the censors themselves were shown an abridged version that did not contain any discussions about Lenin. Nobody dared take the program off the air when the full version was broadcast to Moscow.

The wall of bans was penetrated from the other side as well. Some *Glavlit* censors could see the increasing inability of their organization to cope with the informational flow, and began turning from enemies of journalists into their allies. They tried to reinterpret old rules in a way that would allow publication of as much data as possible (Interview 13). In the late 1980s *Glavlit* instructions were scarcely observed: the Law on Press was under preparation, and censorship was to be abolished by it. Moreover, privately published periodicals, free of any preliminary editing by officials, de facto already existed, and no punitive sanctions were imposed on them. By the time the Law on Press was adopted (Law of the Union of Soviet Socialist Republics "On press and other mass media" 1990) there were about 600 such periodicals; though most of them had quite small circulations, some were published in up to 10,000 copies (Suyetnov 1992). Thus in the USSR, as in many post-socialist countries, alterations in the practices of media control were, to a great extent, prior to legal changes.

One of the reasons why the power elite failed to keep *glasnost* under control was that the elite itself ceased to be a monolith, and could no longer provide its agreed and coordinated image to media (Mickiewicz 1997: 35–6). Heated intra-elite discussions about the ways to reform the USSR poured out into the public domain, especially after the first multi-candidate elections of 1989, which made the elite even more heterogeneous. The main split emerged between Gorbachev and the more reformist political leader Boris Yeltsin, who was removed from all key positions by 1988. His image of the oppressed victim brought him great popularity and influence, and in June 1990 Yeltsin was elected president of the Russian Federation, then a republic inside the USSR; the same day one of his closest supporters, Anatoly Sobchak, was elected mayor of Leningrad, Russia's "Northern capital." This meant that Leningrad television, which at that time covered much of European Russia with its own relay transmitter network, also passed into the camp of Yeltsin's allies. A year later, in May 1991, Yeltsin's team managed to get air time on national *Channel 2* and carry out oppositional broadcasting nationwide.

The split at the very top of the elite was paralleled by splits at all levels between very different kinds of actors. In the late 1980s and early 1990s editorial offices were swamped with a flow of telephone calls from various persons and institutions (Interviews 12, 15) who tried, in commanding order, to establish their direct power over a publication or a program. No special bodies mediated between them and the media any longer, and different groups, split by fighting against each other, gave mass media contradictory instructions. Just following all these instructions at once and thus producing contradictory positions already looked very revealing. Furthermore, such instructions could sometimes be completely ignored: the callers often failed to notice that they possessed no means of enforcing their orders.

Legislation: new rules of the game

In 1990, after lengthy debates in the Supreme Soviet, the first USSR Law on Press and other Mass Media came into force, the earliest draft dating back to 1986–7 (Fedotov 1997: 186). The Law prohibited censorship, and allowed organizations and individuals to set up media outlets aside from the state. Before that the Soviet Constitution had only allowed citizens to *use* mass media, not to establish them; as for special legislation on media, it had not existed at all. In late 1991 the parliament of the Russian Federation adopted the Russian Law on Mass Media (Law of the Russian Federation "On mass media" 1991). Based on its Soviet prototype, it specified rather vague definitions of the previous Law, and rendered some mechanisms of application. However, neither of the laws introduced the notion of media owner and, correspondingly, contained no rules regulating relations between the owner and the media personnel – an omission that turned into a time-bomb.

Still, these laws marked the beginning of a new epoch. Though *Glavlit* continued functioning for some time after 1991, from that moment political control over media was deprived of official status. While in the Soviet Union it had been legitimized by Leninist rhetoric, adoption of Western democratic values made it completely illegitimate. From then on it could exist mainly informally.

Some legalization of state control over media did take place later, when the first law was followed by a large body of various legal acts giving more and more room for the concealment of information and other prohibitive actions (for more details on Russian media legislation see Fedotov 1997; Kandybina and Simonov 1999; Lange 1997; Ellis 1999). In the same way, *Glavlit* was transformed into the Committee on Press in 1992. It became responsible for registration of all media and, crucially, for allocation of frequencies and state funds for media. Furthermore, all media organizations that were not privatized in the early 1990s, remained in the hands of the state.

As can be seen, the old system did have some continuity; however, the state lost its monopoly of control over media. The new legislation predetermined a plurality of agents of influence upon mass media, and made it impossible to create a Soviet-type state-corporation, except in cases when, as happened in some Russian regions, practices were completely isolated from the existing regulations. In all other cases the new laws have become boundaries loosely defining real practices. They have become an environment, which actors have to reckon with in their activities: conform to, infringe, evade, benefit by, mobilize during crises, etc. In other words, the laws have turned into a resource in the hands of various agents, including media professionals themselves. Thus a plurality of agents of power and the informal character of their practices have become the two main constituents of the new system of power interactions in the sphere of media.

Rise and fall of media autonomy

Ivan Zassoursky in his latest study on modern Russian mass media history distinguishes two periods in their development: 1990–5, and the period after 1995 (Zassoursky 2000). The main characteristic feature of the second period is the distribution of media organizations among major business groups and corporations. This event also serves as a division in other periodizations, which contain only minor differences. For example, Laura Belin (1997) considers the presidential elections of 1996 the key event. Yassen Zassoursky offers a more detailed division into periods: he distinguishes the 1996 elections as a separate stage, different from the previous and the future periods, and regards the years 1992–3 as the starting point of media distribution among business groups (Zassoursky 1999: 30–1).

My respondents were also inclined to consider 1993 a landmark; they described the previous period as marked by "maximum freedom of speech" and "euphoria," and the following period – by growing economic dependence. Similarly, respondents in Anna Sosnovskaya's study (2000: 54) referred to the period 1988–93 as *"perestroika,"* i.e. they shifted the boundaries of *perestroika* relative to the standard 1985–91, and did so in order to single out exactly the interval between the age of consolidated state control and the phase of media commercialization.

For my purposes – that is, for tracing the evolution of the major agents of power and their practices in the 1990s – it makes little sense to break this brief period into more than two stages. The first half of the 1990s saw the emergence of those agents as separate social types who were still learning to mobilize their resources. The second half of the same decade was the stage when relatively isolated actors united into competing CIGs as quasi-state, or proto-state structures. The new millennium brought the new consolidation of the State as an institution, which reduced the role of CIGs. This period is beyond the scope of my study, but it is registered as a point against which the previous stage may be clearly distinguished. Table 2.1 outlines the main changes of practices of all power agents throughout the 1990s.

By the very end of the 1980s state-owned media found themselves in a strange position: they were still financed from the state budget, but the old system of state control no longer worked. This unique absence (or rather illusion of absence) of both economic and political imperatives gave journalists the feeling of euphoria that all respondents mentioned. Two events in the early 1990s strengthened this feeling even more. The first one was, as mentioned above, the adoption of the Law on Press in 1990. It cleared the way for the swift growth of a non-state press and the privatization of state-owned media. Until 1992–3 the combination of relatively low production costs with high public interest in social and political problems ensured not only the recoupment of expenses, but also the rapid development of the press. Absolute record-holder was the weekly *Argumenty i Fakty* (Arguments and Facts): in 1991 its circulation reached thirty-three million copies (Ovsepian 1999: 199).

The second event was an attempted overthrow of President Mikhail Gorbachev in 1991, known as the "August putsch." Formed from the most conservative faction of Gorbachev's circle, the putschist group proclaimed itself a new government, justifying it with the inability of the president to fulfill his duties due to a health problem. It would be difficult to overestimate the role of media in this dramatic historical episode. The coup seemed to be poorly prepared: the plotters failed to ensure full control over the media and some other key institutions, such as part of the military and of the regional establishment. They did manage to isolate Gorbachev and to announce a State of Emergency through the media, as well as to order the television director to follow only their instructions. However, journalists of the news program "Vremya" – the symbol of Soviet officialism – disobeyed, broadcasting some accurate reporting. Among other things, they showed numerous protest actions of people in the streets and the trembling hands of the coup leader at his press-conference. This betrayed the plotters' inability to control the situation and encouraged resistance throughout the country. Many regional media carried opposition publications either at their own risk, or at the risk of regional leaders covering for them. The most important among them was the widely received Leningrad TV supported by the mayor Sobchak who, together with his senior political partner Yeltsin, strongly opposed the coup.

Thus, struggling against the putschists, Yeltsin unintentionally turned from Gorbachev's main opponent into his defender. Yeltsin's vice-president, military pilot Alexander Rutskoy, personally flew to rescue Gorbachev from his isolation at a presidential summer residence on the Black Sea coast. After that the plotters were arrested, and Gorbachev lost any political influence. A few months later Yeltsin, together with the Ukrainian and the Byelorussian leaders, declared that their respective republics would leave the USSR; leaders of other republics did the same. President Gorbachev, left without a country to preside over, had nothing to do but resign.

After the coup the last, as journalists believed, barrier was broken, and the long-awaited era of complete freedom of speech began; of freedom, that, in the words of one of the respondents, had "never existed in any country of the world" (Interview 3). However, this widely spread vision seems to exaggerate the freedom of that period. Even then mass media cannot boast of any large-scale investigations concerning contemporary elites, not just their history. Perhaps the feeling of freedom was so intense because the new situation contrasted so much with the previous epoch of closely censored Soviet media. Besides, the freely chosen position of most journalists at that time was to support reforms, and this coincided with the new government's policy; potential conflicts might therefore have been

Table 2.1 Evolution of major agents of power in post-Soviet Russia

Interaction of agents	1991–5/6	1995–6–mid-1999	Mid-1999…
	Atomization of agents, mastering and constructing new rules	*Formation of cross-institutional power groups (CIGs)*	*Decline of CIGs, rise of more traditional institutions*
Agents of external influence			
"State" agents	Loss of old power resources, confusion, disintegration of the State, internal competition	Atomized practices in use of various public resources, clientelist relations with extra-state partners	Consolidation of the State, mobilization and combination of resources
Agents of open violence	Illegal: little interest in media. Legal: ineffective management of violence	Inclusion into competing CIGs, legalization, enforcement of CIGs' decisions on media	Formal institutionalization of violence within the State, decline of extra-state violence
Owners	Category undeveloped, privatization and founding media by journalistic collectives with limited resources	Purchases of, sponsoring and founding media outlets by CIGs, "informational wars"	Tendency towards nationalization of media, grassroots of "internal" ownership
Advertisers and their representatives	Before 1992: undeveloped, media live on subscription and State funding. After 1992: scarce, spread of hidden advertising	Slow growth of advertising, mostly foreign; professionalization of Russian advertisers, rapid growth of political advertising	Sharp decrease in commercial advertising (after crisis of 1998) followed by slow growth

Sources of information	Mastering new rules of communication with media, atomized defensive tactics	Professionalization of sources, emergence of press-services, PR and advertising agencies	Emergence of hierarchy of sources according to their professionalism and other resources
"Representatives" of audience	Emergence of audience research	Institutionalization and concentration of audience research in Moscow	Spread of audience research to the provinces
Audiences	Before 1992: extreme interest in political media. After 1992: sharp drop of purchasing ability, exclusion	Almost excluded from media production; media as means of intra-elite communication and struggle	Slow indirect inclusion into commercial media production; grassroots media activism
Agents of internal influence Top-managers of media organizations	Strategies of creation of financial autonomy of the media	Search for any sources of funding: owners, sponsors, advertisement, both official and hidden	?
Rank-and-file journalists	Identity of bearers of press freedom and democratic reforms, practices of autonomization	(Re-)emergence of instrumental professional identity, contradictions between identity and practices	Disintegration of professional solidarity and high level of anxiety

Source: Koltsova 2001b: 85–6.

avoided. Conditions for pluralism in national TV were actually reduced after the coup: both *Channel 1*, formerly Gorbachev's, and Yeltsin's *Channel 2*, were now held by Yeltsin alone.

Market reforms, so vigorously supported by many journalists, required abandoning government's total control over pricing. However, "liberalization of prices" in 1992 and the following galloping inflation hardly made media the winners: most of them immediately became unprofitable. Circulations of newspapers and magazines decreased considerably compared to 1990. By 1996 the circulation of *Trud* (Labor) newspaper dropped from twenty million copies to 1.2 million; circulation of *Izvestia* (News) – from ten million to 600,000 copies (Lange 1997: 188). Circulation of the most popular *Argumenty i Facky*, which had been thirty-three million at its peak, shrank to 5.5 million in 1994 (Mickiewicz 1997: 220). State funding of media was repeatedly cut. In 1994 it made up about one-fourth of demands of national television; it caused *Channel 1* to split into a number of small independent studios who made the lion's share of its production (Mickiewicz 1997: 170). Each of them was separately looking for advertisers; however, revenues from commercials seldom covered production costs. By 1996 state funding of *Channel 1* almost ceased, and covered only about 30 percent of expenses of *Channel 2* (Bystritsky 1994: 9), although both channels have been always indirectly subsidized by not fully paying for transmission of their signals (Interview 35).

However, breaking all classical Western market laws, the number of mass media outlets did not drop and even continued growing. In 1992–3 private TV channels started to appear, proliferating every year. For instance, in St. Petersburg and its region only one private channel was founded in 1992, two channels in 1993, and five – in 1995.[1] At first glance, the growth of media outlets in such an unfavorable situation may seem a paradox, but there were several reasons for it. First, "privatization of the State"[2] and power led to the emergence of new players who were willing and able to use mass media as either a commercial or a propaganda resource. As mentioned in Chapter 1, the second category prevailed, partly because the 1990s were the time of primary privatization (in its direct meaning) of a vast sector of State property necessary to give a start to market competition. The problem encountered by the government was that in a country where everything had belonged to the State, there was no class who could buy large portions of property. Therefore, distribution had to be based on some other ground, but often was just arbitrary. In this situation the ability of mass media to influence decisions on privatization was sometimes crucial, or at least looked more promising than prospects of media business as such. At the same time, journalists were interested in keeping their jobs, and media top managers in staying at the head of their organizations. Consequently, instead of going bankrupt or even merging, media managers chose to provide propaganda weapons to various external actors. Thus the interests of all parties coincided, and sponsoring, concealed to varying degrees, became a common source of media income.

This is one of the major reasons why reliable media statistics, especially concerning their financial states of affairs, do not exist in Russia. Only in 2000 the Russian Union of Journalists, together with a number of other organizations, managed to bring together various experts who estimated some values for media budgets. The total advertising budget of Russian media for that year was assessed as amounting to between US$1.1 and 1.4 billion; profits, including official state subsidies and sales, constituted about US$7 billion, and costs – about US$10 billion (Yakovenko 2001). Thus, about US$7 billion, or 70 percent of funds, were received by media from unknown sources. Some of them were, of course, revenues from "hidden commercial advertisement" (see below). However, Igor Yakovenko, General Secretary of the Russian Union of Journalists, claimed that the major part of these hidden profits were earned from the so-called "political order" (Yakovenko 2001).

The word "order" is the closest English translation not only for the Russian *prikaz* (command), but also for *zakaz* – goods or services bought and sold in the preliminary agreement. In media production the word *zakaz* has come to mean an ordered media product, a euphemism for hidden advertisement – a journalistic piece that is paid for by the advertiser and covers something or somebody in a favorable way, while presented as "genuine" news or independent commentary. *Zakaz*, or hidden commercial advertisement, then, is a story latently promoting goods or a service, while a political order/*zakaz* is any media product paid for by and promoting political, often state, agents.

Whose media: cross-institutional groups

Having agreed to work as propaganda weapons for various clients, media managers first tried to treat them as customers, preserving control over their "sales policy." But very soon many sold themselves "wholesale", becoming subordinate to one single client. Thus by 1995–6 most media organizations were divided among major cross-institutional groups (CIGs) who either bought the shares of media outlets or controlled them informally. Some of these groups owned giant media holdings. This does not mean that no further redistribution happened later, but such redistribution was rather a form of development of an already established system of relations than the emergence of a new one. In reference to the second half of 1990s, Alexei Mukhin distinguished nine groups of national significance (Mukhin 2000: 78–230). Of those, the following had special relevance to media:

- A group centered around Moscow mayor Yuri Luzhkov, an influential politician who was going to run for the Russian presidency in 2000 and established a number of media organizations, including *TV-Center*.

- The alliance of entrepreneur and political adventurer Boris Bere-zovsky and the businessman Roman Abramovich, one of the owners of a big oil company *Sibneft*. Berezovsky's control over *Channel 1* will be closely examined in Chapter 5.
- *Media-MOST* media holding and its leader Vladimir Gussinsky, the only powerful actor who tried to treat media as a business as such.
- Rem Vyakhirev, director (not owner!) of the Russian "semi-state" gas monopolist *Gazprom* who played an essential role in ruining Gussin-sky's media empire in 2000–1.

The most influential were those who possessed control over national TV channels: Berezovsky with *Channel 1* (which from 1995 became a semi-privatized structure named *ORT*) and Gussinsky with the wholly private *NTV* – the heart of the *Media-MOST* holding established in 1993. *Channel 2*, renamed *RTR*, stayed within the State, but the political elite failed to use it effectively. Luzhkov's *TV-Center* and St. Petersburg television, although they tried to play in this big game, were much less influential.

Other classifications of power groups (Fossato and Kachkaeva 1998, 1999; Zassoursky 1999: 155–91) give a similar picture, with little variation in the exact number and membership of the distinguished groups. The few groups listed above demonstrate that it was not institutions that were the centers of power, but particular individuals, who possessed different resources and were able to make different alliances. It is these individuals who served as the core of the CIGs and determined the "behavior" of respective media. Differences in media content of that time reflected splits between the CIGs. This period was marked by the emergence of such terms as "informational wars" ("media wars," "*kompromat* wars") – wars of discrediting/compromising materials published in media outlets con-trolled by hostile groups in order to influence each other or third parties. The neologism *kompromat* became so common and popular, it even gave the title to a later well-known www.compromat.ru on-line digest and archive, which collected various compromising publications about all sorts of high-ranking officials, celebrities and other public persons. If there were media wars, there were "media killers" – this expression appeared to mean a popular journalist being the main "storm-trooper" of a fighting media organization.

Since CIGs regarded mass media mainly as a propaganda resource, they considered the media's ability to cover their costs no more than a means to make CIGs' propaganda weapon cheaper. This was one of the major factors that hindered development of media's financial autonomy. At the same time, it was CIGs' demand for propaganda services that created their supply and contributed to the proliferation of media organizations, as well as to survival of many who would have otherwise perished.

Division of media among power groups also had a geographical dimension. First, an important factor was the location of all the major CIGs in Moscow. In 1998 the share of Moscow-based media in the (legal) national advertising budget was about three-quarters (Grozny 1998: 16–18). It shows up the tremendous gap between the national and the regional levels of the media system, and it is not surprising that influence spread only in one direction: from the former to the latter. While uniting around CIGs, media also expanded beyond Moscow. Looking back at the St. Petersburg example, we can see that since 1995 the number of TV channels there was increasing only because of local affiliates of Moscow companies. Such affiliates, being independent of any regional agents of influence, often became powerful players in the local media game. At the same time, local media landscapes varied greatly and depended on regions' economic situations, on the number of major agents of power and on the strategies they used in relations with media. Regions dominated by one agent who preferred force to compromise produced monocentric "authoritarian" models, isolated from the national media space. Where several CIGs were struggling for resources, media content became diverse and scandalous. More details on regional media situations will be given in Chapter 10.

Two other events also played an essential role in the development of mass media in the second half of the 1990s: the first Chechen war and the presidential elections in 1996. It was the first war (started in autumn 1994) that showed what role information management could play in the new media system, and what devastating consequences the sources of information could face, if they failed to practice such management. One of the two major sources – the Russian government and the military commandership – refused to provide any "positive" information to media. Since it could control neither media production and dissemination nor the actions of competing sources – Chechen separatists – the latter ruled the roost. The Chechen side succeeded, if not in creating a positive image of the separatists, than at least in constructing a negative image of the military campaign. And *NTV*, when feeling an insufficient supply of objective information on the media market, quickly captured the vacant niche of a national "independent" TV company. Its immense popularity that followed made Vladimir Gussinksy one of the most powerful people in Russia, able to influence even Boris Yeltsin.

The presidential elections of 1996 to a great extent were the result of the Chechen war, and its mistakes were taken into consideration. Withdrawal of troops from Chechnya was said to be a major electoral strategy of Yeltsin's team. But the most remarkable feature of the elections was the consolidation of the major CIGs (and their media) around Yeltsin. *NTV*, from Yeltsin's most severe opponent turned into his "mild" supporter; the withdrawal of troops made this transformation look more or less legitimate. Different supporters of Yeltsin had different reasons to stand by him: some people surrounding the president benefitted from his sickness and inability to withstand various influences; others regarded him as the only alternative to communist restoration (for a brief description of the Russian political spectrum of the 1990s see note 3); many journalists simply feared losing their jobs if the communist candidate won. Anyway, many of those who had before regarded support of Yeltsin a matter of their free choice, in 1996 started to believe they were used to serve the interests of elite groups much more than those of the public.

Simultaneously, many media people clearly saw that elections were a good occasion to improve their financial position. Thereafter it became common practice for media top managers to initiate cooperation with candidates. The latter, on their part, did the same: pre-election periods became a time when numerous new media were founded. Many did not outlive the immediate electoral cycle; others hardly made ends meet in inter-election periods. Many, especially minority and neighborhood media, survived only due to the continuous support of future candidates, usually incumbents.

At the same time, electoral strategies were becoming more and more sophisticated. After 1996 electoral campaigning quickly developed into a separate profession and produced a whole class of experts rendering their services to politicians and CIGs. Together with such political consulting, advertising and audience polling enterprises formed a triumvirate of activities adjacent to media. They experienced a rapid growth in Moscow and to less extent outside it. Here it is worth mentioning that, while in 1995–8 the national advertising market was dominated by two media-selling advertising agencies – *Premier SV* and *Video International* – after the financial crisis of 1998 the latter monopolized the market. What consequences this had for the media system, we shall see further in this chapter.

Consolidation of state agents

Summer 1999, remarkable for Vladimir Putin becoming Prime Minister and for the outbreak of the second Chechen war, was the threshold marking the "decline and downfall of the era of oligarchs" (Kachkaeva 2001) and the beginning of a new period – the period of State consolidation. It is since then that the State has started gradually regaining the traits of a stable social institution.

First of all, the Russian government at last developed an agreed information policy, i.e. a complex of relatively coordinated and non-contradictory actions concerning its public presentation. Virtually for the first time concealment of negative information was supplemented with professionally created positive information flow. Putin, assisted by his supporters, began to generate nearly all known types of incumbent news: "merely official" actions (official trips, visits and meetings), statements and commentaries on various occasions, and, finally, photo-opportunities (such as his flight to Chechnya on board a fighter).

At first, intensive production of positive information seemed to be the main tactic of Putin in his work with mass media. For instance, a respondent who visited Chechnya in autumn 1999 noted that the military officials were more cooperative with journalists than during the first Chechen war (Interview 21). But soon it became clear that Putin and his team were mobilizing all resources to which they had access: informational, economic, "state" and open violence. This fact became obvious after the 1999 elections to the *State Duma*, the lower chamber of the Russian parliament, and was related to strengthening of Putin's position.

The return of the State did not happen all of a sudden; the signs of this process may be traced in the previous years, but it is not until 1999 that they became widely acknowledged. Since 1998 the Glasnost Defense Foundation has been documenting a trend of (re-)nationalization of media outlets at the regional level. This was usually achieved either by forced replacement of a private founder with a state body, or by creating an environment in which a private media organization could not survive and had to "voluntarily" surrender to the state. Regional CIGs that were not centered around either the governor or the mayor of the region's principal city were in many cases removed from the media stage.

A tendency of state consolidation at the national level could be observed around the same time. In mid-1997 the transmitting network of *Peterburg – 5 Kanal*, the only one of all the national channels headquartered outside Moscow, was subordinated to *VGTRK* – All-Russia State TV and Radio Company. By that time Moscow-based *VGTRK* already included *Channel 2* (renamed *RTR*) and two state radio channels. Using the new network, *VGTRK* launched the channel *Kultura*, while St. Petersburg TV was left to broadcast only within its region. A year later *VGTRK* was transformed into a "State Media-Holding." It, first, took effective control of all its regional TV and radio affiliates that, although already belonging to it, in fact had often been managed by the local governors. Second, it incorporated a network of state terrestrial radio and TV transmitters which before had either acted on their own, or obeyed the governors (who often ordered them to block unfavorable *RTR* broadcasts).

The initiator and main executor of this centralization was Mikhail Lesin (Fossato and Kachkaeva 1999) whose biography is full of interesting coincidences. First, he had been one of the founders of the above-mentioned *Video International* advertising agency, which, to recall, became a monopoly after 1998, covering 75 per cent of the national TV advertising market by 2000. Among other things, it acquired exclusive rights to sell *VGTRK* advertising time. Second, Lesin had been one of the key creators of Yeltsin's election campaign in 1996, and later the head of his public relations department. Third, by the time of transformation of *VGTRK* into a holding, he was its vice-director. Finally, in summer 1999, shortly before Putin became prime-minister, Yeltsin appointed Lesin the Minister of press, TV, radio and mass media. The ministry itself was simultaneously created in place of the former Committee on Press. One of Lesin's first decisions was the decree about the Federal Tender Commission responsible for allocation of frequencies, its members being appointed by the Minister himself.

Thus in 1999 the mass media stage saw the entrance of a new actor with great power resources, a "private-state" monopolist who was "able to combine his own interests with those of the State" (Interview 29). None of the respondents took on the responsibility of explaining exactly how the new minister, who had officially left all his positions at *Video International*, combined these interests, although all thought it was obvious that he did. One can only speculate: some events (which will be considered in further chapters) indicate that *Video International* must have had some of its privileges paid for by support of Putin in his presidential campaign in 2000.

Lesin was also an active participant in the successful post-election campaign of consolidation of state control over national television. It consisted of three parts: further reinforcement of the financial position and organizational structure of *VGTRK*, weakening the leading role of Boris Berezovsky at *ORT*, and – the most divisive part – subordination of the opposition *NTV*. Why Vladimir Gussinsky's *NTV*, having supported Yeltsin in 1996, refused to support his successor in 2000, is beyond the scope of this study, but the detailed story of the anti-*NTV* campaign will be described in Chapter 12. The campaign resulted in decomposition of the *Media-MOST* holding and the forced replacement of the board of directors at *NTV*. After that the core of its journalistic team left the channel. Gussinsky himself, prosecuted by the Russian judiciary, had to escape abroad. The second key media baron, Boris Berezovsky, although he had done his best supporting Putin and attacking *NTV* before the elections, gained nothing from it afterwards. Unlike Gussinsky, he escaped abroad without a struggle and surrendered *ORT* to the state before criminal proceedings were instituted against him.

Summary

I would like to finish this chapter by highlighting once more the major changes that the Russian media system experienced, in terms of power relations, throughout the 1990s. First, a formerly quite stable and well-balanced system of relations was replaced by a poorly predictable situation, which led all the actors to employ short-term strategies. Second, the Soviet corporation-State as a centralized agent of power fractured into a number of relatively autonomous agents. Third, State censorship lost its official legitimate status. Many government officials kept the resources provided by their positions but, when trying to influence mass media, they now had to use these resources in ways different from those prescribed. Economic agents and sources of information emerged as quite new agents. Unaccustomed to new rules and roles, different agents continually attempted to redistribute resources and redefine rules for their own benefit using the transitional nature of the situation. This resulted in high level of conflict.

At the same time, the lack of clear rules was actively maintained by the stronger actors, including the very top of the political elite. This allowed problems to be solved according to the exigencies of a particular moment. Such decisions were far from comprising a consistent policy. On the contrary, the State and its power were "privatized" by competing cross-institutional groups. They were based on temporary alliances of individuals with different resources (political, economical, etc.) and included mass media as one of the resources, namely as a weapon of propaganda (in far fewer cases – as a source of income). Another dimension of State decomposition was geographical; this led to the emergence of very different regional media-political configurations.

The relations of all kinds of influential agents with media should not be regarded solely as the restriction of activities of already existent media that would otherwise have been freer. On the contrary, many media might have otherwise not existed at all. In creating demand for propaganda services, CIGs supported the multiplication of media which thus became accountable not to the declared audiences, but to CIGs as their primary clients. At the same time, once founded, media organizations seldom limited their activity to their clientele's propaganda and usually produced a whole range of journalistic products.

Vladimir Putin's accession to power marked the decline of the epoch of CIGs and the new consolidation of the state. It also brought more stable rules of the game, both their formal and informal institutionalization. Renationalization of major media was a part of a broader policy of the Federal elite to concentrate various power resources in its hands. Another aspect of this policy put an end to regional "feudalism" in many spheres, including the media. However, market imperatives were not erased from media production; they just became used for the benefit of those who could adapt to the new situation.

Part II

Agents of power

3 State agents

Even in the most stable and well-structured societies the State never forms an ideally consolidated group smoothly directing all its actions to the same goal. Any modern state is a complex institution that embraces multiple organizations, which turns out to be both its strength and its vulnerability. As mentioned above, sometimes the people constituting institutions act against the ability of the latter to survive. When such actions prevail, an institution either dissolves completely, or becomes "hollow" – that is, while preserving its formal structure, the institution ceases to fulfill its declared functions and serves the interests of some of its individual insiders and their external partners. This phenomenon is close to Hallin and Papathanossoupulos' notion of clientelism, defined by them as "a pattern of social organization in which access to social resources is controlled by patrons and delivered to clients in exchange for deference and various kinds of support" (Hallin and Papathanossoupulos 2002: 184). However, what I am talking about is a much broader and pervasive phenomenon. While clientelism is a more or less voluntary and equivalent exchange between the parties, private use of institutions may include exploitation of institutional resources independently of the will of others: it is especially true for representatives of enforcement bodies who learned to apply their access to open violence to the solution of their individual or team problems. Private use of institutional resources may also occur not only within public institutions, and not only at the top of the society, but at all of its levels and clusters, simultaneously subverting and supporting "host" institutions. The latter supply their internal opportunists both with resources and the legitimate façade necessary to maintain their covert practices. Therefore, such a process may be best termed the hidden privatization of Russian institutions.

Privatization and feudalization of the Russian state

Among other institutions the Russian State, supposed to be "the most public" of all, is the one that experienced the most visible privatization in the 1990s (for a detailed account see Volkov 2002). All its major structures, and the resources provided by them, were in place, but the way they were used played to the benefit of separate state officials and their strategic partners outside the state. These partners, from "criminal" groups to small-scale businesses to huge CIGs, on their part, used state officials and their resources as a means of competition with each other. Moreover, services that state agents could provide were also rendered by actors outside the State, often more successfully. Thus the State lost its monopoly on the creation and enforcement of rules, the provision of security for business transactions, other uses of legitimate violence, taxation and some other traditionally state functions. As a result, state agents found themselves contending not only with external competitors, but also with their "colleagues" inside the State itself.

While this decomposition of the State may be described as privatization, its geographical disintegration is often called "feudalization," though, in part, figuratively. Of all Russia's provinces, only Chechnya went as far as armed separatism and internal war. Other regions, although not without hesitation, limited themselves to bargaining with the "Center" for various degrees of autonomy within the Russian nation-state. The struggle was waged over both the economic bases of such autonomies (control over local natural resources and industries) and traditionally state functions, such as taxation, legislation and enforcement of rules. Depending on the region's resources and the strategies of its leaders, some regions were more successful than others. Thus, in certain provinces Federal laws were largely ignored by local legislatures; others demonstrated more compliance. Furthermore, regions ranged from those with quite consolidated local elites to very fractured ones.

It is not surprising, then, that the plurality of agents and their groups, produced by these multi-dimensional splits, became connected by very intricate relations. Competition and struggle often prevailed over cooperation. In the sphere of media, a good illustration for that is the story of *Peterburg – 5 Kanal* described at greater length in Chapter 11. It reveals a number of informal groups, as well as individuals, struggling for the channel's relay transmitter network: some of them acted at the national level, others were bound to their regions; some represented different "parts" of the State, others stood outside it, still others chose to cooperate across this border. In this particular case the struggle took place mainly in "cyberspace": since in the end everything depended on Yeltsin's decision, the victory was to be won by the one who gained better access to the president and accomplished more effective strategies of persuasion. In other cases the range of resources available to state agents was, of course, vaster.

Since it is resources that determine the shape of practices of interaction with media, on the exterior there is little difference between officials' actions aimed at maintenance of the State as an institution and those serving the interests of the officials themselves or of their extra-state partners. Subsidies or license withdrawals look the same in both cases, but their consequences for media development are different. This may be clearly seen from the comparison of Russian regions where, as noted above, the degree of State decomposition varied greatly. Where it hardly occurred, and most actions of state agents constituted parts of a consistent policy towards media, the latter most often became effectively subordinated to the local political elite. I have no data from examples of a consolidated elite voluntarily carrying out a policy aimed at a decrease of its influence on media production. However, when actions of state officials reflected the interests of various competing groups both within and outside the State, media content became more diverse. Sometimes this diversity spread not only to the coverage of political events, but to other aspects of media production.

Examining each particular practice, it is often hard to trace the aims and motivations of its user. When traced, they are even harder to prove. This is especially true for the cases when state agents service their extrastate clients: in doing so, they benefit in a number of ways, such as "voluntary donations," but it is very difficult to establish the connection between these benefits and the actions preceding them. The example of Mikhail Lesin has already been given in Chapter 2. Still, the general contours of these concealed strategies may be sketched.

Under some circumstances state agents may combine all kinds of resources as listed in Chapter 1. However, some resources are more specific to state agents than others: above all, they are access to material public resources, creation of official rules and open legitimate violence. The latter will be considered in Chapter 4, together with other practices of violence. Here I shall turn to the first two, widely practiced both in the 1990s and nowadays.

Practices based on access to public resources

Material resources, and exchange relations resulting from them, are definitely used by nearly all actors, but only state agents are in the position of being able to (legitimately) spend money which is not from their own pocket. Though the public pocket is not bottomless either, access to it gives them a significant advantage against others. Of all material resources available to state agents in Russia, the most important for media production are real estate, communications and public financial assets. Their use appears where violence and the direct creation of rules is impossible. The latter are preferred because they do not involve the loss of material resources associated with spending, but involve only bereavement.

Real estate and means of communication play an important role in all countries with a large state economic sector, including Russia. As Russian private enterprises, particularly media, are very young, many of them, especially small regional media, cannot buy offices, and have to rent them from the State. After the collapse of the state monopoly for business and public activities, manipulation of the terms and conditions of lease quickly became one of the most powerful methods of influence of state agents on any of their interactants, and media organizations were no exception. While "good" media get favorable rent conditions, such as payment discounts or even free accommodation in the premises of local administrations, "bad" media are treated in quite the opposite way. GDF monitoring is full of stories of how state actors use their ability to selectively worsen rent terms for "bad" media (e.g. increase rent payments, offer obviously unsuitable offices, refuse to extend rent contracts or just annul them, sometimes driving media organizations out by force etc.). Acting as private lessors, state agents hardly trouble themselves to justify their negative decisions. Termination of a leasing contract can be legitimized, for example, just by "the newly emergent necessity to use the premises for the needs of the city administration," as happened in Dzerzhinsk, a town on the Oka river in the Volga region. The cited explanation was received by the director of *Oka-TV* from the committee of municipal property, one of the channel's founders (GDF 18.03.1999).

While on the surface such stories look like the shameless repression of press freedom by the State, often the situation is more complicated, since one or both sides may act not, or not solely, on their behalf, but on behalf of their external partners. Although, as noted above, it is hard to prove, let us venture to consider one such GDF story. In late 1999 in Novokuznetsk, a city in Kemerovo region in South Siberia, the city administration demanded that *Apex*, a local TV company, leave its rented office, although the lease was still in force, and the payments were being made. Journalists connected this decision with their truthful coverage of the situation at the *Kuznetsk Metallurgical Complex* (*KMC*) (GDF 09.12.1999). What was this situation?

KMC, one of the leading industrial enterprises in the region, was at that time under the external control of the *Metallurgic Investment Company* (*MECOM*) headed by entrepreneur Mikhail Zhivilo. Information circulated widely in the public domain that he, a typical Russian nouveau riche, and his CIG made widespread use of illegitimate violence. Late 1999 was the peak of his conflict with the Kemerovo governor, Aman Tuleev, elected the year before. The new regional leader accused Zhivilo of robbing *KMC* of all its potential income and accumulating it in foreign banks. Zhivilo was alleged to have launched a large-scale media war against Tuleev; although this could never be proved, many media did cover the situation to *MECOM*'s benefit. Tuleev, for his part, developed a plan to merge *KMC* with *West-Siberian Metallurgic Complex*, which the governor had come to control earlier, and to appoint a new external manager. The official goal was the struggle with capital outflow, which is, of course, an action contributing to consolidation of the State. But an even deeper layer of the story reveals the interests of those who, supported by the governor, finally gained external control over *KMC*. Among them there was one of Zhivilo's old rivals who had suffered much from his uncompromising business methods (Nechitaylo 1999, Gotova 2000). The change of *KMC* top management took place in November 1999 – shortly before *Apex* was offered to leave its office.

Had *Apex* played in Zhivilo's team? Probably not. And the significance of this story is not that this coincidence is too suspicious to be just an accident, but that such coincidences are numerous enough to represent a typical pattern.

Similarly to real estate, the State also owns the majority of the means of communication, including most radio and TV signal transmitting networks, telecommunications and national postal system, as well as many printing houses. In some cases regional elites acted as a consolidated institution, effectively preventing certain newspapers from being printed in local printing houses or denying certain TV companies access to transmitters. The same can be said of funding the whole network of regional minority newspapers. Other cases are more multi-faceted and resemble the *Apex* example. For instance, in January 1998 president Boris Yeltsin signed a decree guaranteeing equal signal transmitting terms for all TV and radio companies, with the exception of the three TV channels qualified as "national" (*RTR*, *ORT* and *NTV*) who got significant discounts (Nivat 1998: 42–7). On the one hand, *NTV*, the only private channel in this list, had supported Yeltsin in his electoral campaign in 1996, and thus this action could be seen as an act of informal exchange between "the State" and the partly independent business. However, both the owner of *NTV* and the backer of *ORT*, along with half a dozen other leaders, at that time *constituted* the single business-political elite; the process of political decision making obviously exceeded the formal boundaries of the State. Thus it is hard to say whether "the State" influenced *NTV* by purchasing its support, or the very emergence and functioning of formally state agents were produced by the loosely coordinated oligarchy. While transactions in the Soviet economy are often compared with moving money from one pocket to another of the same person, the current situation in Russia may be compared to barter exchange within one family (and indeed, Yeltsin's closest circle was often informally referred to as The Family).

One reservation I would like to make here concerns the goals of state agents in their actions similar to those considered above. It is certainly not always the case that they are aimed at hidden and/or indirect change of media content in favor of those agents. Thus, taking TV companies off the air due to their debts may *sometimes* serve as a method of such change. But in other cases such actions have purely economic reasons: for instance, they may be used by telecommunications people to get paid for their services. The years 1995–6 were marked by a whole series of transmission breaks and warning strikes in transmitting stations which had received no payments for a long time and could not pay salaries. Cessation of transmissions is also caused by absent or incorrect documents (such as permissions for the use of transmitter, license, registration etc). Of course, the Russian bureaucratic system is so complex that it may be easily used against anyone in a perfectly legal way, but cases where license and related rules are ignored for no legitimate reason are hardly less numerous.

The last indirect method of influencing media content I would like to mention here is the management of state financial resources. As a rule those media are subsidized where government bodies are (co-)founders and therefore have extra sources of power. Selective funding of mass media gives a visible advantage to those who have privileges, decreasing the chances of the remaining media for successful competition. Selective funding is primarily used by legislatures of different levels who control local budgets; in this case it serves the State as an institution. However, individual decisions concerning subsidization are often made by officials with executive power, as well as deputies who have their own funds. This opens up wide possibilities for state agents to service their external partners (e.g. media organizations whose backers have brought a particular state agent to power).

A reverse action – selective recovering of debts – is well-known not only to media organizations. The hyper-inflation of the early 1990s meant that nearly all economic actors were debtors of each other. Furthermore, the economy in general was desperate for investment and, taking into account some peculiarities of the Russian legal system, such investments, once accepted, could be also treated as debts to be repaid immediately. The most significant example here is again connected with *NTV*. In summer 1999, *Vneshekonombank*, after consultation with the head of the president's administration, refused to extend credit to *NTV* although this had been agreed on before. At the same time, *Vneshekonombank* did not claim for a comparable amount lent to *ORT* (Varshavchik 25.05.2000). The difference between the two was, as previously mentioned, that *NTV* refused to support the new candidate to the Russian presidency.

State agents can give or deprive of subsidies in forms other than money. Barter deals are available to a wider range of state agents than direct monetary funding, which is why they are quite common at all levels, including small-scale transactions. GDF reports of a characteristic case in the popular resort town of Sochi. The city's State TV and Radio Company was guilty of informing its audience that the case concerning misallocation of federal resources by the Sochi administration had been sent to the Procuracy.[1] After that the mayor came to the TV studio and declared on air that he was going to take back the car, air conditioners and TV equipment that had been given to the TV company by the city administration when it was one of its founders (GDF 09.04.1998).

Barter deals produced by resources available to state agents are nearly endless. Among them are:

• allowing the use of elite facilities, such as a special Kremlin telephone line, or communication by military messenger;

- access to closed state bodies and to confidential information – not to be published, but for use to the benefit of the journalist;
- personal privileges, officially registered as, for example, social welfare: health and other consumer service and free tours etc;
- involving journalists in all kinds of commissions and committees, where a media professional is given power and private interests inside the client state organization (cooptation) (Dzyaloshinsky 1997: 11).

Such types of deals should not be seen as the initiative of the external agents only; everything connected with exchange relations is usually initiated by both sides. For example, the *Vesti Starograda* newspaper was very careful in its reporting about the traffic police administration of the city. The reason, given to me by one of the respondents, was that all the journalists wanted to pass the annual technical examination of their cars without problems, and in fact did so – due to their chief editor's acquaintance with the above-mentioned administration (Field notes 1). Another revealing example concerns the newspaper's relations with the Federal Security Bureau (FSB, the KGB's successor), particularly in reference to the so-called Nikitin case. Alexander Nikitin, a Russian officer accused of disclosure of state secrets to the Norwegian ecological organization *Bellona*, became internationally known as unjustly persecuted by the Russian judiciary and the *enforcers*.[2] In the story, documented in my field notes and cited below, the chief editor "Nikolaev" and the head of the department of politics and economics "Golubev" touch on this case in a seemingly unrelated context:

> May 19. Planning Meeting.
> "Nikolaev" said that someone named "Chagin," from FSB, helped "Polozov" [a journalist in the observed newspaper] to draw up a passport for going abroad. "Polozov" had left for Samara and on returning found his documents made incorrectly. The following day he had to leave on a business trip for Italy.
> "Nikolaev": I made a call to the passport department and they promised to do everything possible, but it takes a week for the documents to pass through the FSB. I gave "Chagin" a call and he helped us.
> "Golubev" (gloomily): Yes, and we helped him with Nikitin's case.
> "Nikolaev" (with indignation): You are talking nonsense! We have never helped him. We acted as a democratic newspaper: we gave both opinions.
>
> (Field notes 1: 19.05.1997)

Again, there is a coincidence: shortly before the described meeting GDF had published information about this newspaper. It reported that the chief editor had killed a story by another journalist about Nikitin's press-conference, cutting the piece out from a prepared proof sheet. He did it on the ground that Nikitin's case was still sub judice. The author of the article explained the accident with the strong influence of FSB upon the editorial office.[3]

Journalists' exchange relations are not limited to state agents, but it is these relations that are usually the most asymmetrical. Above all, they are hard to avoid. When asymmetrical exchange is offered by an advertiser or a source, it may be declined, and another advertiser or source may be chosen instead. But it is almost impossible to choose contacting a deputy of a local legislative assembly instead of a license commission officer. At best, the latter may be influenced through the former, but not ignored. Even when in principle avoidable, state agents still have monopolistic or at least privileged access to many resources that makes them stronger inter-actants. Of course, one can reject state funding, but only at the cost of a clear disadvantage relative to one's competitors. In some societies with a high degree of formal institutionalization, access to various public resources is carefully regulated, and thus their selective use is to a significant extent limited. However, Russia of the 1990s is exactly the opposite case.

Practices of creation of rules

To limit the actions of state agents by formal rules, it is necessary to obtain access to the creation of such rules (e.g. laws, decrees, resolutions, instructions), as well as to their interpretation and application. But those who have such access are state agents themselves; so, when old rules are dismantled, and new ones are still not in existence, it is very unlikely that these agents will develop them to their own disadvantage. Their ability to impose rules is, of course, not unlimited and they face disobedience, both within and outside the state, as well as alternative – unofficial – rule-making and informal institutionalization. As noted in a popular Russian saying, "The severity of Russian laws is compensated by their non-observance." Indeed, the complex of laws and regulations that has resulted from post-Soviet legislative activities may be called simultaneously superfluous and insufficient: below I shall try to explain both terms.

Superfluity means that all the relevant rules taken together turn out to be entirely or almost unobservable. Thus, it is widely acknowledged that throughout the 1990s the amount of taxes to be paid by any given business unit, if counted in accordance with all relevant laws, approached or even exceeded 100 percent of its profit (see Dolgopyatova 1998: 43–4). This is complicated by internal inconsistencies in Russian legislation. Earlier I pointed out the extensive contradictions between Federal and regional laws and regulations, but no less significant are contradictions within the legislation of the same level. Such legal stalemate automatically makes any relevant actor an offender: obeying one norm, s/he inevitably breaks another. The consequences of such a situation are not difficult to predict. On the one hand, since most extra-state actors cannot comply with all the norms, each case is resolved through individual bargaining with the respective state agent – this is the forced exchange that I mentioned a few paragraphs above. On the other hand, when applied as a concerted whole, such legislation may remove almost any actor from the game, and thus is used as a punishment or a method of competition.

I would, however, refrain from viewing this situation as a result of a coordinated state plot. Rather, it is a product of the chaotic creation of rules at different times by different actors and for different purposes. In the early 1990s a head of a local sanitary inspectorate, inventing a new regulation, was more likely to be thinking about the amount of bribe that could be immediately obtained for non-observance of this regulation, than about the long-term consequences of such rule-making. But very quickly more powerful state agents learnt to mobilize various inspections and bureaucracies to influence their interactants, media organizations among them. Sanitary inspection, although it may seem insignificant at first glance, became one of the most typical resources to mobilize, along with tax police and fire control (the list, of course, was always proliferating).

Examples of such strategy are legion: "a man with a warrant for sanitary inspection came with twelve gunmen to close a TV company in Rostov because the temperature in its office was two or three degrees lower than the norm"; "representatives of the chief board of the State Fire Department ... checked out the building of the *Kommersant* publishing house and found out some noncompliance with fire safety regulations. The office was sealed up and production of the *Kommersant Daily* newspaper stopped" (Yefremova and Ratinov 2000).

In contrast, the absence of controlling actions or their ineffectiveness can be a type of a positive practice. One of the most famous examples here is the constant auditing of the financial activity of *RTR*, the second Russian national TV channel, by the State Auditing Chamber throughout the 1990s. Each time the Chamber drew up a long list of serious violations, sent the documents to the Procuracy, and each time the story had no outcome (Rykovtseva 1998: 13–17). The resources of the company, owned by the State, and the funding it received, were widely used for the private needs of its insiders, but since the state funding was incomplete, this must have suited the political elite, thus turning it into a form of indirect payment for the channel's loyalty.

Another common practice of the selective use of rules, based on their superfluous character, is connected with broadcasting licensing. The number of claims to mass media in respect to licenses and other documentation is constantly growing, and most of them are judicially grounded. The majority of the grounded claims refer to interruption of broadcasting for a period of three months or more, or unofficial cession of broadcast to outside companies. Both actions are prohibited, and most of the time they are means by which media producers try to keep their licenses when they appear unable to produce TV programs for some time, in most cases because of lack of funds. Since the procedure for obtaining a license is also quite laborious, many media do infringe the respective regulation, but only some pay for it.

A classic story occurred in 1996 in Syktyvkar, the principal city of the Komi republic in north-east European Russia. The director of the *Svyaz* telecommunications company shut down the "*Telecourier*" TV program as having no license. The program was registered as a separate media producing company, but not as a broadcasting one. Meanwhile Syktyvkar *Channel 3* and *NEP-Plus* channel in the neighboring town of Ukhta went on working, though neither had broadcasting licenses (Panfilov and Simonov 1997: 164).

Another story, more frequently discussed, concerns the extension of a license to *TV-Center*, the channel of Moscow administration and the mouthpiece of the capital's mayor Yuri Luzhkov. By the end of Boris Yeltsin's rule, Luzhkov's political influence was so strong that he could hope to win the presidential elections in 2000. Therefore, as mentioned in Chapter 4, he opposed the pro-Putin party in the parliamentary elections in late 1999, and was completely crushed by the big guns of *ORT* and *RTR*. Luzhkov did not even try to run for president; *TV-Center* got two warnings from the Minister of media Mikhail Lesin, for different violations during the 1999 campaign, and thus lost the right for an automatic extension of its license. The tender was scheduled for May 2000; the members of the tender commission, one recalls, were appointed by Lesin personally. Luzhkov announced that he would like to solve the problem "not in court, but through negotiations" (Varshavchik 12.04.2000). According to Varshavchik, since Lesin and Luzhkov could not agree on who should come to whom, they decided to meet at a neutral territory and chose a café on Tverskaya street, the main avenue of Moscow, where they spent about 2 hours. In May 2000 *TV-Center* won the tender.

Superfluity of rules, allowing for their selective use, has been paralleled by their insufficiency – that is, the absence of rules where they could have brought more predictability of state agents' actions and, consequently, more security for their extra-state interactants. For instance, while in some regions the system for the local funding of media is closely regulated by the law, in others it is arbitrary. It is not hard to guess that in the latter cases state agents are interested in maintaining the indeterminacy of rules rather than in their clarification.

Perhaps, the most serious omission in Russian media legislation is the absence of the law on TV and radio broadcasting which was worked on from spring 1993. In this case it was the president personally who played the main role (he vetoed the draft law approved by the *Duma* in 1995). He did however also have some allies, for example in the Soviet of the Federation, the upper chamber of the Russian parliament, which rejected the draft law some time later, after the *Duma* had ignored the president's veto in 1996 (Lange 1997: 157–8).

As a result, the key problem for electronic mass media (i.e. allocation of transmitting frequencies and granting broadcasting licenses) in the 1990s was handled on the basis of the president's decree of December 1993, relevant government resolutions and respective Regulations on granting TV and radio broadcasting licenses (Edict of the government of the Russian Federation No. 1359 "On licensing…" 1994). With its many omissions, the Regulations allowed the Federal TV and Radio Board to grant the licenses arbitrarily. For instance, the Regulations allowed but did not bind the Board to organize tenders for applicants for a particular frequency. Recommendations of the Commission on broadcasting (a public body) were not obligatory. The resolution about obligatory tenders and establishing a Federal Tender Commission (1999) did not change the situation, since the members of the Commission were to be appointed by the Minister for press.

Such institutionally vague determination of rules is ideal for ad hoc decisions. Thus, Yeltsin alone decided to give the frequency occupied by a state educational channel to the private *NTV* (1996) – or at least he did not agree it with the Federal TV and Radio Board. The same is true for the *Peterburg – 5 Kanal* transmitting networks given to the *Culture* channel. Moreover, while frequency allocation was, as a rule, under the authority of state agents at the Federal level, decisions on taking frequencies away, as can be seen from the Syktyvkar case, were sometimes within the power of regional officials.

So far I have mostly been addressing practices of selective application of existing laws or use of their absence. An important practice both relying on inconsistency in Russian legislation and promoting it further is the "autonomous" creation of rules – disregarding legislation. *Public expertise*, a large-scale research project carried out in eighty-seven of eighty-nine Russian provinces in 1999–2000, revealed that only about 60 percent of regional laws on media conformed to the relevant Federal law. Local laws on state support of media, complying with the relevant Federal legislation, comprised less than one-fifth (Yakovenko 2000).

Many examples of such autonomous rule-making may be also found in the development, situational interpretation and application of regulations referring to journalists' accreditation. Unlike allocation of frequencies or licensing, it is available to a wide range of state agents and therefore has been much more extensive. The institution of accreditation is a complex of rules regulating the presence of journalists at locations where admittance is limited – primarily state offices or state-organized events, as well as areas of disasters and military actions. In the early and mid 1990s, when the institution of accreditation was a novelty in Russia, ad hoc decisions on admitting particular journalists or media companies were most common. Later, state agents became more and more inclined to set up rules restricting admittance in the way most convenient for the corresponding organizations. Such practices include: limitation of the maximum number of admitted journalists, of video and audio recording, denial of the right of accreditation to certain groups (e.g. part-time journalists) or certain types of media organizations, requirements to indicate data about journalists and media organizations not required by law (such as personal data) etc. Thus, in 1998 Alexander Lebed, the governor of a South-Siberian region of Krasnoyarsk, signed the resolution which, among other conditions of accreditation, included the journalist's "professional training or sufficient experience, competence in problems being covered, ability to analyze information received, compliance with journalistic ethics" (GDF 17.08.1998). The years 1998–9 were a period of sharp conflict between the governor and two groups of media backed by his main rivals: the mayor of the Krasnoyarsk city and the leading local CIG. The resolution betrays lack of resources and of an adequate strategy rather than an abundance of power.

Creation of illegal rules is, of course, supplemented by practices of selective refusal, suspension or termination of accreditation of particular journalists or media companies at particular events or with particular organizations. Reasons for that (if any) are usually that the media company covers the activity of the organization in the wrong way. While wrong coverage is to be proved by judgment of a court, this norm, according to GDF monitoring, is most commonly ignored.

Crossing the boundary of legality, state agents have little reason to limit themselves to establishing norms and regulations referring only to legitimate categories, such as licenses or accreditation. Sometimes official rule-making is not connected to any existing legislation at all. A champion in this activity is, perhaps, the municipal council of the small town of Dolgoprudny in the Moscow region. In 1996 it issued an instruction stipulating that any organization intending to perform video-recording in the town had to obtain approval from the town authorities and pay a daily fee of from five to fifteen minimal monthly wage rates (Panfilov and Simonov 1997: 247). Unfortunately, I have no data on how this instruction was observed, but my guess is that it wasn't.

It is not difficult to see that the practices described above, though indirect, are at the same time not too carefully concealed. While use of material resources and selective application of rules is a more covert way of demonstrating power, illegal (or, more precisely, extra-legal) rule-making is a quite direct exercise of power. The degree to which the goal of a power practice is opened loosely corresponds to the amount of resources available; this correspondence increases throughout the 1990s. If the resources are limited, state agents would prefer to combine exchange relations with relatively mild expressions of their will, such as hints, instructions masked as receptions or parties, limitation of the number and contents of questions at press-conferences and the like. As long as the amount of resources grows, presentations of the agents' goals would move from milder to harder forms: phone calls and letters in recommendatory tone, demands to be interviewed only by certain journalists, demands to mention or not to mention particular persons; and finally the demand to agree all or a part of materials of some periodicals with the authorities. When the latter demand takes the form of an official written rule, it means that the process of the imposition of will has reached its logical end: the institution of censorship. The available data do not contain such examples, but cases of establishing censorship de facto are reported by GDF. For instance, in 1999 the head of the Press Board of the Belgorod region administration (who combined this work with the post of Chairmen of the local Union of Journalists) gathered editors of the regional newspapers for instruction. In particular, he recommended them not to publish critical pieces against the governor, who was running for his second term. As for articles about other candidates, he suggested they were faxed to the regional administration and published only after correction and editing (Yefremova and Ratinov 2000).

4 State and non-state agents of violence

If fulfillment of a decision is not bought with material or symbolic resources and not ensured through an ideology, it must be enforced. In consolidated states enforcement exercised by state agents is not usually objected to by the majority of society, while the use of violence by anybody else is not approved. According to the famous Weberian definition (Weber 1990: 651), the monopoly on legitimate violence is a constitutive feature of the State as an institution. In Russia of the 1990s, as I have already mentioned, the state/non-state distinction and boundaries between legitimate and illegitimate were blurred. The actions of state agents, supposedly legitimate, were very often far from being regarded as such, even when the former acted within the bounds of the official rules (e.g. arrest of Gussinsky). On the contrary, with a general lack of consensus on common rules, the actions of non-state agents of violence were often legitimized by "the code" – an alternative system of rules shared both by the "mafia" members and the businesses dependent on them. The mechanisms by which boundaries between the state and non-state violence became transparent in Russia are well studied (Volkov 2002). Here it will be appropriate to sketch them only to the extent that they determine media production.

Demonopolization of "legitimate" violence

Volkov, who examines the socio-economic aspects of legal and illegal use of violence, calls both state and non-state exercisers of violence "violent entrepreneurs." This term is really helpful: certain features of the Russian legal system, discussed earlier, make it very difficult to put each empirical actor either within or outside the sphere of legality. Thus such oppositions as "gangsters vs. businessmen" or "criminals vs. policemen" are often misleading. Therefore, I shall prefer the terms "users/agents of violence" and "violent entrepreneurs" to more traditional labels.

Violent entrepreneurship is a phenomenon essential for understanding the process of state decomposition and the nature of the use of violence in the 1990s. Its start dates back to late 1980s, when private business was finally allowed in the form of so-called cooperative property enterprises (usually small-scale trading or food producing entities). It was then that certain individuals, usually former sportsmen and the enforcers, united into racketeer gangs that quickly spread throughout the whole country. At first they did nothing but extort money from regular entrepreneurs, but soon they faced the necessity of protecting "their" businessmen from competing gangs. This already looked like a service; it became called "roofing," the gangs themselves being called "roofs." Competition led roofs to expand the range of protection services, defending their clients also from police and other controlling state bodies and from unconscientious partners. After changes in legislation in 1992 protection and enforcement services were legalized in the form of private protection companies (as well as the latter often ended up with roofing). It was then that representatives of the police and other enforcers realized that they were very well placed to render such services and started competing or merging with the private roofs.

The next stage – approximately in the middle of the 1990s – came when some roofs began investing accumulated capital into the protected enterprises and starting businesses of their own. Those who did not either ceased to exist or stayed limited within traditional illegal businesses, such as prostitution or the fake vodka trade. Those who did invest experienced increasing pressure of the market economy and started gradually turning into regular entrepreneurs. In order to make their business prosper they had to comply with the existing laws to a greater extent than before. It also made sense to distance themselves from their most criminal-looking activities, and to seek new kinds of connections with the state agents. First, this could be entirely informal cooperation in the form of bribery and joint business with state officials. Second, there was lobbying for the interests of violent entrepreneurs through their representatives in both legislative and executive bodies – this can be called "influencing the State." And the third was "becoming the State": many violent entrepreneurs were successfully elected into legislatures at different levels. Thus Anatoly Bykov, known as the master of Krasnoyarsk Aluminum Plant and the local godfather was elected a deputy of the Krasnoyarsk Land legislative assembly in 1997. One of the most famous failures were the four unsuccessful attempts of Alexander Khabarov, the leader of another nationally known "organized criminal group" *Uralmash* (Yekaterinburg, the Urals), to become a deputy of the State Duma for his home district.

This last stage of cooperation with state agents was marked by formation of full-size CIGs, some of whom had grown directly from violent entrepreneurship, while others had added it in the form of security departments later. At this stage the difference between state and non-state violence is especially difficult to discern. Consider such method of competition as the armed takeovers of industrial enterprises, quite frequent in the late 1990s and still practised. These can be seen neither as wholly criminal attacks nor as purely the enforcement of legal decisions. Suppose that two CIGs clash in a conflict over an enterprise. One of the possible scenarios for the new group would be first to organize the election of a new board of directors and its chair. Since both the "old" and the "new" sides may succeed, this may even lead to the emergence of two chairs elected by different groups of shareholders. Then, if the competing director resists, a court decision is acquired ordering him to leave his post and his office. With this decision the new director, accompanied by his private security group and a "friendly" department of police (or other enforcers) takes the office by force. In this way the director's office may change hands several times. The final victory depends on many factors – in particular, that side may win who has mastered the production of an image of legitimacy in media.

It was the CIGs who could first afford to found their own media or include existing ones as their departments. On the whole, for CIGs media have been peripheral structures that are not always utilized. Therefore many preferred interacting with media people only occasionally, when needed. At the same time, non-state agents of violence had needed media not only at the stage of CIG formation.

Initially media provided the gangs with a good service, frightening ordinary people and competitors and thus giving them an image of almighty villains. Journalist Alexei Khokhlov has told a story about a gang who offered to get restarted his criminal news program, which had been suspended by the local authorities (see Chapter 7). After entering regular business, violent entrepreneurs needed media to distance them from their past and to legitimize themselves both with the public and the commercial elite. One of the criminal groups of the Urals megalopolis Yekaterinburg even hired a popular local journalist who wrote a book presenting the group as a winner in a healthy commercial competition (Lemberg 2000). Finally, violent entrepreneurs would need media both to influence state agents, to enter their ranks through the mechanism of elections, and to retain their positions within the State once they have got them. To give only one example, Anatoly Bykov, mentioned above, was elected into the legislative assembly of the territory holding a blocking interest in a popular local channel *TVK*. (For more details on non-violent strategies of "criminals" see Chapter 7.

Thus, for CIGs, open violence has been only one of the means to control media production. But when non-state violent entrepreneurs do engage in violence, their actions are not only indiscernible from those of state agents; it is often unclear where a particular violent action has come from – from within or from outside the State. In some cases it is unknown, but in the cases where CIGs stand behind those actions it makes little sense to differentiate state and non-state violence.

Certain difficulties also appear when one tries to determine the limits of the term "violence": the difference between "violence" and, for example, "indirect pressure" is rather conventional, and an in-between zone exists. So I will consider the problem by starting from the most obvious point, i.e. cases of journalists killed, and then, step by step, I shall move to more contentions situations.

"Hard" violence practices

As a rule, little is known about the circumstances in which journalists have perished. Throughout the 1990s a large number were killed in military conflicts, along with ordinary people; in the Russian case this happened above all in Chechnya. Others died in incidents which can for certain not be related to their professional activity. Indirect indication that such connection existed is usually provided by threats which had been addressed to a journalist killed later, other persecutions he/she (or the media outlet he/she had worked with) had suffered, or critical stories the killed journalist had published. In 2000 eighteen journalists were killed (Interview 39); according to the experts of the Union of Journalists, the death of four of them was definitely connected with their professional activity; in four other cases a connection to the journalists' professional activity is suspected. The number of murders in the previous years is comparable to the year 2000: nine in 1999, eleven in 1998, fifteen in 1997, nineteen in 1996 (Simonov 2001: 40; Simonov 1999: 52; Avdeev *et al.* 1998: 117; Panfilova and Simonov 1997: 358). Before that there are no reliable statistics.

The first nationally significant story was the murder of Dmitri Kholodov, correspondent of a popular newspaper *Moskovskii Komsomolets*, in Moscow in October 1994. Kholodov acquired a suitcase from a person who had claimed to have material for his journalistic investigation. When opened, the case exploded in the journalist's hands. Years passed before the case got to court. Several acting and former servicemen from airborne troops were accused, but the Moscow military court found all of them completely innocent in June 2002. The General Procuracy objected to the judgement; however, sentences over the military are extremely rare, even when the General Prosecutor is involved. As for those who might have taken out a contract on Kholodov, no information about them has ever surfaced.

The second significant murder was that of the newly elected director of *ORT* and the national star anchor Vladislav Listev in March 1995 (see Chapter 5). He, however, was most probably killed because of his business rather than his journalistic activities. In any event, the case has not been even brought to court.

A third well-known, though less discussed murder was the killing of Larisa Yudina, the editor-in-chief of *Sovetskaya Kalmykia Segodnya* newspaper in June 1998. This had been the only opposition paper in the republic of Kalmykiya (south-eastern part of European Russia). Yudina's case was, if one may say so, lucky: her main "opponent" had been the republic's president[1] Kirsan Ilyumzhinov, somewhat out of favor with the Federal elite, while the paper was supported by one of the most influential right parties in Russia. Quite soon Ilyumzhinov's advisor was convicted for Yudina's murder, although the governor himself did not lose his position (for more details see Chapter 10).

Unsuccessful assassination attempts on media people can usually be attributed to their professional activity more precisely because journalists who have survived can sometimes shed light on the causes of the incident. One of the most scandalous stories is an attempted assassination on Yakov London, a leading journalist and media-owner from the city of Novosibirsk.[2] In early 1998 he was attacked near the entrance to his flat by a gunman who shot him six times. Heavily wounded, he spent a year undergoing medical treatment and became an invalid, though he did not leave the business and even strengthened his position. President of *NTSC* TV company broadcasting to four neighboring regions, vice-president of *NTN* regional TV and the head of its *Channel 4*, co-owner of another two channels, one of the establishers of the *Video International – Siberia* advertising agency (the affiliate of the national monopolist), in 1999 London was appointed by the governor as the chairman of the local affiliate of the state *VGTRK*, the second national TV channel. But achieving an even greater profile than this monopolization became the arrest of three suspects in March 1999. All of them were London's colleagues from *NTN* TV and a related media company.

When it started in 1992, *NTN*, London's primary affiliation, contained only one channel; later it split into *Channel 4* and *Channel 12*, but remained as a single legal entity. In 1997 London sold the controlling share of *Channel 4* and *NTSC* to *Media-MOST*, the media empire of Vladimir Gussinksy. After that, for unknown reasons, relations between *Channels 4* and *12* became very tense, while the position of the latter inside the new company was growing stronger. The suspects who were arrested for the assassination attempt on London in 1999 were the head of *Channel 12* Yevgeni Kuzmenko; an *NTN* shareholder and the director of the *Uniton-video* corporation Andrei Lyubimov; and the former head of *Uniton*'s security department Boris Vlasov. Top management of *Channel 12* immediately claimed that this arrest was a method of unfair competition in media business. Yakov London, for his part, made a public statement that in 1998 one of the arrested had come to him with "convincing evidence" of the guilt of the other two, and offered to "liquidate" them. According to London, he decided not to ignore this information and reported it to the police. While Lyubimov and Vlasov were sentenced in 2000 (surprisingly soon), London's main rival Kuzmenko was released in ten days and became the head of *NTN* in mid-1999 (Rapoport 1999, 2000; GDF 02.01.1998; 14.07.2000).

Whether or not the sentence was just, this story, compared with the murder of Larisa Yudina, shows not only that the practices of influence of state agents on media have been similar to those of violent entrepreneurs, but also that media insiders themselves have been practicing violent entrepreneurship.

Yakov London is one of a few who were left alive unintentionally. Cases in which journalists exposed to violence have been deliberately left alive are greater in number: murder is an extreme measure even for those who practice it. In most cases milder punishments, such as a beating up, are considered enough. Among them, two categories can be conventionally distinguished: cases where the identity of subjects of violence is concealed and those where it is disclosed – straightforwardly or by hints. GDF monitoring shows that most cases of the latter category during the period studied were actions of state agents and, as a rule, of representatives of the enforcers. Indeed, this group has the best opportunities to present its violence as legitimate and avoid subsequent potential sanctions. Non-state agents of violence, not surprisingly, were representatives of security departments of private organizations or of separate protection companies. All these groups acted similarly: beating journalists, especially cameramen, as a rule during or just after recording; damaging and/or taking away cameras and tapes. Below two examples are juxtaposed: one involving state agents, and the other dealing with non-state sources of violence.

- In January 1998 a cameraman from the *Dialogue* TV company was beaten by soldiers of a military base near Nizhny Novgorod when he tried to film a fire at this base. His camera was also broken by the soldiers. The action was justified by the secret status of the military object, although the cameraman stood outside its territory (GDF 16.08.1998).
- In the town of Morshansk, Tambov region, two journalists tried to switch on their camera at the central market and were detained by security. Then one of them was taken to the director's office and beaten for being the author of other TV stories about the market (GDF 14–16.03.1997). In this case criminal proceedings were instituted – a consequence that according to the monitoring, is very seldom encountered by representatives of state bodies.

Despite their similarities, both cases provide enough evidence to identify the agents of violence as belonging or not belonging to the state. An example of a story in which identification appears nearly impossible deserves special attention and precise quoting from the GDF monitoring:

In the town of Achinsk (Krasnoyarsk territory) unidentified people wearing masks and camouflage uniforms broke into the building of the administration of the local alumina complex and caused a fight on the ground floor. Alexei Semyonov, journalist of *TVK – Channel 6* TV company, who happened to witness the event, was thrown out of a window. Luckily, he only got his clothes torn.

(GDF 12.10.1999)

This story makes little sense if one is not familiar with the political situation in Krasnoyarsk territory and the meaning of the appearance of the camouflaged masked people. For those who can decipher the event, it is obviously a typical armed takeover of an enterprise, the general pattern for which was described at the beginning of this chapter. Krasnoyarsk territory, already mentioned several times, is unlucky to have many rich enterprises, a large proportion of which, including the Achinsk alumina complex, in the mid 1990s came under the control of Anatoly Bykov's CIG. But later, as in the Kemerovo region, the governor of Krasnoyarsk united with Bykov's numerous competitors and destroyed his CIG. The change of owner at the Achinsk alumina complex, closely followed by Bykov's arrest, took place exactly in the fall of 1999. By a strange coincidence, *TVK – Channel 6*, for which Alexei Semyonov worked, was controlled by Bykov. Thus, irrespective of Semyonov's professional beliefs, "unidentified people" were more likely to throw him out as a soldier of the propaganda department of a competing CIG rather than as a press freedom seeker.

While attacks on journalists during recording can be characterized as immediate punishment, another group of assaults takes place at the stage of data collection by a journalist to prevent their publication. In this case the identity of the attacker is also sometimes disclosed: this can be necessary to make the aim of the assault understandable for the journalist. However, in the majority of such cases the agents of violence do not identify themselves. In these cases the connection between the assault and the journalist's professional activity can only be conjectured, and journalists have to trace it themselves. Again, in most cases they point at state agents, sometimes – at violent entrepreneurs. Cases in which journalists blame those who could be called "purely criminal actors" (e.g. drug dealers) have been quite rare. All the assaults have similar scenarios. As a rule, the assaulter calls the journalist by name, and hits him or her as soon as the journalist turns to see who is calling. The assaulter does not take money or valuables, and often gives indirect instructions "to keep silent," or "not to write too much," or that "one should not say everything he knows."

"Mild" violence practices

Among milder practices of intimidation, assaults by phone have been very common, both anonymous and with declared identities. Such assaults do not imply that their source has the capability to apply any sanctions, since oral threats require no resources, except the phone. But because the threatened person does not know that for sure and cannot calculate the risks, such methods can be effective (the same is true of phone calls stating that editorial offices have been mined). Even during my short journalistic career I was once threatened by phone.

I was making a small-scale journalistic investigation of a story that on the surface looked quite innocent: I wanted to find out why a building, considered an "architectural monument of Federal significance," had been not restored for years and was gradually falling into ruin. The investigation uncovered an acute conflict about the ownership of the building. Endless court and administrative decisions led me to a non-government organization established "to protect the monument." It was the head of the latter who very aggressively asked me by phone whether I wanted my children to be OK. I finished the work anyway, but told my boss that I did not want the article to be signed with my name. He ignored the request, and though nothing actually happened after that, the happy ending could not have been predicted for certain.

All real threats, phone, personal or in the form of publishing discrediting materials in media, are measures prior to real violence, aimed at avoiding it. Even purely "criminal" agents find threats useful. Alexey Khokhlov, TV journalist and editor of a criminal news and investigative program, told a fantastic story that involved the leader of the largest criminal syndicate in St. Petersburg, Vladimir Kumarin, and soldiers of *SOBR* and *OMON*, famous police departments specially trained for armed operations:

> We had a conflict with the leader of *The Tambovians*,[3] Kumarin, the master of Petersburg, real master. This is the gang which controlled Sobchak [former mayor] and brought the present governor to power. So . . . it was rather serious. So, Mister Kumarin did not feel offended when we told the public about his . . . deeds and so on. He was offended when we called him a cripple. He really had been seriously wounded during an assassination, two years in Switzerland, half-invalid. We had a six hour meeting with him, about a hundred *SOBR*ians and *OMON*ians covered us. And we – I decided it was my duty to apologize to him as a person. . . . Well, in general, in the criminal world – unlike our corrupted politics – there is *the code*. Quite a definite system, clear system of their own laws. Well, so according to *the code* you may tell anybody anything about their activities . . . and so on, but you may not humiliate their dignity.
>
> (Khokhlov 06.07.1998)

The fact that a journalist could mobilize a hundred elite police officers for his defense poses a question about his independence from the latter. At the same time, the need to apologize to Kumarin, for whatever reason, also questions Khokhlov's (or even his protectors') independence from the criminal leader. Indeed, the fact that the police found Kumarin dangerous enough to be opposed by a hundred armed men, but did not arrest him, indicates the scope of his power in the city. Actually, in this story *SOBRi*-ans and *OMON*ians behaved not as the police, but as a classical roof.

Preventing access of journalists to the locations of news events is another relatively mild practice involving violence. Though it can be classi-fied as a practice of negative informational management, which is con-sidered in Chapter 7, it is carried out either by police officers (in state organizations) or by the personnel of security departments (in private companies), and is connected with physical violence – for example, with cameras and video materials being taken away, or with threats to use it. Cases where journalists are not admitted to court sessions or sittings of government bodies, or to the scenes of murders or military actions are the most common. At a criminal trial that I witnessed during my observation at TV none of the numerous journalists even tried to object to the barris-ter's demand that they leave the court room. Another situation I observed was resolved, one could say, successfully. Two TV journalists, filming a story about a medical research institute, decided to get a picture of its sign-board – a huge Soviet construction that embraced all the roof of the shabby four-storey building. However, its front was leased as a luxurious office to a local parliamentarian known for his close ties with the leading city godfather. As soon as the cameraman put up his camera on the oppos-ite side of the street, the security guard at the doorway of the office motioned him to stop. After a short discussion between the journalists, one of them approached the guard and, explaining his needs, asked for permission to shoot. He did get approval, with the reservation that the deputy's office was not to get into the picture (Field notes 2).

A last group of power practices that I want to consider here comprises violent actions towards the property of media organizations (often used together with physical violence and assaults). It includes deprivation of representatives of mass media of editorial, printing and journalistic prop-erty (thefts, burglary, robbery), its destruction or damage (explosion, arson, devastation of premises and machinery), and withdrawal of docu-ments, materials, technical facilities. Cases of stealing video facilities, espe-cially thefts of journalists' personal property from their apartments, are not always connected to the professional journalistic activity of the victim, except when such actions are combined with other measures that make this connection obvious. When taking away editorial property state agents again enjoy certain advantages: they use legitimate procedures, registering the process as a search and seizure, arrest or confiscation of property. The same is true for seizure of transmitters and printed matter, though where editions just "disappear" from editorial offices, printing houses or in transit, taken by "unknown" people are more common. "Disappearance" of an edition is easier to present as a robbery than the disconnection of a transmitter. However, cases are known where cables and wires, connecting studios with transmitters, are just physically cut. An almost humorous example was given by Mikhail Malyutin, one of the few respondents who agreed to disclose his identity. He referred to the period of the 1998 governor's elections – again in the Krasnoyarsk territory – in which the incumbent Valeri Zubov lost to General Alexander Lebed:

> [*Sfera*] was the only channel, which even when channels *Afontovo* and *GTRK* forsook Zubov and in fact took the side of Lebed – so, it was the only channel that told everything it considered necessary to tell about Lebed in a rather tough manner. Finally, *brothers*[4] came and cut the cable. It was at that time when Zubov was formally still in power. But because those were foolish *brothers*, they cut the cable of *TV-6*.[5]
>
> (Interview 40, January 2001)

Maliutin is cautious enough to use the vague slang word "*brothers*" which refers to usually low-rank members of criminal groups and loosely to gangsters in general. Indeed, people who illegally cut cables can hardly be called other than gangsters, but if Malyutin had used this word, he would have inevitably connected the name of the future governor to this illegitimate term. *Brothers* was the word that allowed him to hint cautiously, but clearly, at the transparency of the boundary between "gangsters" and state agents.

The story of radio *Titan*: return of consolidated state violence

While throughout the 1990s actions of state and non-state agents of violence have demonstrated many similarities, here I want to indicate the point from which they started to diverge. Conventionally, it happened when the state reappeared as a social institution able to exercise concerted policies and campaigns, in which the entire range of methods, from exchange to open violence, could be used. As it turned out, such large-scale campaigns are not available to anyone outside the State, even to the most powerful CIGs, and anyone who thought otherwise would lose. The most significant case is, of course, the story of *NTV*, although it involved only very limited violence. Much more threatening is the story of radio *Titan* dating back to 1998; if it had not passed unnoticed by the journalistic community, it could have become an eloquent indication of future changes.

The story of *Titan* occurred in the republic of Bashkortostan, a region between the Volga and the Urals, formerly populated by Muslim nomads, and one of the Russian provinces where the state was far from breaking up even at the peak of Federal turmoil in the early 1990s. *Titan*'s story may be fully understood only in the context of the Bashkortostan's politico-economical situation and, in particular, in the context of the local presidential elections of 1998. The full details are given in Chapter 10; here I want to focus on the methods by which the oppositional *Titan* was defeated by the governor (Makarov 1998: 49–55; GDF 27.05, 08.06, 15.07, 21.07, 31.07.1998, 4–28.02, 02.03, 30.04.1999).

In 1997–8 *Titan*, located in Ufa, the Bashkir principal town, was several times taken off air, together with other media outlets broadcasting in Bashkorstan (including *ORT*, *RTR* and *NTV*). The conflict reached its peak just before local pre-term presidential elections scheduled for June 1998, in which the incumbent Murtaza Rakhimov was running for office. At that time *Titan* turned out to be the only media outlet providing airtime to opposition candidates, with critical pieces on all other media outlets being effectively excluded.

The anti-*Titan* campaign began on May 19, 1998 and gathered speed every hour. In the morning the Mayor of Ufa summoned the lessor providing premises to *Titan*, and insisted on termination of the rent agreement. At the same time the State Telecommunications Inspection, *Gossvyaznadzor*, started inspecting the first studio of the radio company, and several hours later a sanitary inspection began its work in *Titan*'s office. In the afternoon Bashkortostan State Secretary phoned Altaf Galeyev, the president of *Titan*, saying, "don't criticize Rakhimov's administration." On May 20 *Gossvyaznadzor* inspected the second studio of the company. On May 21 *Gosenergo*, the state electric power supplier, carried out an inspection and concluded that many *Titan* employees had no certificates to work with computers. Police began drawing up to the city district where the studio was located. On May 22 a program on *Russian Radio – Ufa* broadcast a piece about *Titan*'s personnel being mentally disordered: it was claimed they were drugged. Meanwhile, Altaf Galeyev kept *Titan*'s listeners informed about the situation, with his radio station gaining more and more public support. The same evening people in semi-military uniform cut the electric supply cable to *Titan*'s office. Next day electricians from *Titan* technical support repaired the cable. At 10.20 the telephones were switched off.

On May 25, at 8 a.m. *Titan* broadcasted a program about corruption in Bashkortostan government bodies. At 9.20 *Titan*'s transmitter installed in the building of the Social Service Committee was cut off, and the chairman of the Committee told *Titan* to remove their transmitting equipment. At 4 p.m. the water supply was cut off; at 7 p.m. – the general power supply. Officials of the Ministry of Interior forbade the tenants of a nearby dormitory to provide any help to *Titan*'s journalists, who by that time hardly left their office. On May 26, the executive director of *Titan* went to take the transmitter, but found out that it had already been seized by police. In the evening the power supply for the whole neighborhood was switched off. The traffic police cordoned off the block around the studio and let in only the cars of registered residents.

On May 27 *Titan* started up its own power generator and broadcast over the neighborhood through outdoor loudspeakers. In the afternoon officials from the local Procuracy tried to enter the company building, but the journalists blocked the door from inside. More and more people supporting *Titan* were gathering around the cordoned block. By 5 p.m. the police closed off traffic, arriving in several buses. Policemen started seizing people, beating up those who resisted and taking them away in cars. About fifty people dressed as civilians tried to kick in the blocked door but failed. Galeyev fired a blank from his own gun in the air through a window – according to his version, in order to attract attention to the fact of his studio being stormed. A voice coming from a megaphone outdoors ordered the journalists of *Titan* to cease fire and informed them about the arrival of a special police group trained for armed seizures. The journalists surrendered. At the Police Investigation Department they were offered ... coffee. After that they felt and behaved strangely, their state reminiscent of drug intoxication. The police officials made blood tests without completing the documents necessary for the procedure.

During the next three days everybody, except Galeyev, was released. In June Rakhimov won the elections. In July *Titan* was officially wound up by the Arbitration Court for "infringement of sanitary norms and regulations" and abuse of freedom of media "in the form of appeals by the president of the company Galeyev, A.G." who "called for change, by means of violence, of the state system and Constitution, and aroused hostility in the society." The latter accusation referred to Galeyev's public appeals to defend *Titan* from the authorities. Galeyev was charged with armed hooliganism. Since his gun was duly registered, illegal purchase, keeping and use of weapons were no grounds for incrimination. Galeyev was kept in prison from May 27, 1998 till April 30, 1999; then he was released on condition that he would not leave the city. The case was returned many times from the court for additional investigation. Neither GDF monitoring, nor the monitoring of Oleg Panfilov (which has separated from that of GDF in 2000) gives any information about the end of the story.

Concluding remarks

For both state and extra-state agents, violence is not the only mode of action, and most actors combine it with exchange relations. The proportion of actions involving violence is difficult to determine in terms of figures. On the one hand, such actions are often concealed. On the other hand, any negative action is more easily identifiable, while positive actions serve just a non-active background. Also, violence usually attracts more public attention than non-violence. Therefore, only very general conclusions may be drawn on this matter. First, when compliance with rules is not ensured by tradition, and when the rules themselves are unclear, the level of violence is higher than in more stable situations. Second, while in the beginning of an unstable period actors tend to make use of the opportunities to solve everything by force, very soon all parties come to understand that a decrease in violence is in their common interest. Although the statistical validity of GDF data should be considered cautiously, it shows a visible decrease in the share of violent actions in the general number of conflicts connected with media: 25 percent in 2000 compared to 47 percent in 1996 (Simonov 2001: 19). The decrease of violence may mean both compromise and suppression of some actors by others. Though, again, it is hard to say what tendency has prevailed, the chapters devoted to more peaceful interactions (especially Chapters 7 and 9) may shed some light on the processes of compromise and compliance formation.

5   Owners

Economic agents, whose influence has become apparent only after the abolition of preliminary censorship, are the ones who have been in the centre of the most heated public discussion in Russia in the first post-socialist years. Because censorship had been the major mechanism of control in the Soviet period, it had been seen as the only obstacle to freedom (although, of course, the Soviet system of control included an economic component, but this was "hidden" behind its administrative exterior). Thus, since economic influence has come as an unpleasant surprise, it has been described in largely negative terms. This attitude is not unique to Russia: those countries in which private television was introduced relatively late (for example, France) have experienced similar tensions. A more detailed analysis of Russian media ownership shows that it has been even farther from providing ideals of "freedom" than classical profit-oriented ownership is.

Is "external" ownership – ownership?

Theorizing economic influences, it is always very easy to slip into purely economic terms – especially if one looks at economic agents only. But even looking at media production in general there is a temptation to regard it "economically": the whole field is permeated by various exchange relations. However, here I consider only those actors whose major practice is explicit exchange, and whose material funds are the basis of their resources.

Ownership, the subject of this chapter, is also not an unproblematic term. Ownership, as ability to exclusively possess, enjoy and dispose, may exist only when certain relevant rules are accepted and generally observed by a society. First, the very idea of division of resources into such exclusive clusters must be regarded as legitimate; second, their de facto distribution among individuals or groups, and the procedures of re-distribution must be also accepted. The first idea – i.e. the idea of private property – became legitimized long before the collapse of the Soviet Union, and thus new Russian legislation had only to legalize what had been long awaited.

However, the second group of conditions was – and still is – widely discussed. In the absence of established rules of re-distribution of huge amounts of state property, nearly all procedures, once applied, and all transactions based on them, could be later questioned and regarded as void. Consequently, often more than one actor would claim exclusive rights for the same item of property, which produced fierce struggles, both within and outside the sphere of legality. Their circumstances, together with the desire to avoid arbitrary taxation and other state controlling activities, led economic actors to conceal their transactions and made the general structure of ownership in Russia very opaque. All this applies in full measure to media. Obtaining data about media ownership, mergers or bankruptcies, as well as media budgets, is difficult not only for researchers, but for participants of the game themselves. They therefore often have to act in a murky and unpredictable environment, which makes their relations quite intricate.

Another difficulty with the specific concept of ownership appears when it comes to owning organizations. In this case ownership gains an additional feature: an owner can not only use and dispose of material objects or financial assets, but also regulate behavior of people employed in their organization, by creating rules and controlling their execution. This, in particular, is what differentiates media owners from advertisers: while the latter can base their relations with journalists mainly on various kinds of exchange, the former have the resources to influence actions of their employees directly and explicitly. The legitimate limits of such influence are also a matter of discussion – if not by the wider public, than at least by the journalistic community. In the Soviet state-owned media the controlling practices of the owner were considered obviously illegitimate, but recognition of private property, though much welcomed, soon trapped journalists in an unexpected confusion. In 1990 the authors of the Law on the press did not introduce the category of the owner at all, because, as they acknowledged later, it did not occur to them that it could be important. This lacuna in legislation led to the informal institutionalization of owner-media relations. Generally, the ability to regulate people's behavior inside media organizations passed to those who paid the money, independently of its (il)legal form. The scope of power loosely corresponded to the share of the input resources. Thus advertisers, sponsors, investors, owners and media top managers have come to form a borderless continuum rather than five separate groups, with the middle category of investors melting into either of extremes. The vague system of rules also promotes the partial fusion of these types of actors.

However, what differentiates owners from advertisers, as well as from all other external agents (apart from ability to directly administrate), is their interest in the survival and general success of their media organizations, which makes them similar to media top managers. This feature raises the question: to which group of agents should owners really be ranked – external or internal? Russian experience shows that there are different kinds of owners, some of whom are closer to one category, and some – to the other. I will call "internal owners" the ones who own only media organizations and have no interests (especially political) outside the media industry, their goals being limited to getting income from their media business. "External owners" here will be those who, on the contrary, are interested first of all in their political capital or in development of other kinds of business for which they need the advertising-propaganda resource of mass media. They are not interested in the profitability of their media organizations as such. "Internal owners" are, therefore, inclined to practice financial control while leaving content and format to those who are authorized to be experts in it. "External owners," on the contrary, rather exercise control over content, only loosely overseeing commercial activities of media executives and sometimes even allowing for a certain "misuse of money." An example of an intermediate case is ownership of neighboring branches of industry (printing houses, telecommunications, paper producing enterprises etc).

This classification cuts across a more traditional typology of state, private and public media ownership. While the latter type is virtually unknown in Russia, the boundary between state and private domains, as shown in the previous chapters, was to a great extent blurred throughout the 1990s. Often a single media outlet was officially owned both by state and private organizations, which usually (though not always) meant that it was informally administered by a CIG as its real external owner or backer. However, the state-private distinction was still important when it came to limitations on the owners' influence. The character of these limitations is predominantly economic: when a private owner's expenses for a media organization exceed a certain threshold, it becomes unreasonable trying to influence it, for it no longer brings either economic or symbolic profit. State owners do not experience this kind of limitation. While state agents hold their positions, they always have their resources at hand and, therefore, may persist with their strategies much longer – this advantage finally made them the winners in the struggle for media, although this happened after the period studied here.

Back in the 1990s, Russia presented quite a specific, albeit not a unique combination of all listed types of ownership. In the West, when ownership is external to a media organization, it is usually in the hands of the State; or, if publicly owned, such media are nevertheless usually connected with the State through informal mechanisms. Private ownership is mostly internal; owners have no interests outside the media industry and thus do not use media as a vehicle for promotion of those interests. Influence patterns within these two formats have been widely studied: e.g. Schlesinger (1987) on government control; Tunstall and Palmer (1991) on business control. By contrast, cases of external private ownership (like *General Electric* and *NBC*) are less well studied. According to available data, it may be concluded that in the West interaction of private owners and the state takes place mostly through legal channels. For example, *CNN* (through *Time Warner*) has official representatives in the consulting committees of *USIA* (United State Information Agency), the essential propaganda organ on the USA (Winseck 1992). These representatives not only "consult" *USIA*, but also fund its programs (in this sense the situation is the reverse of that in Russia).

In the degree of formalization, interactions between Russian media barons and state agents resemble not those in the USA but rather those in Latin America, where such relations are shaped as situational negotiations, often between relatives. They only vaguely resemble formalized communication between the representatives of impersonal structures. In Brazil, for instance, frequencies were originally distributed without any legal rules, in exchange for political services (a similar situation could often be found in Eastern Europe in the 1990s (Sparks 1995: 13)). Furthermore, though the constitution of Brazil prohibited foreign investments in media, one of the companies, TV *Globo*, obtained such a privilege nevertheless. As a result it gained almost a monopoly position in the national media market – of course, in exchange for loyalty to the ruling elite (Fox 1997: 58).

Parallels with Russian practices are obvious. I have already mentioned signal transmission privileges for the three national TV channels, license extension to *TV–Center* and others; similar cases are met at all levels. All daily newspapers in St. Petersburg receive some form of support either from the governor or from the city council or from the administration of the representative of the president of the Russian Federation in the North-West region. Thus in Russia the stream of material support is directed not from the media representatives to state agents, as in the USA, but, rather, from state agents to the media.

One of the reasons for that is the different economic situation. In the USA some media corporations are so rich that state agents, perhaps, need them more than media need state agents; or, at least, they are equal partners. In Russia, media organizations are relatively poor, so that state representatives can and have to offer them financial support. Otherwise Russian media would first, have, partly died out, and, second, have turned into a yellow press, ignoring politics and depriving state agents of a propaganda channel.

However, a second and a more important reason is that in the 1990s Russia was mostly a country of external private/mixed ownership. Thus, respondent "Nikolai Bazarov," the chief editor of a Moscow newspaper, said:

BAZAROV: Our owner bought our newspaper to influence competitors, authorities, others, depending on interests...
INTERVIEWER: And then to convert it again into his income?

BAZAROV: Exactly. But already not in media business, but in – oil. To participate in privatization auctions and gain a ... milliard at once. In this sense Mister Berezovsky has a wonderfully profitable business. He bought newspapers to influence the authorities, to pressure the authorities, and from them he got all those commercial privileges that later turned into live money. And the fact that his paper or television he kept was unprofitable, did not bother him much. Especially because part of the losses, primarily on television, were incurred by the State, not by him personally. And he, at the State's expense, was broadcasting with Dorenko's[1] lips.

(Interview 36, January 2001)

Describing Russian media ownership, Brian McNair (2000: 88) compares Berezovsky and Gussinsky with other "global media barons such as Conrad Black, Rupert Murdoch, and Axel Springer" who also "hope that their newspapers influence the political climate in the countries where they operate, in ways favorable to their media businesses." But the important difference between Russian media owners of the 1990s and Murdoch *et al.*, noted by respondent Bazarov, was that the former often did *not* care about their media businesses: instead, they had their media organizations as intermediate keys in the chains of actions that were to lead to profits in quite different spheres. A first, positive, strategy here was to sell the loyalty of their publications to state agents in exchange for various benefits that they got from these agents and that had nothing to do with media. Another, negative, strategy was to "blackmail" or racketeer state agents and other competitors through their media, launching campaigns that either ruined the plans of their opponents or made them agree to compromise or comply.

The early 1990s was a brief period of conversion of media into what was planned to be a classical internal private ownership. The late 1990s, on the contrary, were dominated by nationalization of media. While representatives of unprofitable media usually did not mind being "swallowed" by the state, their more successful competitors (e.g. *NTV*) often showed resistance.

The mid-1990s, unlike the beginning and the end of the decade, was a time of division of media among CIGs, that is to either private or mixed (cross-institutional) external ownership of informal character. Such owners – apart from establishing their own media – recruited their "propaganda departments" from those media that had failed to survive as autonomous businesses. The recruitment might be of very different character – from completely enforced to completely voluntary. Thus, journalists of one of the St. Petersburg newspapers were urged by a "friend" of the deputy editor to donate him their shares in exchange for future investments that were promised orally but never followed up. The only columnist who objected to this project had to leave her job (Field notes 1:

17.01.1997). The indicative example of *Nezavisimaya Gazeta* is described by Ivan Zassoursky (1999: 60–80). *Nezavisimaya Gazeta* (*Independent Newspaper*) (*NG*) was established in 1990 when political independence was probably the most saleable product at the market of media products. Its initial circulation was 150,000 copies. After liberalization of prices and decline of popular interest in politics, *NG*, as all the others, faced dire financial straights. Its poor financial position caused a team of leading journalists to leave it and establish a competing publication that took a half of *NG*'s readership. Reluctant to sell the newspaper to a single external owner, its chief editor Tretiakov tried to maneuver among various sponsors, until in mid-1995 *NG*'s publication had to be suspended. A group of journalists headed by the deputy editor rebelled, organized voting for Tretyakov's dismissal and initiated negotiations with some of the most influential CIGs, in particular, with *ONEXIMbank*. Luckily for Tretyakov, *ONEXIM* also had competitors, who at that time were personified in Boris Berezovsky. The latter offered the dismissed editor his conditions, and they were accepted. After some legal procedures Tretiakov returned to the newspaper which reappeared in the fall of 1995.

I observed the outcome of a similar story in the *Vesti Starograda* newspaper, who had "got" a new chief editor half a year before my arrival. Despite general openness, none of the journalists dared to speak about his accession to his position, except a seventy-year old reporter "Semyon Starozhilov" who had begun his career under Stalin. Even he talked without recording. According to Starozhilov, when *Vesti Starograda* (*VS*), an old Soviet newspaper, was made a joint-stock company in early 1990s, it turned out that due to some mistakes in the documents the newspaper premises and equipment stayed the property of the city administration. This gave it the possibility of becoming one of the newspaper's founders and of appointing the chief editor. *Starogradian*, the local bank, became the other founder in exchange for future investments. But before anything could be accomplished, a group of *VS* journalists rebelled. A classmate of one of the rebels at that time occupied the position of the deputy mayor and, when the mayor went on a trip abroad, he issued a decree which replaced the old chief editor "Polkin" by the rebels' leader "Volosov." Polkin was not even informed about the decision, until the next day, when in the midst of the making-up process Volosov showed up in his office with the decree. Polkin gathered a meeting of the journalistic collective who voted against the new editor and managed to bring the mayor to one of the meetings upon his arrival from abroad. The mayor revoked the decree but, perhaps because the story took place half a year before the 1996 mayor elections, the rebel Volosov soon regained his position. In Starozhilov's view, Polkin himself contributed to the situation by being too tolerant: he had not fired the rebel team. The bank top management, who, like many *VS* journalists, regarded Volosov as a poor professional, suspended its investments. Before the elections *VS* published a number of articles of doubtful accuracy against the mayor's main competitor, but it did not save the incumbent from losing his position to the newcomer.

The new governor, in Starozhilov's opinion, was quite kind: he did not fire any of the newspaper workers, except Volosov. The latter was replaced by a candidate proposed by the bank, Nikolayev, the one who was imprudent enough to let a sociologist inside his editorial office. Niko-layev, for his part, quickly got rid of Volosov's team and brought in a whole bunch of new people. Those who remained got higher salaries, and the bank recommenced its investments. In the *VS* case, however, the mayor and the bank did not form a CIG and soon quarreled: the mayor, in fact, was a part of another CIG, which included another bank that had funded his electoral campaign.

ORT, *RTR* and *NTV*: the three differently owned giants

While the *VS* story illustrates the formation of one particular kind of media ownership (mixed state-private), the three national TV channels – *ORT*, *RTR* and *NTV* – are a good example of all major kinds of ownership and of the dynamic in this sphere in the 1990s, including such important patterns as privatization and nationalization. At the national level there was probably only Vladimir Gussinsky (*NTV*) who represented internal ownership and regarded his media holding as a source of direct income, although there is no reliable data on that. Some respondents claimed that Gussinksy was just as much a media-racketeer as anybody else, but was more cautious (Interviews 35, 41; Pankin 1999: 166). If so, there should be some signs of Gussinksy's successful business outside media, but there are none. The story about media-racketeering itself appeared during the anti-*NTV* campaign in 2000 in the rival media: *Media-MOST*, Gussinsky's holding of which *NTV* was the core, was accused of organizing an illegal intelligence service which was said to collect compromising data on many elite members. As noted in previous chapters, intelligence was a typical activity for security departments of many CIGs and, moreover, was neces-sary for the survival of any large-scale business – the business of selling "objective" news was no exception. Another condition for survival of busi-ness at the level for which Gussinsky had aimed was an alliance with powerful state agents – alliance which *Media-MOST* chose to be involved in, despite a risk of being later subordinated by its allies. To be fair, there is no convincing evidence that for Gussinsky it was just an inevitable evil, and not the final goal.

On the other hand, there are some facts indicating that Gussinksy's final goal was indeed internal ownership of the Western type where media production was to become a source of profit, and the objectivity of news was to turn into a product to exchange for ratings, and then to revenues from commercials. Gussinsky would hardly have begun building a full-scale media industry around *NTV*, if he had not viewed it as a commercial enterprise – at least his colleagues who made media business as politics, did not develop it in such a way. Gussinsky, on the contrary, started a cinema studio and serial production, a design studio, a number of distributor firms; his holding was the first to launch a private satellite and to start satellite TV. As a Moscow journalist noted, "Otherwise why were they going to put *NTV* up to the New York exchange by 1998? Quite consciously they were moving to a more or less transparent budget, and clear financial indexes, and to possible profitability" (Interview 35, January 2001).

Thus, *NTV* leaders tried to rely on various resources not controlled by the Russian government – foreign support: symbolic (received for the image of fighter for press freedom), financial (search for a buyer for *NTV*'s shares in the West) and other (e.g. dual citizenship of Gussinsky, his status of the Gibraltar tax resident). The launching of their own satellite is a link in the same chain: it could have provided independence from the State signal. Ironically, it became the reason for *NTV*'s major difficulty: it was for this project that *Media-MOST* received credit from *Vnesheconombank*, that a year later demanded it back ahead of schedule. So, if *Media-MOST* was an attempt to develop a large-scale media syndicate as a predominantly commercial enterprise, it may be considered unsuccessful.

Another national TV channel, *RTR*, is a classic case of external state ownership. In the new economic situation its management faced the same difficulties as similar companies in other countries: a combination of financial self-support with the informational will of the owner. As Yuezhi Zhao has put it with reference to China, such media have to dance "skillfully between the party line and the bottom line" (Zhao 2000: 12). Unlike their western colleagues, many Russian journalists regard both goals legitimate: some sincerely believe that the State has a right to carry its opinion to the people and, therefore, to own and control the media (Interview 19 and other interviews; see also Yuskevits 2000). Besides, unlike state-owned media in some other countries (e.g. *Doordashan*, an Indian state company), for *RTR* economic goals were secondary throughout the 1990s. Perhaps a partial explanation is that state agents, while being able to entirely control content, have had few resources with which to punish economic "misbehavior": *RTR*, or *Peterburg – 5 Kanal*, or any other such company, cannot be announced bankrupt or otherwise closed down, since this would deprive their owners of a channel of propaganda. One can, of course, change top executives, but Russian experience suggests that the newcomers would be hardly less likely to "misbehave" financially than their predecessors. Furthermore, quick rotation of top managers, produced by the owners' desire to find the right figures, usually reduced both the economic and the information efficiency of the company. The new head usually brought personnel changes and other reorganization, while their use of funds for the company's development was not guaranteed.

Thus, in 1998 the State Auditing Chamber revealed that during the previous six years, *RTR* had participated under three different heads in the starting of fifteen firms and made "monetary and estate contributions" to their authorized capitals. Investment records had not been preserved, and *RTR* had received no dividends. By 1998 *RTR* office also housed eleven exterior firms that paid no rent (Rykovtseva 1998: 13). It seems plausible that such favorable conditions were not given to these various organizations as humanitarian aid. Furthermore, it can be assumed that the potential to profit from access to public resources was granted to the State media executives deliberately, as a kind of payment in the situation of shortage of official funding from the state budget: the continuous absence of punishment for financial "misbehavior" suggests this conclusion (see Chapter 3).

The case of Berezovsky, backer of *ORT*, the third national channel, unlike the two analyzed above, looks like neither external nor internal ownership, and thus deserves special consideration. In the mid-1990s, when Berezovsky's influence at the channel was at its peak, he could hardly be called an owner at all, since formally his share in *ORT* was relatively small: from 8 percent announced initially to 21 percent later (Interview 35; Mukhin 2000: 108). Throughout the second half of the 1990s there were no reliable data on Berezovsky's share; rumors circulated saying that this figure could have reached a much bigger proportion, e.g. through dummy persons and firms. The situation remained unclear until in 2000 Berezovksy was "invited" to sell his share to the State and shocked the public by professing himself the owner of a 49 percent share.

Until then, Berezovsky's practices, originating from Soviet traditions of political communication, had been based on manipulation with complicated exchange relations between multiple actors, usually individuals. The profit was absorbed mostly from the result of this intermediary activity, not from monetary investments. Like the state agents, he regarded television not as a source of direct income, but as a means of getting information/symbolic advantages that could be later converted into other kinds of capital. Berezovsky was one of the first to start actively attaching media organizations as propaganda appendages to his cross-institutional group. This strategy was extremely successful until Putin's accession to power.

Again, there is a shortage of reliable evidence about the concrete mechanisms of influence employed by Berezovsky on *ORT*. Expert opinion has been based mostly on assumptions and on shared beliefs that circulated among the Moscow elite; it was considered so obvious that it did not need any proof. On the one hand, it was widely believed that Berezovsky exchanged loyalty of *ORT* to the government for privileges for his business. Evidence about these privileges is openly available: enormous import taxes on foreign cars gave a big advantage to *VAZ*, the nearly monopolistic Russian producer of outdated automobiles, and to *LogoVAZ*, its dealership founded and headed by Berezovsky. This was combined with exclusive tax privileges awarded to *LogoVAZ* for … import of the very same cars, in the first instance – elite models (Lilin 1998: 52).

On the other hand, in order to sell loyalty of any media organization, one has to control it. How can this be accomplished without significant monetary or property investments? On this matter, there was another belief that Berezovsky ensured such control through his advocates in the Kremlin, which leads to a paradox: if both privileges and control over TV were received from Kremlin officials, what did Berezovsky offer them in return?

Even high-ranking Moscow journalists and experts close to the elite were not sure in answering this question. They usually came out with some general phrases, surprised at the question itself: the situation seemed so natural for them that explanation was not needed. One of the respondents, a chief editor of a Moscow newspaper, said thoughtfully: "the State can't box your ears when it doesn't exist," and later he added "Under the condition of a disintegrating state, rules do not exist. That is why he [Berezovsky] owned something like a 20 percent share of *ORT*, but everybody said it was Berezovsky's channel. While the controlling share belonged to the State. The State did not take care of it, but Berezovsky did" (Interview 36).

One possible solution to this paradox is pointed at by Ivan Zassoursky (1999: 148): to control a media organization without much investment one had "to buy people, not the company" which is much cheaper – according to Zassoursky, this was the essence of Russian privatization in general (cf Hallin's clientelism and "privatization of the state" addressed in Chapter 3). He points at the system of "double salaries" at *ORT*; generally this meant that official salaries were supplemented by "black cash" payments for "good" employees; this is, of course, by no means characteristic only of *ORT*. In this case the serious support of state agents might have been needed for Berezovsky only at the decisive moment – the moment of privatization of the channel.

A more convincing explanation, though not contradicting Zassoursky's, is offered by Anna Kachkaeva (2001): Berezovsky "was allowed to use *Sibneft* to fund *ORT*."[2] *Sibneft*, one of the richest oil companies in Russia, was in the 1990s owned by Berezovsky together with Roman Abramovich. The expression "was allowed to use" suggests Kachkaeva was referring to some extremely favorable conditions in the privatization of this enterprise that Berezovsky might have received in exchange for something – for example, an obligation to rule *ORT* "in the right way." That the biggest state enterprises in Russia were privatized for prices much lower than their real value is generally acknowledged, so the deal described does not look unrealistic. Bearing in mind its hypothetical character, the story of the *ORT* privatization may be reconstructed in the following way.

As described earlier, late 1994 to early 1995, when the privatization of

Channel 1 was being fought over, was a time of increasing lack of funds for both national state channels, and of Yeltsin's decreasing popularity. It was even more undermined by the start of the first Chechen war and by the negative reaction of the more and more influential *NTV*. Meanwhile, the presidential elections were to take place in early 1996. In this situation the president was offered a promising and democratic looking plan: state-owned *Channel 1*, the most popular TV channel in Russia, is transformed into *Public Russian Television* (Russian abbreviation – *ORT*), and a popular talk-show host and political commentator Vladislav Listev with a reputation as an independent fighter for press freedom is appointed the General director. This is the "democratic" part of the plan. The rest is: the controlling share stays with the State (which makes the term "Public" in the title of the new company hollow); a 49 percent share is privatized in favor of certain persons and organizations; in exchange they promise to provide Yeltsin with a good rating through the right use of the half-privatized channel. *Channel 1*, by that time fragmented and poorly admin-istered, could not have fulfilled this task. Therefore, there might be a hope that private managers would make the then messy organization a prof-itable one, so that Yeltsin's team could get a propaganda resource for free.

The first holders of the privatized share of *ORT* became Boris Bere-zovsky's *LogoVAZ* (8 percent) and the so-called *ORT* Bank Consortium, which included *SBS Agro* bank, *MENATEP*, *Alfa* bank and *Obyediny-onny* bank (Fossato and Kachkaeva 1998). While the latter soon became dominated by Berezovsky, the rest represented other nationally influential CIGs; thus initially the situation did not look monopolized by Berezovsky. However, his closest ally Sergei Lissovsky with his *Premier SV* advertising agency was to become *ORT*'s exclusive media-seller – that is, a structure monopolistically allocating commercials on the channel at a certain rate of interest. Lissovsky also headed a show-business firm *Liss's* which means he might have had an additional interest in access to the most popular channel.

In any case, *ORT* was registered at the Moscow registration chamber as a joint stock company on February 28, 1995. Next day, on March 1, Vladislav Listev was killed, and the investigation on this case has, of course, produced no result. It is known that Listev had stood out for a six-month ban on commercials on *ORT*, and for restrictions on them after that as well – in compliance with the idea of public television. This fact was the reason why after his death the Moscow Procuracy (subordinate to the strongest of Berezovsky's rivals Moscow mayor Yuri Luzhkov) inspected the flats and offices of Lissovsky and Berezovsky, but this was the end of the story. Lissovsky was appointed head of the *ORT-advertising* depart-ment, and in 1996 he became one of the key figures in designing Yeltsin's electoral campaign.

According to Kachkaeva, the amount of money, contributed to *ORT* by Berezovsky in 1995 can be estimated as approximately US$50 million;

they were spent, not as an afterthought, on enormous salaries for key figures of the channel. "And then, as was said by his financial right hand Badri Patarkatzshvili, we did not stop [*ORT*] from investing advertising revenues into its development. But we did not invest ourselves" (Kachkaeva 2001). This, in Kachkaeva's opinion, is one of the reasons why in 2000 Berezovsky was offered exactly the same amount for his 49 percent share, while its real value must have been at least five times more.

The ease with which Berezovsky was removed from control over *ORT* after the advent of a stronger president indicates that his power must have had a poor foundation and might really have been built on manipulating the contradictions in the fragmented elite. As Kachkaeva (2001) put it, "in fact Berezovsky had been only *allowed* to rent the first button of the country. Allowed. Because he had never really funded it.... And when there emerged a need to get rid of Berezovsky's services, he was removed."

Toward a typology of media ownership in Russia

The three different types of ownership exemplified by the three national TV channels do not include private external ownership, widely spread in the media less significant than national television. All types are summarized in Table 5.1.

Among media outlets representing private external ownership in this study, along with many small-scale media established by entrepreneurs usually for electoral purposes, there is the newspaper edited by respondent "Bazarov" who mentioned that his owner was connected with oil. At the national level classical private ownership has been nearly impossible, since any large-scale business in Russia would demand the creation of a full-size CIG. Therefore, private internal ownership also exists mostly beyond large media and beyond politics, and has been more and more represented by entertainment or professional publications. Simultaneously, the proportion of media externally owned by the state has been

Table 5.1 Types of media ownership

Type of ownership	External media as propaganda resource	Internal media as business
Private	Usually small-scale media established by entrepreneurs, as a rule for electoral purposes	Profitable non-political media (tabloids, FM stations, etc.)
State	*RTR*	–
Mixed	*ORT* 1995–2000 "*Vesti Starograda*" newspaper	?
By CIGs	*TVK-6* Krasnoyarsk 1995–2000	*NTV* 1995–2000, *TV-6* before 2001

growing. State internal ownership is a contradiction in terms: it is hard to imagine a State indifferent to its media's propaganda potential, so even if it is concerned about profitability, revenues are a secondary goal. Exceptions may be found only when state ownership turns into a mere formality, but I know of no such examples in Russia, unless they are very marginal. They may however be found in other countries. Thus, Zhao recounts a practice of creation of "quasi-independent" media in China: since only specially authorized state and party bodies have the right to establish media there, in the early 1990s some (in fact non-state) agents tricked the state, unofficially obtaining licenses on behalf of such authorized bodies (for a certain fee or interest), but in fact running their media on their own (Zhao 2000: 8).

Media owned by CIGs may be registered as private, state or mixed, but in fact are managed by the CIG leader through his subordinates and on the basis of CIG's resources, including economic capital and violence exercised, if necessary, by CIG's security departments. If a CIG sees its media only or mostly as a propaganda-advertising resource, such ownership is external; here Krasnoyarsk *TVK* of the Bykov period is a good example. If a CIG sees its media as a business, this is internal ownership. A classic case is *TV-6* of the period when it was owned by Boris Berezovsky, but before it gave refuge to the out-of-favor *NTV* journalists. The almost entirely entertainment channel *TV-6* was a commercial project alien to any information wars.

Finally, *ORT* is such a special case that it has been treated separately in the table. It could be called the television of Berezovsky's CIG, but he did not manage it alone. Alternatively, it could be called the channel of "the main CIG" headquartered in the Kremlin, but Yeltsin, of course, never directly managed it, nor was it managed on his behalf solely in his interests. Thus it can be assigned to mixed or shared ownership of the weak and fractured state, on the one hand, and, on the other, a CIG, that was powerful enough not only to equal, but sometimes to substitute the disintegrated state.

It is not difficult to see that this typology takes account mostly of methods of acquisition of media organizations by owners and of their general goals, but not of concrete day-to-day mechanisms of imposition of owners' will on journalists. Scarce evidence about the latter, obtained through available sources, suggests that this is achieved through editors and other top figures at the media organizations, most often – through their heads. Since it is they, not owners, who are represented in my sample of respondents, I will consider these practices in Chapter 9 devoted to media top managers.

6   Advertisers

"Russian media should shrink by 70 percent," was the verdict of one of my Moscow respondents: he referred to the estimate of legal media profits made by the Union of Journalists in 2000. According to it, as already mentioned in Chapter 2, advertisement and sales revenues together with legal state support comprised only about 30 percent of the total Russian media budget (Yakovenko 2001). Thus in 1990s earnings from advertising were far from covering expenses of the Russian mass media. Even those media that managed to exist on advertising only – i.e. managed to be profitable – could not miss its shortage. These were the media that either avoided support from external owners and sponsors (which was rare), or simply could not count on it because their format was unusable as a propaganda resource (e.g. erotic tabloid or rock-music radio). If they failed to attract advertising, such media, unlike those suitable for propaganda, ceased to exist. This means that for purely commercial media the situation was even more precarious. The practices of media professionals who emerged from this situation are the subject of this chapter.

A meager pie of legal advertising

The modest development of advertising in 1990s has several causes. The main one is that the relatively low (compared to Western countries) purchasing capacity of the population made the promotion of goods ineffective. Second, as a totally new branch of economics and a new cultural form, advertising needed some time to be assimilated both by consumers and potential advertisers. Third, Russian legislation was quite unfavorable to the development of advertising. In particular, it regarded the major part of advertising expenses not as production expenses, but as made from taxable income (Interview 29; Dunkerley 2003). Also, newspapers in which advertising content exceeded 40 percent were taxed higher, although 40 percent is considered quite low even in richer Western countries: there commercial content averages 58 percent (Dunkerley 2003). These restrictions were not abolished until 2002.

Shortage of advertising funds, on the one hand, made media producers agree to terms of advertisers without much bargaining, and on the other – stimulated the latter to look for cheaper ways to inform the target audience about themselves. Combined together, these two factors led to the development of hidden advertising. However, "classical" methods of advertisers' influencing upon mass media also existed. The most common technique, not unique to Russia, has been cancellation of an order for advertising as a punishment for critical statements about advertisers, made in news or publicist programs/articles. There is insufficient evidence on how common these practices have been in Russia; most respondents could not recollect such cases, but not because Russian advertisers are indifferent to criticism. On the contrary, as claimed, for example, by respondent "Pavel Yakutovich," an insider from a leading advertising agency, a critical statement about an advertiser could appear only by mistake:

> The channel won't debate with them [with advertisers], and, of course, if it does such an absurd thing – somebody of journalists says this sort of nonsense, and – this goes on the air, it will be a small conflict they'll try to hush up. To settle somehow ... well, meet – managers will meet with advertisers, will sit together with a cup ... a glass of whisky, and settle everything. It can't be, say, of purposeful nature. The channel won't do that on purpose.... The thing is the advertiser gives it money. And it is so scarce nowadays.
>
> (Interview 29, January 2001)

Another respondent, "Galina Minskaya," made a similar statement and told me a story fully confirming the hypothetical scheme of "Yakutovich." An Egyptian tourist agency organized a free tour to Egypt for a group of journalists. After that all the journalists wrote positive reports, because PR-men "worked them over," except a woman correspondent of a magazine devoted to traveling, who wrote what in her opinion had to be written, as retold by Minskaya: "dirty ragamuffins beg for money, you cannot hide from them anywhere, service is poor, I liked nothing there." The problem of the magazine was that it had signed a long-term contract for a full-page advertisement with that Egyptian company for a large sum. The Egyptian company decided to cancel their advertising order.

> Then [the managers of the magazine] requested an analysis of this article from a research ... institute of sociology, how it affects the reader from the psychological point of view. Because the article was really funny.... Absolutely independent experts wrote: yes, there is something negative, but nevertheless it can draw readers' attention, make them take interest in Egypt; as for the negative aspects mentioned there, they do not ... do not indispose people from going to Egypt. Yes, this is a personal subjective point of view. But you shouldn't make things sweet all the way. OK, our chief editor of that

magazine together with the general director go to the office of the Egyptian agency with this report, well, they had a long talk coaxing them there, and they settled the conflict at last ... and then, at their own expense now, published another article about Egypt, this time what the Egyptians wanted to see.

(Interview 33, January 2001)

This story also illustrates the practice of combining hidden and open advertising, typical for advertisers. Russian media managers also initiated such combinations: they quite commonly urged advertisers to place commercials in their media offering them free "ordered" articles in addition. Thus, in the 1990s the volume of hidden advertising seemed inversely proportional to the degree to which relations in the advertising market were institutionalized; and the institutionalization, in its turn, depended on the amount of money in this market. The most formalized relations in this field were in Moscow, that, as mentioned earlier, accounted for about three-quarters of the country's advertising budget. The situation in the provinces was greatly different and favored development of informal influence of advertising upon news production.

By the late 1990s Moscow boasted of the structure of an advertising market corresponding to "the Western standards," according to which it had been constructed. In such a standard scheme, relations between advertisers and mass media are mediated by three kinds of agencies: media sellers, media buyers and creative agencies. Media sellers buy advertising space or time from media in bulk, and then retail it to media buyers for higher prices. Media buyers represent the interests of advertisers, and try to buy time and space in mass media in accordance with media-plans, developed by them for advertising campaigns for a particular company or a certain product. Creative agencies stand separately; they produce commercials and other advertising products. Existence of so-called "agencies of the full circle" is also possible.

This scheme, even when it evenly balances the interests of all participants, already presupposes compromising between them, and thus gives advertisers room for exercising a certain influence on media content. In Russia the situation was most difficult for media. For them, the ideal scheme would be such a dominance in the market that would make all other participants struggle for advertising space and time despite the possible negative coverage of some advertisers. For the latter, the ideal would be quite the opposite: it is media buyers who should determine where to place advertisements, aiming at the most efficient promotion of products. Instead, the balance of power in Moscow, and later in the Russian advertising market in general, became upset in favor of media sellers (Koneva 1998: 17; Interview 29). First, some of the leading media sellers introduced the practice of buying exclusive rights to sell all advertising space or time of a given media outlet; this deprived media of control of their sales, and of possibilities to balance between different advertisers in order to avoid too much bias in their content. Second, acquiring exclusive rights in a number of media, sellers started making media buyers place commercials of their clients in all media of a given seller, and not only in the media regarded the most effective by those clients. Third, the high profitability of such entrepreneurship soon led to concentration in the media selling sector in Moscow, and advertising time of the national channels around 1997 became split between a duopoly of seller agencies: *Premier SV* of Sergei Lissovsky, who controlled *ORT* and *TV-6*, and *Video International* (*VI*) owned by Yuri Zapol and Mikhail Lesin, who controlled *RTR* and *NTV*. It can easily be traced that in that period advertising campaigns of clients working with *Premier SV* were shifted to *ORT* and *TV-6*, and those collaborating with *VI* – to *RTR* and *NTV*.

Nevertheless, the duopoly aroused a sort of competition; but the events of 1997–8 turned this duopoly into a monopoly. In 1997 information began circulating within the advertising market that the national channels, and especially *ORT*, wanted to get rid of exclusive media sellers and sell their time without intermediaries. In consequence of these rumors, *Video International*, a stronger player, offered *ORT* to sell its advertising time for the coming 1998 at a price much higher than *Premier SV* had suggested. In order to retake *ORT* from *VI*, Lissovsky had to pay much higher rates for *ORT* advertising time and, consequently, to raise prices for advertisers as well. Then the 1998 crisis broke out, the advertising market was devastated, and *Premier SV* went bankrupt (Zassoursky 1999: 200–1). As a result, *VI* got all four channels, plus the *STS* network.

In this situation *VI*'s ability to dictate terms to advertisers increased greatly: now *VI* could give instructions on what channels advertising should and, what is more important, should *not* be placed. One such channel became *NTV* during the campaign aimed at Gussinsky's removal: just before 2000 *VI* unexpectedly terminated their contract with it, still keeping 75 percent of the advertising market (Interview 29). By that time Mikhail Lesin, the new Minister for media, had already left all official positions in *VI*. Nevertheless, analyzing the reasons for this sanction, we come to the production of news and to *NTV*'s political position. Breaking the contract in the middle of the season made little economic sense for *VI*: it lost one of the most popular channels thereby. On the other hand, a political rationale may easily be detected: besieged by politicized creditors and deprived of stable advertising flow, *NTV* had to hurriedly create a media seller of its own. This seller, small and unknown, could not compete with *VI* for advertisers without selling *NTV* time at extremely low prices. Therefore, *VI*, seemingly acting against its own interest, won in the long run: in return for its loyalty its partner within the State (could it be Lesin?) must have provided favorable climate for its monopolistic position and super-profits, supposedly not forgetting to bargain about his own interest. Thus Moscow, the center of market reforms, was also the first to acquire a highly concentrated advertising market merged with the state. Since most national Russian media are located in Moscow, this applied to the national advertising market as well.

Hidden advertising: invisible market of visions

In the regions the situation in the advertising market was very different; in 2000 it still resembled the situation in Moscow in 1993–5. The amount of money circulating in the regions left no space for such a number of inter-mediaries as in Moscow. Channels, as a rule, sold their time themselves, basing on their own rates, which did not always relate to ratings (Pushkarskaya 1998: 20–4). Often separate shows themselves sought for commercials to cover their expenses and to be placed at an adjacent time. Such programs went off air as soon as they failed to find advertising. Many newspapers hardly knew their audience at all, engaging in arbitrary adver-tisement allocation and content production. Hidden advertising, euphemistically called *zakaz*, was extremely common. It mainly existed in two forms: at the level of the media organization's management, and at the level of individual journalists.

The most financially stable media organizations were those where man-agers could control the flow of hidden advertising. In such case revenues could be directed to the development of the company; and success of the company, in its turn, entails a decrease in the share of hidden advertising, first of all, of small contracts. This happens because such a media company is not interested in losing its reputation as an independent outlet for a low price, since "independence" at this stage of development becomes a com-modity and plays its role in providing success. In the opinion of respon-dent "Gorsky," an employee of the public relations department of a big metallurgic company, such a media organization still can be bought, but the price is too high for most claimants to the advertising-propagandist resource to consider the purchase reasonable. Such media resemble those of the Western countries.

Hidden advertising at the level of individual journalists, often labeled by media professionals with the strange word *dzhinsa* (derived from English "jeans," possibly a reference to the function of jeans in the Soviet black market), was a common practice in companies where the manage-ment was unable or unwilling to set up control over it. These, first, were state media where salaries were fixed at a low level, and management was concerned with keeping skilful employees, rather than raising profitability (to which, incidentally, the state owner might object). In other situations, as, for example, in *Nezavisimaya Gazeta* before 1995, the management wanted to keep autonomy of the organization, and so prevented "whole-sales" of advertising space to one big customer. Because of this position of management, the *NG* journalists began writing *dzhinsa* circumvent their superiors, and this also undermined the independence of the paper (Zassoursky 1999: 68–71). In some extremely badly off publications journalists lived almost entirely on ordered articles (Field notes 1: 18.02.1997). Thus, *dzhinsa* is a form of latent privatization of media organizations by individual journalists.

Hidden advertising, as already mentioned, has become a practice initiated by both sides. For advertisers it is cheaper, since instead of a special commercial an ordinary story is produced, its cost being already included in news production costs. Furthermore, many advertisers consider this form of advertisement more effective: a story presented as "genuine" news or independent opinion gains more trust of the audience, so it is easier for media producers to find customers for such advertising. In many media the process of taking orders for *zakaz* quickly became quite open for all interested parties.

In one of the observed TV companies information about "hidden" advertising was placed on a special board in the news room. In the list of other news stories these stories were marked with the word "*zakaz.*" Orders were taken through the commercial department, with official rates and a system of discounts for bulk buyers. Besides small presents from the advertisers (e.g. beer from a brewery), the rank-and-file journalists got a certain percentage from each order covered, up to 20 percent, if the reporter producing the story had found the advertiser him/herself.

Of course, advertisers are often not aware beforehand whether a particular media company takes hidden advertising or not, and if so, whether they have any special reasons to betray the advertiser to the public. Therefore the initial offer is a bit risky as in any illegitimate activity. My respondents recounted that to solve this problem advertisers usually tried to find informal contacts with representatives of mass media. This is one of the reasons why journalists were often taken on as press secretaries and public relations managers: they could use old acquaintances among their former colleagues. However, in other cases deals were made quite openly. A public relations manager from a university in "Starograd" told me how she got involved in hidden advertising for the first time. Planning a presentation at her university and having no experience in contacting media, she just called one of the local TV companies and suggested this event as the material for a news story, plainly saying she could pay for it. "We talked quite openly," she testified with surprise, "and bargained on the phone." Besides the representative of the commercial department, the reporter and the head of the newsroom took part in the deal. Participants agreed $150 for one story shown twice. They also agreed to mention a firm which partly sponsored the presentation and let the educational establishment "prepare speakers." Thus the story suited the interests of both the TV company and the advertiser.

Would this event have made a story if the PR manager had not offered the money? It might have gone either way. Thus, one of the newscasts of *STV* that I observed, contained two almost identical stories about

Student's Day celebrated in two different universities: one of them was an ordinary news story, and the other – an ordered one. The reason for the different approach was that one of the universities was rich and able to pay, and the other was poor, and journalists had time to fill.

As we can see, at the level of regional mass media it is more difficult than in Moscow to distinguish an advertiser from a sponsor and from a source of information. Sometimes media organizations refused to publish news relating to a "solvent" source, if this source did not pay for it (even if the event met journalists' definition of newsworthiness). In other cases a source refused to give the required information, if there was no promise to insert elements of advertising into the story. For example, *PTV* journalists gave up a soft news story about a famous Christmas tree decorator, because the director of the factory where the man worked demanded a full advertisement of his enterprise.

While the cases that I observed in my research are relatively minor, in the late 1990s, and especially in the beginning of the next decade, institutionalization of hidden advertisement grew to a much larger scale. In 2000–3 it was already vigorously discussed in the press itself; some publications even published lists of informal rates for hidden advertisement in various media (see Punanov and Loginov 2000; Svarovsky 2002; Kornilov and Rzhevsky 2003). Those who published such lists were themselves included in the lists published by others. In 2001 *Stringer* magazine published a whole series of monthly overviews of "PR" campaigns (that is, informational wars with hidden positive and negative advertisements) and their estimated budgets (see e.g. overview of April 2001: "Osnovniye..." 2001). The highest rates were, of course, on national TV and amounted from $3,500 for a story to $35,000 for a whole talk-show. Hidden advertising in the Internet was said not to exceed $50. Regional media costs were much cheaper. According to my observations, in St. Petersburg local TV news the amount could be $100–150 for a story. My observation also gives a crude idea about the share of hidden advertisement in the total amount of news: stories were ordered quite often, but not every day, and not more than one in a newscast. Of course, this does not represent the general situation in Russia.

A brilliant proof of the pervasiveness of hidden advertisement in media was a story that became known as the *PROMACO* provocation. In February 2001 the *PROMACO* public relations agency from St. Petersburg offered twenty-one national and Moscow newspapers a fictitious story about the opening of a new electronic supermarket at a non-existent address. Thirteen newspapers published the story as hidden advertisement – that is, having got the payment, they presented it as genuine news. Three newspapers recommended that *PROMACO* place the story as a legal advertisement, four requested additional information, and one published the story for free. After that *PROMACO* disclosed its action in the press, publishing the rates of all thirteen newspapers and the wording used by them in their contracts with the agency. The definitions given to the published product by the newspapers involved ranged from "news story" to vague "publication" to plain "advertisement." The list of those who used hidden advertisement included the two leading Russian "yellow" dailies and the leading "yellow" weekly, several supposedly "high quality" newspapers, and the official newspaper of the Russian government. *PROMACO* addressed the Ministry for antimonopoly policy with a request to punish both the agency itself and the thirteen media outlets. The agency also held a press conference explaining the goal of the provocation. In the opinion of the agency representatives, PR information should be published for free, but having discovered that this was definitely not the practice in Moscow, the agency decided to attract public attention to the problem.

The story indeed was full of resonances. However, its consequences were, perhaps, not exactly what *PROMACO* had planned. First of all, hidden advertising, of course, did not cease to exist; on the contrary, it became a more overt practice. The amount of fines that media could be charged by current legislation was far less than the amount of their revenues. Second, although the agency managed to attract some attention to itself, this did not last long: very soon *Kommersant* publishing house was being accused by other media of the organization of this provocation, while *PROMACO* was said to be a puppet firm. For this, however, only indirect evidence exists. *Kommersant Daily* newspaper was the one which covered the story earlier and in more detail than others. Furthermore, none of the *Kommersant* publications published the story for money, and only one secondary magazine *Client* published it for free, which gave *Kommersant Daily* a basis for its claim to objectivity. Unlike hidden advertising, free publishing of such materials is not illegal, so, if indeed the action was generated by *Kommersant*, its risk was minimal.

Throughout the 1990s, especially at the beginning of the decade, and especially in poor markets, advertising for money co-existed with different non-monetary forms of exchange, by which mass media or individual journalists were provided with services (medical, transport, information etc.), depending on the resources the source possessed. Usually this method of payment was used by state agents, but the story of the Egyptian tourist agency shows that private sources could act in a similar way as well. Until 1995–6 this situation was typical not only for the regions, but for Moscow as well. According to Sergei Dorenko, a popular *ORT* anchor, around 1992–4:

> ... the stories went on the air in exchange for a car to be repaired; when the boss said, "Valya is moving to a new flat, she needs furniture to be carried, so we are putting this story in the newscast. She'll get two thousands dollars. She'll take one and a half, and give five hundred to our fund." There were special managers responsible for

corruption. I personally attended a meeting at a TV company, where corruption managers reported: "the number of stories produced is this, the number of our children sent to summer camps for this money is that, the number of protective iron doors installed in our employees' flats is . . . etc."

(Dorenko 1998: 10)

Political promotion: advertising or propaganda?

Finally, a few words should be said about "hidden political advertising," widely spread both in Moscow and beyond, and, according to experts of the Union of Journalists, constituting a lion's share of the concealed 70 percent of media budgets. Political advertising is usually referred to as propaganda, but the mode of its existence in Russia has been very similar to that of any hidden advertising. Journalists themselves have come to call it with the same word – *zakaz* – adding the adjective *political*. Political and commercial advertisers have often been serviced by the same public relations and advertising agencies. However, some differences may be also observed.

Being cyclical, political advertising intensified during elections and decreased between them. Pre-election periods were a time of fierce struggle not only of political players for media, but also of media organizations for political advertisers. Some outlets welcomed everybody who paid, others tried to make exclusive contracts. As a Krasnoyarsk political consultant claims, not without approval, some advanced media offered "package services," not only providing promotion of the advertiser, but also promising to block publication of any discrediting material about him/her (Agafonov 2000). Various forms of barter deals have already been described in connection with commercial advertising earlier in this chapter, and in connection with state agents in Chapter 3.

Pre-election periods were also a time of proliferation not only of "genuine" newspapers that, although established for political reasons, sometimes endured and collected some readership, but also of entirely "fake" publications. Once in the *Vesti Starograda* newspaper I witnessed a conversation between a journalist and her friend, a sociologist, who said she had been offered "to falsify a newspaper." When asked what it meant, she explained she had to make an edition with fictitious readers' letters and sociological polls, entirely supportive of a candidate to the local legislative assembly. The paper then had to be distributed for free (indeed, on the eve of elections mail boxes are usually full of such free politicized press). She regretted that due to some legal reason the elections were being postponed, together with the enormous honorarium promised to her. Having listened to the sociologist, the journalist said she had also done this kind of work, but only once and for "a decent person" – and she named the leader of one of the most established reformist (democratic) parties in Russia. She was proud that sometimes she could speak to him in a very tough manner and edit his texts (Field notes 1: 18.02.1997).

Political advertising, characterized by bigger stakes and, therefore, by more aggressive strategies, seldom involved exchange relations only and often produced various coercive and semi-coercive relationships. Exchange could be imposed not only on media by state agents and other political advertisers, but visa versa as well. Agafonov (2000) describes the practice of media using their informal connections with candidates to pressure their electoral headquarters to work with them. One of my respondents also told a story that when a person he knew decided to run for mayor in a small town, he was visited by representatives of a local newspaper who demanded $250,000. Otherwise they threatened to drown him in *kompromat*. If paid, they promised not to publish anything bad, though they warned him that for this little money nothing good would be published either.

Owners, advertisers and sources: separate groups or a continuum?

Upon a closer look at two groups of economic agents – owners and advertisers – it becomes apparent that they have many similarities. Simultaneously, anticipating the next chapter, I would like to draw a parallel between advertisers and sources of journalistic information. Advertisers, therefore, are an intermediate category. Weak advertisers are closer to sources: although the former use economic capital, while the latter do not, both directly provide material for media content. Engagement of both in intricate types of exchange with journalists (including barter, unequal and delayed transactions) blurs the boundary between the two. The advertisers–sources continuum is shown in Table 6.1.

Although empirically hardly separable, hidden advertising should be analytically distinguished from unrecognized exchange with sources. The former is explicit exchange, concealed from third parties, not from the participants who recognize it as illegitimate. The latter is most often an implicit exchange aimed not at the benefit of a particular journalist, but at a "better" organization of news production. If such exchange is recognized, it is usually interpreted as friendship or mutual help and thus

Table 6.1 Advertisers–sources continuum

Mode of payment	Resulting product
Open (legal) payment	Advertisement
Concealed payment	Hidden advertisement
Unrecognized exchange	Bound news/comment
Free	"Genuine" news/"independent" comment

regarded as quite legitimate. These relations will be considered in further detail in the next chapter on sources, and in Chapter 8 on rank-and-file journalists.

Strong advertisers are closer to owners, especially if we juxtapose hidden advertising and external ownership as shown in Table 6.2. Divorcing "classical" advertising and owners is less problematic: though both "own" economic capital, owning money and owning an organization, as already noted in the previous chapter, is not the same. The latter involves much more enforcement than the former. It is true that an owner of an organization interacts with the rest of the market on the basis of exchange, but in his communication with those "owned" exchange relations are supplemented, if not substituted, by those of subjection/subordination. So, while an owner can impose his/her will on all subordinated and, as one might say, on the organization as a whole, advertisers can control only its "pieces," certain time and space slices. That is why in its classical form advertising resource is much weaker.

The existence of hidden advertising and external ownership makes the situation much more complicated. "Retail" hidden advertisers hardly differ from their legal "colleagues." But when a media outlet starts offering "exclusive package services," taking obligation not to publish anything negative about an advertiser, and especially when such services grow into long-term contracts, the advertiser gradually turns into a latent sponsor or backer. At this stage s/he already engages in giving direct instructions concerning media content and personnel, that is, does what a regular owner would also do. However, this kind of sponsor cares little about the media organization's ability to make ends meet, and prefers to buy another one if the previous one has gone bankrupt. The media organization, in its turn, may at any time choose to change its strategic partner and, for example, sell itself to a competitor of the former sponsor. So these relations are still relatively loose.

Advertiser's use of media organization's propaganda-advertising resource becomes even more effective if s/he gets a tighter control over it

Table 6.2 Hidden advertisers–external owners continuum

Form of "sale" of media's advertising resources	Resulting form of influence upon media content/media organization
Unofficial "retail" sales at the individual level	*Dzhinsa*
Unofficial "retail" sales at the organizational level	Informally institutionalized hidden advertisement
Unofficial "wholesale" of all space/time of the media outlet	Latent sponsorship/backing
Official (though usually concealed) sale of a media outlet to an advertiser	External ownership

and makes it one of the departments of his/her organization. Therefore, at some stage an advertiser-sponsor may decide to buy a media outlet officially and thus turn into an external owner. Actually, nothing prevents him/her from developing into an internal owner as well, but in this case s/he completely ceases to be an advertiser. An external owner, on the contrary, is akin to an advertiser, since s/he uses her media outlet for the same purpose: for advertisement or propaganda of his/her interests, and not for getting profit, as a "genuine" owner would do.

7 Sources of information

Journalistic sources of information have deserved much attention from researchers, although mostly without connection with other agents of influence on media products. Meanwhile, information, as opposed to economic or political capital, is a specific resource of the mass media sphere and the main raw material for a news producer, and thus cries out for conceptualization in terms of power relations.

Some concepts: sources as disclosers, hiders and producers

Among the studies applying the concept of power to interaction between journalists and sources, the one I have chosen as a starting point for this chapter is that by Richard Ericson and his colleagues (Ericson *et al.* 1989). Based to a significant extent on Erving Goffman's notions of front and back regions, this study offers an elaborated classification of sources' strategies. Since Goffman was primarily concerned with individual interaction, Ericson redefines his concepts with reference to organizations. Back regions are understood as places where organizational work transpires and decisions are taken but which are open only to the purview of those who are officially or informally authorized to be there. Front regions consist of those areas where the public business of the organization is transacted. According to Ericson, two major types of practices of handling with information, or signs, may be employed in both regions: *enclosure* and *disclosure*. Intersection of all four categories gives four typical actions, represented in Table 7.1 and illustrated by my examples.

Enclosure refers to efforts to limit or extinguish the signs that are given out. An effort to keep signs or knowledge from another is an attempt at *secrecy*, and is usually reached by excluding from back regions those people who want to give the information away. *Censorship* is a restriction on publicizing more broadly something that is made public in one narrower context, i.e., information is present at the front region but not allowed to be disseminated outside it. Disclosure entails efforts to communicate signs. An effort to communicate to the unauthorized something that is normally communicated only to the authorized, with the

Table 7.1 Ericson's practices of sources

Area of communication	Mode of handling of signs	Resulting practice	Examples
Front regions	Enclosure	Censorship	Ban on recording at a public event
	Disclosure	Publicity	Press conference
Back regions	Enclosure	Secrecy	Ban on attending an event by journalists
	Disclosure	Confidence	"Closed briefing" for journalists

expectation that it is not to be made known to others, is a *confidence*. "Closed briefings," given in Table 7.1 as an example of confidence, are meetings where journalists are provided with information they are not supposed to publish; they are a subject of further consideration in this chapter. Finally, *publicity* is an effort to give out favorable information in the front region to be communicated further without any limitations.

Numerous examples of all four types of Ericson's practices can be found in Russia, but I would like to slightly shift the angle of conceptualization of sources. Ericson mostly talks of strategies towards information as if information is something that already exists independently of the source's will, like a physical body, and that can only be hidden or disclosed. My respondents, both sources and journalists, preferred to talk about the *production* of events, along with the production of image, of trust and of other symbolic goods. While Ericson's vision may work well with, let us say, lay sources, who let information emerge and function without regard to their will, more experienced and professionalized sources may be better described as information producers. Furthermore, for lay sources this latter definition also seems applicable. By its mode of functioning in the media sphere, information is a product that, after being shaped, is offered for free, exchanged, sold, or imposed. As a product it demands effort in its manufacture. Not only is giving out information of one's success a product that should be adequately packaged to be sold, but hiding information about one's failure is also a product, it is also a version of reality that is *produced*. Moreover, there are events that are produced or staged specially for media and that, if media suddenly disappeared, would have no sense and just would not happen. Finally, one should not disregard the creation of false information which occurs quite frequently, especially when it comes to information about competitors/opponents. When an informational war unfolds (in Russia) actors usually do not care if the *kompromat* is true, false or "half-true," so one can hardly trace the boundary between production/manufacture and disclosure.

Thus it seems plausible to talk of three major strategies of sources: production of positive information about themselves, production of absence of negative information about themselves, and production of negative information about competitors. Although analytically it is possible to distinguish more kinds of practices based on the parameters involved in this typology (see Table 7.2 at the end of the chapter), it is these three practices that have shown themselves to be the most typical. The classification itself does not contradict Ericson's. Both will be further integrated in this chapter.

Sources' professionalization and stratification

As mentioned in Chapter 2, a very specific situation with reference to sources development existed in Russia for a short period of time: in the late 1980s–early 1990s, when the institute of official state censorship was abolished. This institute had mediated the relations between media professionals and their sources; and after its abolition these two sides appeared to stand face to face, without any skills or rules of mutual communication.

However, both sides soon became professionalized, mostly having adopted foreign models. This resulted in rapid emergence of a hierarchy of sources, which has not undergone any changes since the 1990s and is still in place. At one extreme are powerful organizations with their professional press-services and PR experts, and at the other – common people, casual participants of news: witnesses, victims, passersby, and "typical representatives of common people" (selected by journalists). The preference given by journalists to institutionalized sources in comparison with non-institutionalized ones is well documented (e.g. Hall 1977: 315–48, and Table 8.1 in the next chapter); the existence of such a selective attitude is a main cause of sources stratification and, consequently, of differences in their strategies towards media. The group of "common people" hardly has any strategies of influence on mass media at all, since its only resource – information – is temporary, casual. These agents are the weakest; they can not get access to mass media on their own, to say nothing of influencing the interpretation of the situation created by them. Since they demonstrate no recurring practices of power, these sources are not studied here, but they deserve a brief illustration. Since no data on them could be found in other studies on Russia, I have picked an example from Nick Couldry (2000: 273–87), who developed this subject on British material. One of his respondents, "Rachel," who had watched a protest action in the town of Brightlingsee in 1995, was greatly surprised at a local TV story reporting that public order was provided by twenty-six policemen without special munition, though she had counted twenty-three police vans with specially equipped people. Making a call to the editorial board, she learned that the journalists had used information provided by the police press-service; she asked to be able to give her own account to disprove this information, but was refused. For any media producer, the reason for this is obvious: sources, who cannot confirm their trustworthiness either by status or by long-term relations with journalists, have to be excluded because journalists lack both time and desire to check all of them. The flood of such calls and messages is scarcely manageable, and thus exclusion of some sources in favor of others is structurally determined; all that journalists can change without unreasonable losses are the criteria of choice.

A more advantageous position is occupied by individuals whose knowledge is in constant demand, e.g. experts. Starting from this group, the main (and increasing in strength) motivation for "mediatization" of sources is self-advertising. Such sources may be called purposeful producers of coverage either of themselves or of their clients. This category is close to Molotch and Lester's term of "event promoters" (Molotch and Lester 1974), but embraces a broader set of activities: purposeful sources are involved not only in promotion, but in production, and not only of events, but of other kinds of raw material for media. The prevalence of advertising motivation among such sources is one of the reasons why they are hardly distinguishable from "genuine" advertisers. For instance, experts' strategy arises from this motivation to put himself/herself forward as the best specialist. Combined with the desire of journalists to create permanent networks of easy-to-get sources, the result is the emergence of an enclave of experts in every field, who constantly fill their respective informative niches in mass media and block access by other experts to media. Experts can also use third parties, who offer them access to mass media in exchange for the required statements. For example, a forecast of a share price increase concerning a particular company can bring this company substantial profits ("Fyodor Ozersky," Interview 24). According to Ozersky, the activity of a representative of such a company, both in connecting media with the expert and in agreeing about his/her statement, is not necessarily formulated as an open and crude deal. Presented like this, it would resemble hidden advertising and, being perceived as illegitimate, would tend to deter some potential participants. Often a company press-secretary would act as a "friend" recommending a good expert to a good media organization and "helping" the good expert to express what is mutually agreed to be close to his own point of view. This secures both journalists and experts against loss of self-esteem and of symbolic capital (image of independence, professionalism, etc.)

To ensure regular access to mass media, experts have to keep abreast of current events and become active participants in them, thereby coming to be potential personalities in future news stories. If individuals join groups or organizations, they become able to produce events for mass media themselves. In this case to get coverage is still easier than to get an opportunity to interpret the event as desired by sources. For example, a demonstration produced by a large NGO has a good chance of being covered in the news, but the demonstrators can be mocked at or condemned by the reporter, an expert or a "witness." Thus, during my study I was present at the shooting of a story about the first congress of a youth organization. The ceremony was very solemn, the governor was present. The reporter skeptically remarked to me that this was all part of the governor's election campaign. In making the TV story, he emphasized in his voice-over that some participants did not understand their role in this congress, accompanying this comment with a picture of a group of adolescent navy cadets.

Influence upon the interpretation of events is provided with the help of more complex information management techniques available to the sources who possess resources enabling them to professionalize this activity. In Russia, as elsewhere, professional information management exists in two main forms: in the form of press-services (or press-secretaries), as a structural part of an organization-source, or in the form of autonomous PR-agencies. The latter form is the final stage of professionalization in this sphere, when work with information is separated from the information source, and becomes a service, for which fee is charged (Manheim (1998) has called it a "third force in newsmaking").

From its very emergence in Russia (in Moscow, to be exact), PR began to join, merge and take over adjacent activities: political consulting, marketing and applied sociology, and partly audience research and advertising business. In the late 1990s, when the rest of Russia was just developing the institution of press-secretaries, Moscow was full of companies offering the full (or nearly full) range of the services mentioned. People dealing with these activities formed a common professional community, or at least freely circulated from one sphere to another. Thus, one of my respondents first worked with the President's press-service, than was engaged in political consulting for parliamentarians, and after that joined a PR department of a private oil company. The head of that PR department was at the same time the director of a PR agency of his own, and one of his friends, who had dealt with the organization of regional election campaigns, was promoting a metal mining company on the market.

During 1990s, the image of the Russian PR man became demonized in journalistic and popular culture which presented him as an omnipotent villain able to "make any vagabond into President" (Interview 37) through manipulative media technologies. This belief is not entirely groundless. After the dismantling of the Soviet propaganda machine, that had long been ineffective, Russian audiences unexpectedly faced a new type of information manager with new techniques, for which audiences were nearly unprepared. However, the possibilities of informational management are also not unlimited, and this will be addressed further below.

Production of positive information

According to my interviews, PR professionals do not see a significant difference between the promotion of a product, a firm, a candidate or a political party. The difference lies only in particular methods, but all these activities are perceived as branches of information management. Respondent "Ozersky," an employee of a PR department of an oil company, said that during his work with a private PR agency they were "leading" a vodka brand and several ministers and ministries (Interview 24). According to this and other interviews, whether it is a single advertising campaign, or the everyday "leading" of a client, political or commercial, public relations in the end always proceed from the available budget, on the basis of which a "media-plan" is developed. Official advertising, *zakaz* and the creation of unpaid newsworthy events may be part of this plan as its components, and are not mutually exclusive. Besides them, a whole range of typical techniques may be named: buying experts (mentioned above), establishing friendly relations with experts and journalists and making them allies; corporate discipline ensuring filtration and coordination of outgoing information; coordination of format and time of output of information with format and rhythm of mass media and with journalistic notion of newsworthiness; "production of events"; and, finally, production of information products by PR-teams themselves – both commercials and "news" stories, which later are inserted into mass media schedules without alteration. The cluster of those practices that violate the law is often called "black PR."

Full-scale PR requires sufficient financial resources, and this, along with journalists' selectivity towards sources, is another major cause of the stratification of sources. In Russia the biggest consumers of PR services among political actors were candidates to positions of mayors and governors,[1] and among commercial agents – primarily representatives of raw materials, heavy, power, and transport industries. For example, in 1998 the *Transneft* oil company spent (officially shown only) US$458,000 for information pieces in press (Yevgenieva 1999: 32). As respondent "Gorsky" noted, "officially three rubles are transferred to [the customer], but actually – three hundred."

Small firms, though spending for "information pieces" less funds in absolute figures, seem to need them to the same extent, especially companies producing popular consumer goods and services. During my study in TV newsrooms, I saw hidden advertising of beer, watches, furniture, medical services, educational services, and commercial exhibitions. Even those sources who have access to open violence often try to increase the effectiveness of their interaction with media using hidden advertising or other positive techniques. According to Alexey Khokhlov even "gangsters" use not only negative strategies when dealing with mass media:

[A]fter one of our stories ... our program was suspended. For two weeks. So they suspended the program, and the first call offering help was, however strange it is, from gangsters. From the very same *Tambovians*. And they said, "What d'ya need? We'll buy ya a heap of air

time ... and that's that." Then I asked them, well, [weren't] they glad
the program had been closed? They say [makes a characteristic gang-
ster gesture], "are you dumb, brother, who'd show us on TV then?"

(Khokhlov 01.07.1998)

Thus, PR activities, as listed above, are a complicated aggregate that
includes both "genuine" information management and practices undistin-
guishable from hidden advertising. Their final form, that completely
expropriates control over media content from journalists, is production of
articles and programs by advertisers themselves. It is also the final form of
the merging of advertisers, sources and producers. It is not very typical for
general newscasts, but paper articles and specialized TV news (as well as
game shows) are often produced by various companies or their PR-
services. For example, a St. Petersburg computer shop produces a program
devoted to computers: it includes news, games and competitions, and goes
into the general background of advertising of this firm. Employees of the
traffic police prepare and anchor radio news reports on road accidents in
the city. One of the elite Moscow universities launched a quiz show for
high-school students, the winners of which were accepted into this university without entrance examinations, obligatory for all the rest. The show
was anchored by a university professor.

However, even those sources who have managed to gain full control
over news production, to say nothing of less powerful ones, use different
adaptation techniques and at least to some extent try to comply with journalistic notions of newsworthiness. Otherwise they risk – or may be con-
vinced by journalists that they risk – missing their target audience. One of
my respondents gave an example of such an adaptive scheme. Since journalists, naturally, rate information on events of "public significance"
higher than direct information about organizations, a company – for
example, a manufacturer of water treatment filters – can develop an
"independent" analytical report on water pollution in the region, timing it
to a certain ecological event or date, and present it to journalists. Using it
as a source of information, mass media will produce programs on ecological subjects, where the manufacturer will be mentioned as a secondary,
but positive character. In this case the filter producer has a good chance to
gain exposure in media without paying.

Production of negative information

Bad news is a common media product that usually increases ratings and
thus stimulates journalists to seek for such data. However, what I want to
address here is a slightly different matter. Lecturing to young journalists,
investigative reporter and editor Alexey Khokhlov warned them against
confusing journalistic investigation with what came to be known in Russia
as "leak of *kompromat*":

[K]ompromat does not appear in mass media just by itself. It is always somebody's *zakaz*. For example, the case of Kovalyov [Minister of justice who had to resign because of discrediting publication], if people think it is a struggle for uprightness, or, say, "purification of ranks" – far from that. If you know, after his resignation the Ministry of Justice got reformatories and prisons under its jurisdiction ... and this is tremendous money. So dealing with such subjects you'd be very cautious, so that they won't use you blindly ... Currently a scandal is developing in [N-town], with real estate agencies. There are two [competing] groups there. Unfortunately, one group is *roofed* by regular police, and the other – by the regional department for the prevention of organized crime. They have their own interests in these groups of real estate firms, and they in turn discharge *kompromat* to mass media, and use journalists.

(Khokhlov 01.07.1998)

Unlike "genuine" news, sought for by journalists, leak of negative information about competitors is a sources' tactics opposite to production of positive information about oneself. For wide audiences such leaks both in the 1990s and later have been the most visible part of professional informational management: while hidden advertising needs to be specially sought for, scandalous "exposures" and "investigations" were eye-catching. Furthermore, they usually appear as concerted (dis-)information campaigns simultaneously in different media and then disappear as unexpectedly as they popped up. The visible part of these campaigns is of course only the tip of the iceberg. First, leaks of *kompromat* are a central, but not the only method of such "informational wars," while the whole range of information management as a rule is used. Second, the logic of the appearance of *kompromat* in media and disappearance from them follows the logic of struggle between various actors and teams for economic and state resources. Since media are mostly helpful in acquiring those state resources access to which is provided through elections, it is with them that the second type of information wars was mainly associated in the 1990s and later. These campaigns are aimed at potential voters and usually operated with *kompromat* that exploited popular phobias and prejudices (typical were proclaiming an opponent to be homosexual, Zionist, too rich, or connected with criminal activities). The "economic" type of wars, throughout the 1990s connected chiefly with privatization and further redistribution of business units, at that time targeted an elite audience and thus operated with more complicated symbolic products. For such audience homosexuality was not an issue at all, and connection with criminal activities, given the general situation with illegitimate violence described in Chapter 4, could hardly frighten it either. What could work for this audience was, for example, understatement of value of a company before its privatization or hostile takeover; or questioning the legality of unfavorable auctions, mergers or other transactions; or accusations of unfair taxation or customs duty policy etc. In such wars the wider audience hardly even understood the subject of the dispute, if it consumed the respective media products at all.

A separate type was information wars in which mass media defended their interests and interests of their owners, such as the anti-*NTV* campaign of 2000 described in Chapter 12. Some wars were more complex in character. One of the most high-profile scandals erupted in early 1999 when *RTR* broadcast a low-quality tape which showed "a person looking like General Prosecutor" Yuri Skuratov having sex with two (alleged) prostitutes. The prosecutor's reaction was frantic: he first sent in his resignation, then changed his mind claiming he had been pressured by some of those who were under his investigation, then he made a number of contradictory statements and, finally, was dismissed by President Yeltsin. The circumstances of this story are very strange. Immediately after the broadcast criminal proceedings were instituted against Skuratov in which he was accused of exceeding his commission and obtaining fourteen men's luxury suits for free (allegedly as a bribe). Given the scale of activity of Skuratov's suspects, as well as the general level of corruption and financial fraud of that time, this accusation looked ridiculous. The leads in some of the cases Skuratov was then investigating were said to extend as high as to Yeltsin's Family. Whether this is true or not, broadcasting of a tape that discredited an officer of General prosecutor's level on the state-owned national channel could be sanctioned only by very high-ranking officials. Later one of the taped women was interviewed by the notorious anchor Sergei Dorenko at *ORT* – the most popular national channel that was then controlled by Boris Berezovsky, one of whose companies had also been under investigation by Skuratov. The woman publicly confirmed the identity of Skuratov. After his dismissal, however, the accusations about the prosecutor were withdrawn; neither his identity on the tape nor the authenticity of the tape itself were ever proved. Thus, much indicates that the scandal had been specially designed to dismiss Skuratov. Although, given the informal organization of the federal elite, it is unlikely that Skuratov had been really independent in his investigative activity and he might have been serving the interests of one of the competing groups, in the context of media research this is not central. What is important is that this case illustrates the scale and the "genre" composition of the flow of *kompromat* at that time. The ethical side of the broadcast was discussed in the journalistic community for a while, but in a few months it was drowned in streams of *kompromat* leaked during the parliamentary elections of late 1999.

Another important question is how the tape could appear at all. One of the versions that favored its authenticity pointed to a number of persons in elite circles who specifically enticed high-ranking officials into a "bad flat" in order to pressure them later.[2] The taping equipment was, of course,

illegal. The interviewed woman also claimed that many high-ranking officials used to visit the flat, albeit not all of them engaged in sex. Although
none of this was ever proved, the very emergence of this version is indicative. As discussed in Chapter 4, the role of private protection companies
and of security services of private firms in the 1990s was very important.
Since both an actor's physical safety and the security of business or position in the state body depended on knowledge of the current balance of
power in the environment, gathering various information about partners,
competitors and other potential interactants of the client became one of
the central activities of protection organizations. The information
obtained might be just stored or used privately, but at certain moments it
could be leaked into media as well.

Autonomous searching by private enforcement bodies was complemented by another source: investigation carried out by enforcers themselves. Given the clientelist relations of legal enforcement bodies with
various external partners, it is not surprising that results of their work
became available outside those bodies, under various conditions. Some
materials had to be specially ordered, but often already existing dossiers
were sold. One database containing information about high-ranking politicians and businessmen, including transcriptions of some of their paging
messages, was said to be in circulation throughout Moscow for a few years
and once even to have appeared on the Internet (Fomin 2000). Less
sophisticated databases have been freely sold at flea markets along with
pirated films and music CDs; they include lists of private and corporate
telephone numbers and addresses, people's passport numbers, family
members, car accidents, owned real estate and cars and related transactions, workplaces and their changes, data on health, individuals' previous
convictions and legal proceedings instituted against him/her, and so on.
While last year's databases are so cheap as to be available to anyone, the
latest data are expensive. Data collection may also be ordered from
private semi-legal investigators who are not involved in the security business and form their own market sector, buying and updating databases,
and maintaining contacts with state enforcement and investigative
bodies (Zakharov and Krivosheyev 2001). And vice versa, the enforcers
are also said to use these investigators in their legal work, because their
services are quicker then making official inquiries to other state bodies
and departments.

In fall 1998, during my research I attended a course of investigative
journalism taught by a famous investigative journalist Andrei Konstantinov at a local journalism school. Once he and his colleague demonstrated
to his students how cooperation with enforcers should be carried out. A
number of such bodies maintained a joint telephone information service
that provided data from some of the above mentioned databases to
anyone with the authority to know the password. The password changed
every day; according to Konstantinov, a list of passwords for the current

month was always hanging in any district police department. So, he told the students, they could even peep at such lists while visiting these offices. But it was better to maintain continuous relations with policemen. With these words Konstantinov's colleague dialed a telephone number and, calling someone by his first name, inquired for a password. Then he asked students if anyone wanted his personal data to be checked; after a volunteer provided his first and last name and approximate date of birth, Konstantinov's colleague dialed another number, gave the password, and immediately got the volunteer's exact age, current and previous addresses, phone, data on family members, and absence of convictions.

General availability of various harmful data on people and organizations, combined with fierce unregulated competition among them and with the readiness of media to disseminate these data, made the information wars almost endless; nor have they ceased at the end of the 1990s. There have been several typical ways of getting these data into media. First, *kompromat* can be published for a fee, but, given the risks for the media connected with such publications, it costs more than positive publications. When the link between the client source and the media organization is effectively controlled, *kompromat* may simply be invented. Respondent "Ozersky" told me that once, to discredit a competing candidate running for the local legislative assembly, his team published a story of him owning a luxurious mansion that he could not have bought on his declared income. According to Ozersky, he knew that the house did exist somewhere, but had no time to look for its picture. "So we just took a picture from a commercial booklet," he said (Interview 24). The high cost of access to courts, their slow work, lack of independence and virtual impossibility of proving the libellous intentions of media, makes such forgery quite a safe strategy. As is shown in the *PROMACO* story, revenues of media organizations from such publications usually exceed their potential losses. On the other hand, since bad news usually has more of a chance to find its way to media than good news, this option is also open to sources, under the condition that the source makes an impression of not being interested in the dissemination of the particular *kompromat*. One way of doing this is to publish defamatory data on a temporary website (e.g. a site of a fictitious media organization) that would immediately disappear after the end of the PR action, and then to give informal hints to journalists on where interesting material may be found (Dragin 2002). Publication of *kompromat* may be imposed or forced as well. First, external agents often find it the only way to respond to similar publications of their rivals. Second, media owners may oblige their media organizations to start an information war. And third, PR agencies or media themselves use it to extort money from various actors by inviting them to order a *kompromat* publication or a whole war, and simultaneously threatening to take a similar order from their rivals.

Production of absence of negative information

A negative practice supplementing the lack of *kompromat* against rivals is production of absence of unfavorable information about oneself. This is not only the concealment of already existing "facts," but a more complex strategy uniting techniques of control of information flow at two stages of its production: *within* the source organization and *outside* it, in the community of media producers and competing sources. The first stage may be divided into three major components:

1   avoiding actions that may serve as material for unfavorable publications (thus, policy makers often refrain from unpopular reforms which they themselves consider necessary but which arouse fear of negative coverage);
2   concealment of those actions once they are committed (Ericson's enclosures);
3   various substitutive techniques, including distraction, redefining "bad" as "good," and others.

Control of the stage of production outside the source organization has shown itself as consisting of dealing with two major situations: first, when journalists possess material for bad news – true or false – but have not published it yet. Here the source's task is to convince them to refrain from publication, typically by involving them in some kind of exchange relation, or by force (the latter has already been considered in Chapter 4). The second situation arises when publication has already occurred, and the task is to stop the further multiplication of publications and to negate their harmful consequences. PR experts qualify this strategy as "crisis management" and offer their client-sources a whole range of techniques, the most important of which may be called reparative framing.

Since the first listed practices – avoiding certain actions – extends beyond information management as such, I shall start from the most obvious practice of concealment of "facts." GDF monitoring reports an abundance of cases of plain refusal to give out information motivated by different reasons. The most typical of them are:

1   the information represents a state, commercial or other secret;
2   the information is not known to the source, or people who have it are not available now (sick, on holiday, etc.);
3   the source is unable to gather the required information;
4   no reasons.

Motives based on the personal and/or emotional attitude of a source to a particular medium are also common; some sources do not even try to mask their unwillingness to give information with any legitimate reasons, which indicates that legitimacy is unnecessary for retaining sources' positions. For example, the governor of the Bryansk region Yuriy Lodkin, explaining his refusal to talk to representatives of the *Bryanskoye Vremya* newspaper in early 1999, said that "this yellow paper [did] not exist" for him, because he did not like the articles and headlines of certain pieces and, besides, *Bryanskoye Vremya* cooperated with radio *Liberty*, funded by the State Department of the USA (GDF 12.02.1999).

A further development of enclosure practice is non-admittance of journalists to sites of events, and is close to the direct violence addressed in Chapter 4. This tactic has a limitation, however. It is most effective against TV journalists who need a picture, and less effective against the printed press that deals with verbal information. Generally, the whole strategy is effective only if all channels of the information to be concealed are blocked – this was often disregarded by sources in the early 1990s, when they still lacked experience of operating in the new media environment. As a rule, concealment of negative information is preferable for the source to the production of positive news because only the former strategy (when effective, of course) liberates the source from the necessity of avoiding certain actions, and thus releases the restrictions that existence in the public domain may put on sources' activity. Often, it also seems cheaper because production of positive information demands some constructive effort, while concealment at first glance demands no action. All this led state sources in the early 1990s to practice, in Ericson's terms, secrecy and censorship, while they failed to notice that alternative ways of acquiring their secrets were no longer under their control. With time sources became more experienced: thus, when Putin became prime minister in 1999 and launched a new Chechen war, his team started its media policy with the active production of positive news about the "antiterrorist operation," and only later, gaining more and more power, it supplemented its strategy with various techniques of enclosure (for more details see Chapter 13).

By the mid-1990s many source organizations learned to control all or nearly all outgoing information. In some organizations, as in the case described below, employees were prohibited to give interviews to journalists, and thus all contacts became channeled through their press-service. For state organizations that are obliged to disseminate certain information, the safest and the most effective way has become a strategy that may be called bureaucratic deceleration: source representatives do not refuse cooperation, but increase the cost of access to information so much that virtually no media can afford such time and labor losses. A vivid illustration of bureaucratic deceleration is the situation I came about during my participant observation at *Vesti Starograda* newspaper when I was told to write an investigative piece on the protection of architecturally valuable façades. An extract from my field notes containing a few episodes from the long story of my communication with the State Inspection of Monuments Preservation (SIMP) is presented below:

On Wednesday June 4 I called the named clerk, Kozlovskaya, every 15 minutes. At last about one p.m. I reached her, and she told me rather sharply she was going to answer journalists' questions only with the special permission of the director, since there is such an instruction. I noted that it was Anna Ivanovna [press-secretary] who sent me to her. She seemed to breathe in as deeply as she could and barked out:

– I am not subordinate to Anna Ivanovna, I obey only Klein [the director]!

I called Anna Ivanovna who was scarcely aware that Kozlovskaya would send me to hell. Press-secretary said the director's instruction really existed.

– You have to write an official request on behalf of the editorial office. . . .

On June 11, Wednesday, I went back to SIMP. It was a day when the office was open, and the reception was full of people. The press-secretary looked at the request: register at the documentation department, Pyotr Nikolayevich will see you on Friday. It's all that can be done today. I went to the documentation office, waited and was told to go to room 403, Sidorov's signature was needed. I went, stood in line, he said: this is not my responsibility. But he was polite, went with me to the reception, waited until press-secretary got free and explained the situation to her. She sent me to the documentation department again. There I joined a line to another clerk, and she registered me without a word. Just before that I had secured a place in the queue for the vice-director who also could sign the request instead of the director (a line for a couple of hours). Just because the line to the director was for previously registered people, and still those at the end were told they would not be accepted that day. . . . I stuck to the director as soon as he went out to the corridor . . . At the staircase when I'd almost lost hope he suddenly stopped, signed and wrote a note "Attn Kirillov." Then asked about the essence of the request and shouted running away "Then it's not to Kirillov, it's Ivanov and Semyonova."

I went to press-secretary, she said: Ivanov is away today, Semyonova is on vacation. I decided to join the queue for Kozlovskaya and got in one minute before the end of her office hours. She read and said: this is not to me, I am not Kirillov. I explained the situation, and she started writing on my request, saying: it is not to Semyonova either, I shall tell you, to whom, and you'll get the director's signature. I asked her, why should I do it again if he had just signed the request. She threw me the request and started shouting: So get out of here, if you can't talk politely! I'm telling you what to do, and you're not listening!

I objected: organizations are obliged to reply, if you don't do it, I shall write that SIMP is preventing journalists from getting information. She howled: do it! She had already stood up from the table.

"And you personally," I added. A pregnant pause followed. I was holding the paper. "Write who should do it," I said not very confidently, but she sat down and wrote barking out:

– Have you registered it? OK. We'll answer in a written form, the period for replies we have is one month.

(Field notes 1. Various dates)

As a conclusion to this story I must say that though the article was finally published the bureaucrats won the game. I spent more than a month on the investigation, got a very modest result, and my remuneration was far less than the effort (I bought a pair of boots for it). So no journalist, unless it was a journalist-sociologist like me, would follow this all the to the end.

Such an increase in the cost of access to negative information is especially effective when coupled with decreased cost of access to positive information. More generally, production of absence of negative information is successful only when it exceeds enclosure techniques and includes some positive, e.g. substitutive, actions. A substitutive character is acquired by positive information when it is produced not to fill an information vacuum, but to replace the flow of negative information; this effect of substitution revealed itself very well during the second Chechen war when the military suddenly became "friendly" and "cooperative" in taking journalists to the sites of events, but started effectively blocking their autonomous travel. Another substitutive technique is the redefinition of potentially negative information as positive. Thus, a merger leading to the creation of a monopoly may be presented as a measure to improve management and to decrease transaction costs. Bureaucratic deceleration, substitution and redefinition are, of course, milder practices than plain secrecy, and their very emergence in the 1990s indicates a shift of power balance from sources to media professionals.

Since full secrecy was usually no longer available to sources in the 1990s, to produce absence of negative information it became more important to control flows of information that had already leaked outside, and of those "facts" and interpretations that originated in the external environment. One of the central techniques here came to be known as "blocking." When a source acquires information that his/her competitor has ordered a *kompromat* piece about him/her in a certain media outlet, s/he can offer the respective media organization more money for not publishing the *kompromat*. While publishing negative information generally costs more than publishing positive, blocking is even more expensive. Although, of course, the source may learn about the preparation of a *kompromat* attack from its security service or through external partners, often media themselves inform potential victims in order to negotiate a better deal. The process may even go through several iterations, thus turning into a kind of auction between the "leaker" and the "blocker" mediated by media representatives. By the end of the 1990s blocking had become included in informal price lists as a regular service along with hidden advertising. It was often offered not only to eliminate separate pieces, but also as a "subscription" – that is, media organizations began taking on obligations to block any *kompromat* against the client during a certain period of time, usually a month.

Consumption of blocking services has been also complemented with sources' strategies of involving journalists in subtler kinds of exchange, from barter deals to all sorts of "mutual help" and "friendship." Friendship-like relations, in particular, are effective since they create ethical obligations, and thus journalists often feel uncomfortable when they "let down" their friends by exposing them to unfavorable coverage. Inclusion in decision making within the source organization and "closed briefings" are other ways to "intimize" the source–journalists relations. At closed briefings, as a press-secretary of a democratic political party told me, journalists are given information not for publication, but for "orientation." Sources understand that overwhelming secrecy may lead journalists to disclose some information unintentionally, because in a situation of information shortage they may misunderstand the source's true interests, as well as wrongly identify the source's partners and enemies, and thus mistakenly praise or criticize actors or actions (Interview 38). The practice of confidence, guarding media producers from such mistakes, also creates an atmosphere of trust between sources and journalists and makes the latter feel exceptionally close to knowledge unavailable to others, maintaining the wish to preserve this unique position.

When negative coverage does happen – either as a result of a leak of "facts" from within the source, or as fake *kompromat,* or as unfavorable interpretation of something already known – special techniques of crisis management are used by sources. Thus, respondent "Gorsky" told me what can be done if a leak of *kompromat* is known about but cannot be prevented:

INTERVIEWER: Have you ever met cases when one and the same media outlet within a short time acted ... sold itself to competing [hidden political advertisers]...

RESPONDENT: All the time. Moreover, often different points of view are published [for money] in one issue. It's a common story.

INTERVIEWER: What about effectiveness of such...?

RESPONDENT: Well, often it is done on purpose. If I am told that material discrediting me is already in the layout, and you can't block it, then the only thing you can do is to put your story next to it – a story which turns this *kompromat* into an absurdity, or at least neutralizes it somehow. So here there are two arguments: for and against, and they are just put together. Merely.

INTERVIEWER: But that means that the media organization has cheated the one who came first...

RESPONDENT: Sure. Sure.

INTERVIEWER: So he won't pay next time.

RESPONDENT: Why not? If it's a popular publication, he'll be even urging them to publish him.

(Interview 31, November 2000)

Like substitution, this counterbalancing strategy is also a kind of production of positive information, although of weaker eliminative power: when the crisis has happened, any methods of information management are relatively weak. Plain denial of compromising "facts," even if it is an official refutation confirmed by court decision, has proved itself particularly ineffective for sources since it arouses a very low level of attention and trust, while its cost is quite high. Redefinition is not often available in the case of a *kompromat* attack – thus, it would be quite problematic to redefine Skuratov's situation as positive. Often the most effective strategy for a source is reparative or compensatory framing: a part of the "facts" – true or false – is admitted, but the scale of the crisis is reduced, or anti-crisis measures are emphasized. Many respondents, including PR professional "Galina Minskaya" stressed that the best thing for sources was crisis prevention, not "repairing":

First of all, you should not let a crisis happen. A well organized PR work of the company's PR department or of an agency that consults this company is to regularly – say, once a year – carry out such monitorings, opinion polls and look for weak points. See if you are having ecological problems, or foreign companies are often accused of robbing our motherland – an image of such a capitalist, rumors about exploitation of Russians in foreign companies and so on. Such things should be learned beforehand. Because a journalist does not take such information from the blue. Information must circulate for a while before it gets into media. And it should be prevented. If possible. But if suddenly such an article appears.... I always recommend that my clients meet journalists. If it is a serious campaign – then give a refutation, but it's the last thing to do, it is only if it's a criminal case, when everything is perverted, then you should give a refutation. But when it is just a mistake, a lack of information, then I never recommend confrontation with journalists. It is always better to send a very polite letter – we, having full respect for your publication, reading it from beginning to end all day long, and always admiring its objectiveness and professionalism, we were stunned – stunned is already a too rude word – we were surprised to see this article, we understand that the journalist just lacking information occasionally made such and such mistakes, and our common interest is to meet and to give the journalist the full information so that in the future such mistakes are never made. And as a rule, since information is food for a journalist, they come and take that information which from our point of view reflects reality. And after that you should make friends with this journalist, invite him for press-lunches, include on trips ... One should make friends with journalists, because companies who do not have such intimate, so to say, contacts with journalists, later they pay for it.

(Interview 33, January 2001)

Along with the above mentioned party press-secretary, "Minskaya" is one of many respondents who specially pointed out the effectiveness of "making friends" with journalists. The pervasiveness of this practice is confirmed by other sources, including Vyacheslav Kostikov, the former press-secretary of President Yeltsin (1997: 44–9). Underscoring the importance of positive actions, especially seen in Minskaya's speech, also shows that production of absence of negative information is indeed a *production* process: it is an on-going activity that demands constant decision-making, time and financial resources. Not all sources engage in such laborious work; many, including the most high-ranking ones, often ignore informational management in non-crisis periods and choose ineffective methods during crises.

One of the best known examples of poor crisis management during the study period was the catastrophe of the *Kursk* submarine in the Barents sea in August 2000. Putin's team, which before had given the impression of a group with a consistent information policy, constantly contradicted itself in its statements. While contact with the submarine was lost on August 12, Saturday, the military first silenced this fact, then, during Sunday, admitting problems, denied the sinking of the *Kursk*, and claimed that it had "lain on the seabed." At the same time Norwegian media revealed that Norwegian seismologists had registered two detonations on Saturday. On Monday the military admitted the sinking, but claimed they established radio contact with the submarine; later they said that they only heard "knocking," while Norwegian seismologists said they could not hear anything. Still denying the damage to the *Kursk*, the military continued trying to give an impression of a successful rescue operation being carried out. At the same time navy experts said that absence of reliable communication with the submarine, and the fact that not one of the crew had used individual life saving equipment, indicated that the damage was so serious that the chance of anybody remaining alive was very low. Later investigation confirmed both the two explosions heard by the Norwegians and the fact that no crew members survived more than a few hours after them.

Denying the scant livelihood of saving the sailors, the military made the Russian audience hope for it for many days; the sharp increase in ratings of all newscasts showed that nearly all the adult population was following the story. This tactic did not add to the popularity of the military authorities, but the most public outrage they provoked was their refusal to accept international aid offered to Russia on the Monday. The official reasoning was that the Russian military had all they needed for the rescue operation. Contradicting themselves, the military did finally accept the aid two days later, when it already hardly made any sense at all. The frantic character of the elite's informational activity was especially obvious against a background of alternative viewpoints broadcast by media, first of all by *NTV* which at that time was in the midst of its conflict with Putin. I have no information as to why, knowing this, Putin's team did not make its actions more coordinated. However, it is obvious that by August 2000 Putin's major strategy of minimizing discrepancy in the coverage of the officials' activities had already gone beyond information management and based mainly on access to direct violence and rule-making.

Concluding remarks

Generally, information management as a distinct practice seems to be possible only in the situation of plurality of agents of power in media production, when sources may be discerned as a separate group and when resources are not held monopolistically either by them or by any other group of agents. The less available is direct violence or coercion, the more there is informational manipulation, and the more sophisticated it is. This, on the one hand, means that the outcome of such manipulative techniques can never be perfectly secured, because no complex action can be always perfectly accomplished, and no complex environment can be always perfectly controlled. On the other hand, this situation leads to increasing professionalization of sources and to reduction of the share of "genuine" news in the general news flow. Following journalistic slang, by "genuine" here I mean just news based on events that "happen" independently of sources' purposive action – without either self-advertising or leaking of *kompromat*. Genuine news, thus, does not demand any source's strategies at all, while its opposite, which may be called "provoked news," does.

Table 7.2 shows the major types of sources' strategies outlined at the beginning of the chapter, placing them into a two-dimensional system of coordinates. This system produces six possible types of practices, but the three major ones, considered in this chapter, are set out in bold. Two of the marginal practices concern production of information not about sources themselves, but about others; they are possible, but not widespread. Production of positive information about the third parties is not common, unless some partnership or exchange forms between the source and a positively described object. Most often this type of production is carried out by public relations professionals, who, on the one hand, are not sources themselves but, on the other hand, are not autonomous agents of power either, but rather representatives of interests of sources as their clients. The same may be said about production of absence of negative information about others; both types have little significance of their own. Production of negative information about oneself hardly exists at all and is

Table 7.2 Purposeful production of information by sources

	About oneself	*About other actors*
Production of positive information	**Self-advertising (publicity)**	Advertising as a service
Production of negative information	Corrective and compensatory framing	***"Kompromat"* discharge**
Production of absence of negative information	**Enclosures "Blocking"-like strategies Substitutive techniques**	"Blocking"-based PR as a service

available only in the form of reparative techniques when some leaked or externally created "facts" are admitted and shaped in a certain way.

The table shows that the proposed classification partially intersects with that of Ericson, but emphasizes other facets of sources' activity. In particular, it disregards the front and back region distinction; it also views sources' activity as a construction of something called "information" rather than dealing with already existing "facts," and thus it pays attention to sources' strategies toward third parties, e.g. their competitors. Ericson's types fall into two of the three major practices: while publicity virtually coincides with self-advertising, both enclosures may be included into the group of practices producing absence of negative information about oneself. Confidence may also be regarded as one of the substitutive techniques. It is thus not hard to see that production of absence of negative information is quite a heterogeneous category; however, since it is not reducible to mere enclosure, it still makes sense to single it out here, while further refinement of the typology demands additional study.

8   Rank-and-file journalists

Practices of rank-and-file journalists where they are focused on the final product are fundamentally different from actions of all other agents: journalists are the only agents whose influence on the final product is not mediated by anybody else and, consequently, this influence does not have qualities of interaction between human beings. Therefore, though practices of newsmaking are generated and maintained almost exclusively by journalists, and thus may be interpreted in terms of agency and action, they have been usually viewed more as a structural influence of "journalistic routines." I do not want to dispute this productive approach here, especially because Russian journalistic routines have not shown any meaningful difference from those described in other studies. Nevertheless, I want to briefly highlight the main components of those routines in order to position them among those journalistic practices that do involve interaction with others.

Although anyone who wants to influence the final product of newsmaking has to first deal with reporters, the everyday practices of rank-and-file journalists are some way from explicit contacts with most agents of influence. As a rule, journalists do not interact directly with owners, advertisers or state agents, unless these actors are sources of information. The role of social buffer is played by the heads of media companies, who try to harmonize the companies' interests with outside pressures, while ordinary reporters seldom have to deal with any agents of power other than sources of information. If a particular source combines several resources, special instructions about how to deal with him are given – again by top media figures.

Most of my respondents considered such events as fights between Berezovsky and Gussinksy (or their alliances) no more relevant than, perhaps, any other people would do, and journalists' everyday lives looked like the lives of ordinary people: rumors, gossip, attempts to reinterpret superiors' instructions or messages of other media. The closer journalists approached to top managers, and the closer a media organization was located to Moscow, the higher was the level of awareness about the balance of power in the organization's environment. Some rank-and-file reporters also took an interest in it, but for most of them fields where the world of journalists' everyday activities intersected with the world of outside agents were not the most significant. This does not mean that outside factors have no influence upon rank-and-file journalists, but often they just do not realize this to the full extent.

Moreover, the influence of media executives is often not recognized as control. This is understandable; when asked what influenced them most, journalists usually started from "the most legitimate" end, saying that nothing limited them except the structure of newsmaking activity itself, thus invoking a structural vision of their routines. Then they admitted, with some regret, that they had to obey their bosses, against whom they had almost no resources to resist. Indeed, in this relationship journalists have little choice other than to obey either "pragmatically" or through the legitimization of bosses' power. Journalists have quite another attitude when they possess power resources of their own, and this often happens when they come into contact with their sources. These agents usually took second place after journalists' bosses and were contrasted to them as an illegitimate, an external interference that should (and could) be resisted.

Being junior partners in interaction with bosses, journalists exercise practices that may be called reactive; therefore, the latter will be discussed in the next chapter after considering strategies of bosses themselves. Here I shall first consider the influence of the structure of journalistic labor, and then look at journalist-source relations from the perspective of the former.

Newsmaking: fixed practices

As all my respondents agreed, an influence journalists feel the most is, in their terms, "production necessity," i.e. of technical, organizational and format/genre restrictions. The way journalists used this expression indicated that for them it referred to a very broad phenomenon, that included such concepts as "media logic" by Altheide and Snow (1979), time-space restrictions described by Tuchman (1978), the levels of media routines and organization influences as discerned by Shoemaker and Reese (1996), and structural aspects of working with sources. The centrality of "production necessity" for journalists, and their explicit awareness about this kind of limitation is, perhaps, a reason why such restrictions are also the first to be noticed by researchers, and consequently are most widely studied. These influences define the general context of actions of all agents, including external ones. Theoretically, a president may have enough power resources to "break in" the news format in a way he likes, but practically the result would be quite contrary to his initial goals. De facto, interference in the news genre is not practiced in most countries, with major authoritarian regimes being a possible exception. On the contrary, all external agents try to adapt to its specific features. And in virtually no countries can agents ignore news programs, even when they do not want to deal with mass media.

News genres and formats, though generated and maintained by the journalistic community, are perceived by media producers as impersonal, because, once introduced, they tend to freeze and become obligatory for the newcomers; in this respect, as I have said, Russian journalists display little difference from their colleagues worldwide. At the same time, the big cultural and social break of the 1990s, which affected media as well, destroying traditional practices and genres, produced confusion and heated discussions among journalists about the foundations of newsmaking. This, of course, does not disprove the structural character of format constraints during stable periods, but tells us something about the roots of such constraints, about journalists as agents who can conventionally be identified as their "authors" and "maintainers," and about the power they exercise over news products. A story that happened during my observation at *STV* is a good starting point for considering these questions.

> By 13.00 I came to the district court to watch TV shooting of a session on the joint legal action brought by two people who suffered in an accident at *Sennaya Ploshchad* metro station, against St. Petersburg Metro administration. I had to wait for a long time for *STV* journalists. I began making notes, so as not to waste time; the plaintiff willingly gave an interview. A journalist turned to me to specify some details, and as soon as I began explaining, a small group of people gathered around me with notebooks in their hands. They were making notes after me. At last *STV* appeared, represented by "Andrey," a cameraman, and "Boris," a driver. The reporter "Kirill," as I found out later, was late because of transport problems. The cameraman told me that another reporter, "Grigori," had prepared for him a written list of questions to be asked. He wondered what I was doing there, and I explained that I was interested in the practical work of journalists. He answered that now I had a chance to work as a journalist, and gave me the list of questions. I arranged it with the plaintiff's attorney; Boris gave me a microphone, and I asked questions – twice as many as there were in the list. I suggested Andrey should shoot the plaintiff, but he did not agree for some reason.
>
> He told me to arrange for an interview with the judge, but she refused. So did the representatives of the Metro administration. I was doubtful if just one *sinkhron* was enough for the TV story, but he said it was quite enough. I wrote down everything that had not been recorded, and Andrey, for some reason, began to shoot the plaintiff giving interviews to other journalists. Later, when he had turned the camera off, reporters from *PTV* appeared, and a woman from the Metro administration began talking to their camera. Andrey tried to switch on his camera, but was too slow doing this, because his camera was rather old. When later we were running downstairs, I told Andrey how *PTV* worked – microphone to a person's mouth, and start asking

questions. That's what we should have done, I said, dealing with both the judge and that Metro woman. Andrey said that it wouldn't have worked with the judge, she was too experienced for that, but said nothing about the Metro woman.

Sitting in the car, he and Boris agreed the event was not enough for a story, just have the anchor give some comments with a couple of pictures. When we came to the studio, "Farkhat" [the head of the newsroom] saw me, and said to Kirill, "Here you are, this girl, Olessia Koltsova, will tell you everything about the court session." Kirill first wanted me to complete my work on the story on my own, but Farkhat did not allow him. Kirill asked me to sit down, sat opposite to me, and began asking for details...

(Field notes 2, abridged, autumn 1999)

While the completion of the work on the news story will be considered in the next section, here I would like to point out at the meaning of the cited episode: several times during the processing of the event "the news" appeared and then disappeared. A TV story was planned first, then, since the reporter was absent, it might have been substituted with a picture series voiced over by the anchor's comments; then, on the basis of available camera shots, my report and archive materials, finally the story was made and broadcast. Such unexpected emergence and disappearance of "news" is not something extraordinary in journalists' work; on the contrary – it is a part of routine. In one case the story of the previous day's event was made with the help of archive materials only, used because there were no fresh pictures (as its author said, "assembled out of nothing"). And, conversely, another time a whole local newscast did not get on air just because the journalists missed the time when it should have cut into the national broadcast. The emergence of the court session as a news story also depended on such factors as availability of archive materials, transport problems, the age of the camera, the experience of the judge with media, presence of other journalists at the event and, finally, presence of a sociologist doing participant observation.

These seemingly accidental and external factors influencing newsmaking are in fact very tightly interwoven in the process. On the one hand, they are the indicators of the constructed character of news, which is often more produced than searched for and transmitted. On the other hand, news owes its sudden births and deaths in the process of journalistic activity to the fact that news is not entirely a construction; rather, its nature is dual. News as a TV product is a commodity that should be supplied to the customer regularly; news as "a fact of life" is an event viewed as significant in comparison with others. Journalists use the word in both meanings, being aware of the gap between them. News as a product should be made at even intervals, but quite often there are not enough "facts of life" for that. Since a journalist is interested in continuous production, many ways to manage with the lack of news can be found. Some possible methods are mentioned in the cited episode, but the main strategy is to plan or predict the event, to make the prediction of the unpredictable a routine matter (Tuchman 1978: 39–63). In particular, some events, dates and seasonal changes are easily predictable, such as annual flu epidemics, or preparation of a municipal heating system for winter. Moving of status figures (both in space and up or down their organizational hierarchy), a constant material for news, also can be followed easily. Besides, there are matters relating to no particular date: generally, these are situations or trends, not events. A set of such subjects or ideas are always "in stock" at any editorial board for "filling in holes."

Unpredictable events are classified and distributed among institutions responsible for them without participation of journalists. Practically all such institutions (law enforcement bodies, fire service, ambulance, Ministry of Emergent Situations, etc.) have their own press service departments. With their help events can be channeled in a way convenient for journalists; permanent channels provide regular production and publication; and "non-channel" information is dropped – as, in particular, is illustrated by the story of Rachel. Journalists usually mention a limited number of source types, listing them by approximate importance as follows:

1   Information agencies. Often used source, though they have two drawbacks: can be late and can give inaccurate information, which always has to be checked.
2   Journalists' personal contacts covering particular subjects. Their information overlaps with that of agencies, but often comes earlier.
3   Information from sources provided by fax or telephone (in case of obvious commercial intention it goes through respective departments). This source is much disliked by journalists precisely because of its advertising character and usually little compliance with a journalistic notion of newsworthiness.
4   Other mass media. Not a very "prestigious" source, because journalists always try to be faster than their competitors, rather than follow in their tracks.
5   Information provided by the public – quite a rare source.

"Farkhat," the head of the newsroom at *STV* – that is, a person responsible for planning and assignment, and editing of the most important pieces – commented for me on three newscasts, indicating the source type for each story. His account, presented in Table 8.1, although not statistically representative, still clearly shows the prevalence of personal contacts and information agencies among other sources.

The network of sources is constructed based on the subjects, topics or themes which are most often publicly discussed – that is, based on past experience. The list of themes tends to freeze (see Table 8.2), and every newcomer of the journalistic community learns firmly what topic can be a subject for news, and what cannot. The "authorship" of the list cannot be attributed to only one group of actors or institutions, it is difficult to find particular authors at all. Thus, the journalistic community cannot be labeled the sole author; one of the reasons for this is that reality is structured not by journalists, but by other actors for other purposes, while journalists use already existing structures for their own purposes. Vice versa, other actors (e.g. press services) try to use mass media to visualize anything of their interest, and this is also picked up by journalists.

Not only is the list of subjects and topics fixed, but the list of types, or genres of facts and events able to be the material for news is closed as well (see Table 8.3). As a rule, journalists most of all pay attention to events connected with high status persons, as well as their specially organized actions, that is, to scheduled events (the prevalence of "routine events" over "accidents" and other unexpected happenings is well documented in other studies, for example, in Molotch and Lester 1974). These events are usually compact in terms of time and space, predictable, and their structure provides journalists with both pictures and text.

As Table 8.3 shows, types of events are closely connected with the genres of news stories they produce. Speaking more generally, the structure of a story is another fixed value, along with the set of sources, subjects and types of events covered. Thus, each TV story consists of the following elements:

- Non-synchronous elements: a number of pictures, 2–5 seconds each, accompanied by an voice-over – a non-synchronous off-screen speech by a reporter;
- Synchronous elements (pictures with original sound):

  a *Sinkhron* – a speaking character;
  b *Standup* – a correspondent speaking at the place of the event;
  c *Inter-shum* – any picture without speech with original sound.[1]

Total duration is usually 1–3 minutes (typical length varies between companies); a story often begins and ends with a *standup*; from two to five *sinkhrons* can be inserted into the body of the story with voiced-over pictures between them; sometimes (but rather seldom) *inter-shums* can be found.

Any agent willing to get into the news should either fit into this structure as a character, or produce an event that can be handled according to this structure. Thus, it is more difficult to cover such subjects as "growth of crime" or "poor condition of environment" (trends and states) in a news story than "Starovoitova's murder" or "breakdown of the *Vodokanal* water supply system." Separate crimes or disasters easily fit into news structure, primarily since they can generate a picture, while trends and

Table 8.1 Subjects and sources of news at STV (an example)

	Subjects' titles in the editorial archive	Explanatory notes	Sources: comments from Interview 25 with "Farkhat Ramazanov"
Tuesday	Nikitin – process	High-profile trial over officer Nikitin accused of giving away a state secret to a Norwegian ecological NGO	Information agency, information had been obtained beforehand through a correspondent maintaining permanent contact with Nikitin's attorney
	Anikushin – the memorial plaque	Anikushin – a famous Soviet sculptor	Information agency; personal contacts also took place
	Lenenergo	Municipal power supply company	Information agency, the subject was constantly checked and followed by personal contacts as well
	Roskomkino		Information agency
	University of Economics – round-the-table discussion – rectors		Information agency
	Gusev – medal – Menshikov Fund		Personal contacts with Gusev and the Russian Museum
	Representatives of the arts – award ceremony		Personal contacts with the representatives of the arts
	Dirty election techniques	Local parliamentary elections	Archive of the information department of the TV company
Monday	Protest action of the Russian students		Press-release received by fax, but one of the journalists knew some people from that movement, and was already aware of the event
	Clinic "C" opening ceremony		Zakaz (hidden advertisement) – placed with the commercial department by "C" medical company

Day	Event	Note	Source
	Latest Bely award in literature, press conference Regional library	Bely – a famous Russian writer	A correspondent's personal contacts
	The Mikhailovsky Castle, restoration	Mikhailovsky Castle is a museum	A permanent contact, established a month ago
	Nikitin		An anchor's personal contacts; Personal contacts with the attorney
	Vodokanal	Municipal water supply company	The head of information service personal contacts
	Elections – registration		City Lawmaking Assembly, information agencies
Friday	Seasonal opening of the bridges over the Neva has finished		Known from previous year's experience, personal contacts with "a guy" from Mostostroy [bridges maintaining and supervising company]
	Anti-governor coalition		Information agencies, personal contacts with politicians "and since all this had been planned beforehand, we had enough time and managed to shoot Sobchak . . . among other things, he answered our questions about today's 'dirty election techniques'"
	Starovoitova – anniversary of death	Refers to high-profile murder of Starovoitova, a Russian parliamentarian and HR activist	"I think everything is clear about the sources"
	Pushkin – memorial museum – restoration	Pushkin – classical Russian poet	Information of journalist responsible for archeology
	Commander-in-chief of Leningrad Military district arrives		Information from the army headquarters, personal contacts of the head of information service
	Radio Baltika – fifth anniversary	Radio Baltika – fifth anniversary	Information broadcast by radio Baltika
	Ivchenko – sixtieth anniversary	Ivchenko – famous theatrical actor	Information from a correspondent responsible for theater

Table 8.2 Subjects of news stories broadcast by PTV (July 1998–January 1999)

Subject (more than one per story is possible)	Quantity	
	Number	%
1 Politics: visits, statements and movements of political figures, elections, political assassinations, financial crisis 1998, government activities, etc.	119	47.6
2 Crime: any violation of law, including assassinations	52	20.8
3 Social: protest actions, strikes, hunger-strikes, financial crisis 1998; matters from the "social sphere"	39	15.6
4 Matters in official discourse called "soul life" or "spiritual life": problems referring to national identity (burial of the remains of the Czar family, the fifty-fifth anniversary of lifting the siege of Leningrad, other memorable dates, awarding ceremonies, etc.)	31	12.4
5 Culture: exhibitions, theater tours, festivals, anniversaries of people of art	30	12.0
6 Holidays and memorable dates	18	7.2
7 Technical: accidents, wrecks, crashes, more seldom – technical and engineering achievements	15	6.0
8 Economics: condition of the financial system (as a rule – crises)	8	3.2
9 Environment and nature (as a rule – natural disasters)	7	2.8
10 Entertainment: curious and amazing events	5	2.0
11 Other	9	3.6
Total number of stories analyzed	250	

Source: Koltsova 2001c: 115.

states are predominantly verbal or interpretative constructions. However, a picture without interpretation has no sense either: if journalists have just a picture of a flood, it is not enough for a story until they have the necessary information about the disaster (location, duration, size, amount of damage etc). Moreover, this information should be provided by respective experts, and preferably given in the form of *sinkhron*. That is why experts are the most common characters of *sinkhrons*; other common categories are witnesses/participants/victims and high-status persons, who make the news just by the fact of making a statement on any subject (newsmakers). If there is a central character in the story, his/her relations/friends/enemies etc., are made to be involved.

Stories, in their turn, are arranged in a certain order within a news program. A typical structure of a "regular" or "ordinary" newscast was described to me by a number of respondents (Interviews 12, 14, 18, 22, 23):

Beginning – politics and economics.
Middle – miscellaneous: community life, international news, accidents.
End – culture and sports, curios and amusing events (soft news).

Table 8.3 Genres of events and news stories broadcast by PTV (July 1998–January 1999)

Genre of story/event covered	Subgenre		Quantity	%
1 Formally organized events, actions, operations or performances			65	26.0
	1a	Events; meetings, congresses, celebrations, trials, burials, cultural events (exhibitions, festivals, etc.)	47	18.8
	1b	Actions: street meetings, picketing, strikes, hunger strikes, spontaneous protest actions	10	4.0
	1c	Press-conferences	4	1.6
	1d	Other operations,: e.g. water supply cut off, fishermen rescued, grants and donations	4	1.6
2 Activities of high status persons			41	16.4
	2a	Statements	19	7.6
	2b	Visits	17	6.8
	2c	Movement in hierarchy	5	2.0
3 Accidents: crashes, disasters, terrorist acts, high-profile crimes			39	15.6
4 Descriptive stories			37	14.8
	4a	Descriptions of new social phenomena or trend: e.g. crisis, defamation during elections	20	8.0
	4b	Descriptions of social conditions or states: life of community or a social group, historical sketches	11	4.4
	4c	Portraits of a person	6	2.4
5 Chronicles: narrations of a sequence of events referring to one subject			22	8.8
6 Complex stories			8	3.2
7 Other			22	8.8
8 No data			16	6.4
Total			250	100

Source: Koltsova 2001c: 116.

The "emotional" structure of an ordinary program was described in the following terms:

Beginning – routine news, e.g. official information.
Middle – culminating point: any event being to a certain extent outstanding against the background of routine ones; aimed at preventing the audience from losing interest in the newscast.
End – routine information again.

Typical reasons for a departure from a "standard" newscast are situations when extraordinary events identified as sensational break into its structure (breaking news). Such news items are always given at the beginning, or at least are announced there, and the whole program is constructed around them: other stories developing the same subject are given, additional details are promised to be given to the audience as soon as they become available before the end of the program, etc.

Newsmaking: contested practices

As already mentioned, all the indicated elements – sets of sources, topics, genres of events and stories, structure of stories and newscasts/print editions – being relatively fixed, present a difficulty with establishing their authorship. Journalists have their own visions on this matter. Many of my respondents were sure that structure and subjects of news are dictated by the interests and specific perception of the audience, though these journalists did not maintain direct contacts with it. Respondent "Mikhail Tarasyuk," a TV reporter, justifying the abundance of crime subjects in TV news, even referred to Maslow and his theory of hierarchy of needs: basic needs are satisfied first, Mikhail said, and secondary needs – after them. As, according to Maslow-Tarasyuk, safety is the main need of any human being, the audience most of all is concerned about crime and disasters. So, he said, "we can't ignore this" (Interview 18). Some respondents (though only answering my questions) pointed out that the rules for media production are rather conventional. A TV anchor said in his interview that journalists follow tradition, and nobody knows what it would be like if they tried to do it differently: "Just there is such an unwritten rule, and nobody has tried to dispute it" (Interview 20).

In some cases, however, the rules *can* be disputed, and change may take place. Such changes, that were particularly intense in the 1990s, shed some light on the authorship of formats and themes. Thematic change, not being a special object of the study, can only be sketched here. For example, criminal news in the format in which it exists in the West was unknown in the Soviet Union. As a former TV and newspaper editor put it, "we were not prohibited to publish it, but it just did not occur to us that a janitor killing his wife with a kitchen knife could be an issue for a newspaper" (Interview 8). It can be argued that such things did not occur precisely because they had once been prohibited, but in any case late Soviet culture ascribed newsworthiness to events having public significance – thus, pilfering at work, inherent to a socialist economy, could be and did become an issue for media. Covering this and other disadvantages of the (post-)Soviet system became especially popular in late 1980s – first half of 1990s – a period that hardly knew any good news at all. 1987–8 were also the years when all media became suddenly flooded with "news" on Soviet history, concerning various previously concealed matters – from Stalin's repressions to Brezhnev's stagnation to Lenin's red terror. Teachers based their lectures on newspaper publications, and the whole country seemed to be taking a history lesson. This agenda was quickly washed away by matters of extremely intense contemporary political and economic life: the growing shortages and armed ethnic conflicts at the fringes of the USSR, the attempted coup and the collapse of the Soviet Union, the liberalization of prices and devaluation of everybody's savings, the bombardment of the Russian parliament by Yeltsin and adoption of the new constitution and so on. Overburdened by political uncertainty and economic difficulties, audiences were virtually unresponsive to culture or sports events.

The mid-1990s were the years of privatization that was almost publicly struggled for by various CIGs through their media, leaving the audiences in the role of a silent witness who hardly defined any news agenda at all. The late 1990s brought to media the general fatigue of a society exhausted with the intense political life of the previous decade, and a decline of the inter-CIG struggle that now allowed room for other topics. Sports, crime and infotainment gradually gained popularity. An indicator of the fatigue tendency is the considerable share of "culture" and "spiritual life" on both state TV (Table 8.2) and private TV (Table 8.3). Respondents, though, also explained this by special efforts of state agents to divert journalists from creating disturbing products and to push news out of the political realm.

Thus, the agenda setting process was not an exclusive product of a journalistic community, but rather followed more general developments in society, coming partly from state agents, CIGs, audiences and other actors. Format changes, however, may to a greater extent be attributed to media-producers. In the late 1980s it was rank-and-file journalists and middle-rank media executives who became major agents of innovation, while top managers at that period had to moderate their initiatives and negotiate them with state agents. It would be also an exaggeration to say that journalists were directly pushed to format changes by audiences. Instead of studying audience perception, they studied the experience of their Western colleagues. Manifesting their difference from the Soviet standard and associating with the Western standard was often considered enough to attract audience attention. To some extent that was true, but the difficulties that post-Soviet audiences experienced in the perception of such innovations are largely unknown. Among the most visible changes was the speeding up of the general tempo of broadcast news, with much faster speech and shorter pictures: 2–5 second shots could hardly be imagined in the solemn Soviet news. Next was the introduction of more personified, informal and often faltering speech – all this, including mistakes, was regarded by younger journalists as an indicator of live broadcasting and, consequently, of the truthfulness of the news item, while the older generation perceived it as absence of professionalism (see more details in Mickiewicz 1997: Ch. 4, esp. 78–9).

Intensive format change was occurring during the time of my observation at the *Vesti Stragorada* newspaper. It took place against the background of the technological innovation that was being introduced by the owner bank. Computer layout was already in place, but journalists wrote their articles by hand, often on the back of old proof sheets, and later they were typed by a typist at one of the few editorial computers. Many journalists could not use computers. Photos accompanied the layout to the printing house in hard copy, because of the absence of equipment that could transfer scanned pictures into high quality images: offset printing was not available. The only computer connected to the Internet was occupied by a special worker who sorted all incoming messages, including news agencies' products and personal correspondence. These innovations, together with complete reshuffling of departments and their personnel, turned the news production process into a mess. People were constantly asking each other who they should ask, what they should do and where should do it. Everybody tried to make last-minute changes in the computer layout since, unlike on paper, it was so easy; the result was that the chief editor often signed off the version of the newspaper that in fact was not final.

Similarly, everybody tried to introduce his/her own notions of newsworthiness and format requirements. The official corporate mission, prepared by the chief editor for the bank, posed two tasks to be fulfilled by the journalistic team: first, to create a family evening newspaper, and, second, "to influence decision-making by the power and business elites" (Field notes 1: 13.03.1997). Translated from the euphemistic language, this mission meant that the second task should have been lobbying for the bank's interests within the local elite, while the first task was aimed at making the accomplishment of the second cheaper through the at least partial covering of expenses by revenues from ordinary readers. These hardly compatible goals led to the situation where, as noted by one of the respondents, "everybody was doing his own newspaper." Family edition proponents promoted infotainment genres, including healthcare and consumer news. The newsroom head stood for short hard news, quickly reported. Since that was practically unachievable because of the slow work of the printing house, others offered to concentrate on "exclusive" news and detailed next-day accounts. One of the journalists, commenting on a story of a dog killing its master's family, said that it was time for the paper to be up to date and, like others, to give juicy details, such as the baby's brains leaking out. The chief editor, however, said it was not their style, and other details should be picked up. The head of the economic and political department thought that style was not really important, if the facts were described correctly. The leading columnist built up a classification of news into *accidental*, like the janitor killing his wife and the dog – its owners, and *systemic* – those that influenced the life of society most of all. According to him, the latter were to be given preference. Lacking common criteria for well executed formats, editors often had difficulties in evaluating journalistic pieces. Older journalists noted that the familiar Soviet system of news genres was dissolving: some formats died out, others emerged, and boundaries between all of them blurred, which posed special problems both for writing and editing.

Thus my observation suggests that format change was predominantly, though not exclusively, a product of the journalistic community. Preconditions for it were set up first by state agents, and later by economic agents, who often even pushed journalists towards changes. The process itself was quite spontaneous and chaotic, especially in the early stages. By the late 1990s a new system of news formats became visible, although the duality of non-contested and disputable elements, as well as those constructed and sought for, was to some extent preserved.

Newsmaking dualities: journalists' attitudes

In handling duality of news, my respondents usually exercised a kind of doublethink, although I do not imply negative connotations here. Quite often journalists easily combined misrecognition of the constructivist component of their work in some cases with the instrumental approach to "reality" in others. On the one hand, journalists used such categories as "fact," "witnesses," "material evidence".[2] On the other hand, stories had to be "assembled" and "manufactured," events had to have been "effectively presented," and interviewees were to be "caught out" and "wound up." Once before shooting, respondent Mikhail Tarasyuk gave me instructions on how to put questions to an interviewee. The main thing was not to forget my initial goal: "to pull out of her the things you need."

Later Mikhail also gave me detailed comments on stories produced by him. If you want your story to be a success, he said, you should previously have an idea, and then pick up material suitable for it. The most obvious method is constructing an idea on simple binary oppositions. He showed me a story intended to be an example. It dealt with so-called *black pathfinders* – people who illegally search for old arms, weapons, or explosives on World War II battlefields and graves. The first opposition was setting the official world of commemorating the Great Patriotic War (World War II) against the world of "businessmen" who dug out old entrenchments and sold arms and elements of munitions found there.

Second, black pathfinders were opposed to the representatives of enforcement bodies. Speaking about the latter Mikhail said: "this cop is just like them – cops themselves are digging there for something to find." But this remark was not included in the story since it could blur the opposition (though the respondent did not give this reason for its exclusion). He emphasized that in this case he did not view either side in moral categories.

In other cases such moral marking was manifest, as in the story about water supply Mikhail showed me. It took place in a town on the Russian-Estonian border, one part of which, called Ivangorod, belongs to Russia, and the other called Narva is located over the river in Estonia. The water supplying centre built in Soviet times for both parts of the town has since the fall of the Soviet Union found itself in the newly independent Baltic state. Commenting on the story about the Narva authorities cutting off the water supply from Ivangorod because of unpaid debts, Mikhail several times stressed:

> All this is combined into solid integral narration in accordance with the major drama theory principle: obligatory opposition of two things: on the one side you have vicious Estonian officials, on the other – those poor, miserable and so on, Russian citizens.... And then everything becomes simple, clear, and, most important, logical and easy to construct.

The key categories of the respondent were *idea, dramatic composition* and *impact upon audience*. I wondered whether the dramatic facet of a journalistic piece does not contradict its factual side. He explained that the journalistic professional task was to compose the story without such contradictions:

> Those old women going with jugs [to the nearest pond for water] – I don't dream them up. And that malicious Estonian plumber who cuts the water supply off, I don't invent him, there he is, that's all true. I mean, if I disguised myself as an Estonian malicious plumber – then, well, yes, that's it, it goes then ... this is called breaking in the structure of the news story.

(Interview 18, January 1999)

Based on my respondents' opinions about the structure of a news story, it appears possible to sketch their professional and ethical stance on the matter in the following way: you can do whatever you want with the initial material, but the material itself should be genuine. That is why, for example, "Farkhat," the head of the newsroom, criticized a story about a city legislative assembly by a famous reporter: he had put a notice "For deputies only" on a public bathroom and shot it as though it was authentic.

Another respondent, a newspaper journalist "Valentina Soroka," condemned "faked" newspapers (see Chapter 6), even despite her own participation in producing one. On the other hand, a story made "out of nothing" but conforming to the rule formulated above is a sign of a great skill. I observed many occasions when such stories were praised by colleagues (e.g. Koltsova 1999: 87–104). The existence of this ethos indicates that journalists do not have the goal of making news a comprehensive model of reality as a whole. Rather, they consider it necessary to reflect the verifiable circumstances of certain events.

Another conclusion that may be made from my observations is that Russian journalists did not demonstrate attempts, either "genuine" or "hypocritical," to separate "facts" from "commentaries," as is common practice, for example, in the USA (e.g. Tuchman 1978: 97–101). On the contrary, ability to combine "facts" skillfully with elaborated explanation or emotional judgment without any evident contradictions is sometimes considered a sign of professionalism. "Vladislav Menshikov," a high-ranking TV manager, responsible for news at *STV*, said:

> We don't have journalism of fact in Russia, and won't have it for long.... Psychology is still such that people rather need to be explained than, eh ... shown. Instructed than shown.... Of course, you may say "show it, our people are not stupid, they'll understand, why are you treating people like this?" But in reality it is not quite so. I think people expect from television some explanation, consolation, something else, but not at all only information.
>
> (Interview 26)

"Menshikov" admitted, though, that there were political reasons for not separating facts from comments, stating that media were, as before, means of struggle.

The most common way of introducing commentaries into news is "turning" them into facts by citing third parties, which is, of course, not unique to Russia. A character's speech is regarded by journalists as a fact in the sense that one cannot deny it happening. This is really convenient: in this case the responsibility rests on the character, not journalists. Moreover, journalists prefer *sinkhrons*/citations to carry emotions, assumptions and other vulnerable declarations, while verifiable statements are kept for voice-over/author's text.

After the news story from the court session I was criticized by the reporter "Kirill" because I did not interview the plaintiff, since "she could have said something emotional" (this, perhaps, would have contributed to the dramatic structure of the story). He told me to view the material and select 15–20 seconds from the interview with the plaintiff's attorney. When I asked what I should choose, he said, "something like how he is going to win the case." I was a bit lost, and explained that I had asked him about "the facts." Then Kirill watched the recording himself, and chose the episode where in the first phrase the attorney *supposed* that other injured people would also bring legal actions, and in the second phrase he already sounded affirmative: "I believe that the other people who were injured, well, they will sue the Metro administration, and the process is on now. The people will, so to say, make claims against Metro for all they deserve." The opposite party – the metro representative – was not given a voice not only because of problems with Andrey's camera: Kirill never expressed interest in it. Acting like this, Kirill did not experience any external pressure – if there was any, it would more probably be generated by the metro administration than by the injured woman. Kirill just insinuated his own attitude to the case into the story.

Generally, the duality of constructed and sought-for facets of news meant for journalists that the sought elements were to be accurately borrowed from the outside, which led to responsibilities and to at least some degree of dependence from external agents. The constructed part of a news story, on the contrary, was something that wholly depended, or was believed to wholly depend, on journalists themselves, and thus was associated with their autonomy, power, and creativity. Therefore, the constructed facet looked more attractive but, unfortunately for journalists, it had little chance to be legitimized in the outside world, which produced the described tensions in journalistic practices and attitudes.

Journalists dealing with sources

Since sources mediate most "events" of "reality" for journalists, they are a constitutive part of the newsmaking process, whether they have any strategies or not. Journalists, on the contrary, always adopt some kind of strategies toward their sources. One major cluster of strategies, concerning recruiting and choosing sources, was already touched on in the previous sections. The building of a permanent network of sources of certain structure solves the problem of finding and choosing off-screen sources – a bigger and a more important group of sources. The "dramaturgical" approach to making stories, and other considerations of format and style, are methods of choosing those sources who get into stories as characters.

Another major cluster of journalists' strategies toward sources stems from a difference in interests between these two groups of actors and concerns the elaboration of "definitions of situations" and their interpretations. Neither the intuitive interpretations of lay sources, nor the deliberately constructed interpretations of professional press-secretaries may become material for news without alteration, unless the story made is a case of hidden advertising. Liberation from sources' interpretations, even if journalists do not support the idea of objectivity, is nevertheless regarded an attribute of "genuine" news, otherwise journalism, as reporter

"Mikhail Tarasyuk" put it, would have become a sort of extension of corporate public relations departments. Alexei Khokhlov noted on this matter that "one should never evaluate the real situation by basing on police statistics. The police statistics reflects the work of the police, not the crime rate" (Khokhlov 1998). Such differences in the goals of sources and journalists make their relationships inherently conflictual.

Perhaps the highest level of conflict between them existed in the early 1990s when sources and journalists were for the first time left face to face. In the previous chapter I mentioned that sources at that time had hardly any experience of interacting with media, which decreased their power. At the same time, journalists either had no critical skills in relation to sources or, more generally, no skills in autonomous data collection, because this had been neither needed nor possible in the Soviet Union. With time, as professionalization and mobilization of resources by a certain class of sources was leading to stratification within this group of actors, journalists became increasingly aware of the power component of their relationship with the former. As I said at the beginning of this chapter, misrecognition of external control when it was mediated by superiors, viewed as internal agents, could easily be transformed into struggle against an agent of pressure, as soon as my respondents identified it as external and, therefore, illegitimate. This is clearly seen, for example, in the interview of respondent "Vitaly Bogdanov" (see Example of annotated interview) where he speculates upon the main types of influences rank-and-file journalists are subjected to. In the discourse he offers, control of their superiors is totally dispersed in the impersonal demands of production, and they both are opposed to external pressure, or censorship, by sources.

Figuratively speaking, the power of journalists' resistance to the influence of sources is inversely proportional to the amount of resources the latter possess. Journalists whom I observed, as a rule, avoided conflicts with those sources who could act as agents of violence, especially of illegitimate violence. For example, the meeting of Alexei Khokhlov, a journalist emphasizing his independence, with members of the *Tambovian* criminal group, finished with his apologies to them (see Chapter 4). During my observation I also came across a similar case. Once journalists from *PTV* were tasked with making a news item about the disappearance of a large credit obtained by a factory from a foreign bank. The same day "Mikhail Tarasyuk" discussed the task with his secretary "Zinaida."

> "Well, generally speaking, one can easily get one's head kicked off, if one goes working with such subjects," Mikhail said, and Zinaida started moaning, "oh, yeah, sure." "But we have to see what it's all about," he added. They agreed that they would say [to the boss] that there was nothing interesting there, or that they didn't manage to find anything, or something like that. Anyway, all their efforts would be in vain. "Let the Auditing Chamber or Procuracy deal with it," Mikhail

said, "at best an investigation piece in a newspaper, but they won't let it be shot."

(Field notes 2: 16.01.1999)

But journalists deal quite differently with those possessing insufficient power resources. The same reporter spoke rather emotionally about a scene he had made in the Russian museum because they had not received him as, he thought, they should have. He had been waiting in the museum for an hour, and it was not a specialist on Surikov painting who at last came to meet him, but the head of the information department. Mikhail shouted at the museum staff, and said that "if they [could] not arrange it all normally," he would not shoot at all; and that it was the museum who was interested in shooting of exhibitions most of all. According to him, the museum officials became extremely worried. Another day waiting for the Minister of the Interior for an hour and a half did not arouse Mikhail's indignation at all.

The majority of sources seem to take a middle position between these two cases in relation to power resources. Their resources are comparable with those of journalists, and the interaction of both parties resembles a constant testing of each other's boundaries of power. For example, during the described shooting of the lawsuit against the Metro organization, its representative first refused to give an interview, but when a reporter put a microphone close to her face, she said a few words in front of the camera. Next time the journalists were shooting in a court room where a closed session was going to start, until the defendants' attorney came and ordered them to get out. When the accused were being brought to the court room, the journalists and other spectators were made go out to the corridor, and police closed the passageway. The cameramen continued shooting standing round the corner and, though they could not catch the defendants' faces, they managed to get some pictures anyway.

Generally, dealing with sources who possessed approximately equal power resources, my respondents used three main groups of methods: exchange of services of access, breaking of agreements with further compensation, and initiation of relations of "friendship." The first type is based on the mutual complementarity of journalists' and sources' resources: the latter have access to information, and the former – to its dissemination. Interests of the two groups of interactants sometimes differ, but nevertheless journalists and sources are still interested in each other, and every party uses the other for its own purposes. Thus, sources sometimes agreed that some information they had little need of, or even did not like, would be published on condition that the matters these sources were interested in would be mentioned. Journalists included such requests in their stories, thus buying the right to cover the aspects they needed. One of the respondents spoke about a case in which the chief manager of an airport allowed a cameraman onto a minister's plane on condition that the signboard of a certain company would be shown in the story. This case could be considered as hidden advertising, but the journalist did not get any reward other than required by "production necessity."

Another time a local FSB official gave a journalist a chance to get an interview with a minister, though he could easily have made the reporter get out. The official seemed to require nothing in exchange. But several days later I heard a phone conversation in which the journalist was arranging for an interview with the FSB officials to provide them with a good chance of drawing the "attention of Moscow" and demonstrating the good work of their department. Thus the exchange of services took a more complicated, delayed character.

Since the interests of journalists and sources are still rather different, journalists often chose to infringe their sources' interests deliberately. For example, in his story one of the observed journalists reported a theft of a computer from a polling station as a political event: indeed, in the light of numerous infringements during that election campaign, the version about a malefactor trying to torpedo the elections seemed plausible. The press-secretary of the respective state body was in a rage, according to the journalist. The reporter risked losing his favor, but next day, in a story devoted to different matters, he managed to make a statement that, according to preliminary investigation, the previous version imputing political motivations to the robber had been disproved, and so the theft appeared to be an ordinary crime. After that the press-secretary forgave the "guilty" journalist, and their relations were restored (all three cases reported after Field notes 2).

Like sources, journalists often emphasized the significance of informal relations for the successful work of a reporter:

> Journalism is a very informal profession.... Arranging informal relations is quite a delicate process: on one occasion you have to drink vodka in friendly atmosphere, on another – congratulate somebody on something. And you shouldn't speak in the tone like this, "How do you do, Alexander Nikolayevich,[3] it is Mikhail Tarasyuk from *PTV* disturbing you. Would you be so kind as to help us in a very important matter..." No, you'd speak like this, "Alex, well, I need it a lot, you know, help me out, mate, will ya," I mean you should seek to turn your relations in the right direction.
>
> (Interview 18, January 1999)

Thus journalists found themselves constantly balancing conflict and cooperation. Friendship-like relations, on the one hand, limited journalists' autonomous interpretative activities, since they created personal obligations and exchanges; on the other hand, friendships with informal sources, quite often helped in obtaining information that otherwise would have been unavailable. First, they speeded up the process of data search and thus allowed journalists to overcome time constraints that in the structure of newsmaking are usually very tight. Second, informal sources often offered alternative facts and interpretations, although usually anonymously. The motivation of such sources might not always be limited to informational wars and sometimes could include their "genuine" desire to reveal some information they were afraid to be associated with. In such situations journalists, of course, risked being sued for defamation and libel, but they kept cooperating with such sources, otherwise they would have obtained only "boring" official statements.

The wish to break out beyond the boundaries of interpretations thrust upon journalists by official sources often motivated them to move from selective cooperation with unofficial sources to accepting intentional *kompromat* from them. This still did not necessarily meant that journalists were taking one side in an informational war. Respondent "Samuel Petrenko" said that he collected *kompromat* provided by all conflicting parties, and then drew his own conclusions. He did not consider this activity "genuine" journalistic investigation, because an investigation, in his opinion, required not only using competing sources relating to the existing conflict, but an individual search for new, concealed conflicts. Such a journalist had to be not only unconnected to either party, but also aware of their interests and thus able to analyze the correlation between the materials provided and the parties' interests. Still, what Samuel did was much closer to a journalistic definition of genuine news than to a leak of *kompromat*. Moreover, like Alexey Khokhlov (see Chapter 7), he took precautions against being used "blindly": this may happen if a journalist agrees to publish a leaked *kompromat* without knowing for whom and/or how it will work. It can appear dangerous for him/her, because being a blind weapon in the hands of one party in a conflict, the journalist can become a victim of the other. Unlike a deliberate mouthpiece, a blind journalist cannot take any precautions against this danger.

Journalists' attitudes toward external influences

An approach that regards social actors as power agents assumes that in their relationships each of them tries to minimize the power of his/her interactant, while seeking to maximize his/her own power, and submits to the will of the other only when this decision brings less losses than benefits. This applies to journalists no less than to anyone else, but because journalists more than many other professionals are expected to make value-based decisions, they less than others may ignore normative discourses going on around them. Knowledge that some of their actions, within certain normative frameworks, are much less legitimate than others had direct impact on the behavior of my respondents.

I have already tried to show that they tended to deny legitimacy to weaker power agents, while actions of stronger actors were more willingly legitimized. The general picture is, however, more complex, and more-over, the very grounds for legitimacy were seriously contested in the jour-nalistic community in the 1990s. When asked about his attitude toward media being used by external agents for their goals, a *TRK Peterburg* anchor "Arseni Kuznetsov" noted: "a journalist doesn't give a damn about what he is lobbying. Of course, there are some matters of principle; for example, I'll never support Zuganov.[4] But at a more dispersed level it's all the same to me: Gorbachev, Luzhkov – what's the difference?" (Interview 17). To be fair, I should mention that Kuznetsov became one of those protesting in *TRK Peterburg* against supporting governor Vladimir Yakovlev, Luzhkov's ally, but that happened a year after the interview. Like "Kuznetsov," TV anchor "Pyotr Senichev" characterized the fact that media organizations served the interests of various external agents as a "normal" thing, although earlier he had delegitimized the influence of sources:

> I don't see anything bad in it at all, because . . . well, it's like a surgeon, well, he sells his skill to cut people's bodies, well, to cure these bodies, to operate on them. A journalist sells his skill to write texts, that's all. Somebody works in one company, somebody – in another. Of course, you may speak about freedom of speech, but it is freedom in one company[5] [laughing].
>
> (Interview 20, October 1999)

The very concept of freedom of speech was seldom used by journalists unless it was provoked by me. However, this does not mean that journal-ists were unaware of the existence of the concept – quite the opposite, throughout the 1990s Russian journalists were exposed to a real flood of Western "preaching on how to work right," as one of the respondents put it. It is not surprising that the inundation of Western "instructions," combined with the contradiction of those instructions with Russian reality, aroused a certain irritation and skepticism in the Russian media community. However, although most of the time respondents considered the concept of press freedom a naive Western ideal, after the first negative reaction they usually admitted their positive attitude toward it.[6] The degree of the naivety ascribed to the concept was also different: some would claim that this ideal could not be achieved in contemporary Russia, while others were sure it was never and nowhere achievable.

Different studies of the professional identity of Russian journalists reg-ister domination of pragmatic constituent as well. Svetlana Yuskevits, a Russian researcher working in Finland, points out that among thirty inter-viewed journalists working in the north-western region of Russia only three defined their notion of "a good journalist" in accordance with the traditional Western ideal of an independent and fearless fighter for objectivity (Yuskevits 2000: 8–11). Other respondents gave definitions in terms of professional skills, talents, or love of the profession. Similar data were collected by Davis *et al.* on the basis of twenty-eight interviews in Tatarstan, an industrially developed region in the Volga basin with a big indigenous Moslem population. In particular, the researchers investigated journalists' opinions on whether Western ideals were applicable to Russia. The main conclusion of the study is that journalists' conformism to social structures imposed on them is a hangover from Soviet times, which is negatively marked in the article (Davis *et al.* 1998). However, since the researchers explicitly asked their respondents about the Western model, the result might have been to some extent distorted by the generally negative attitude of Russian journalists to Western "preachers." Another researcher, Anna Sosnovskaya, who interviewed forty journalists in Petersburg, did not press such models on her respondents; as a result, no concepts of independence and freedom of speech emerged in their discourse at all. Instead, they mentioned the following criteria of professionalism: work in a media organization as the main source of income, relevant education and special training, recognition by the journalistic community, interest in the profession, talent, and several others (Sosnovskaya 2000).

Taking a pragmatic position, however, journalists usually were not willing to give up the notion of press freedom completely and often attempted to marry it with their real practices. TV journalist "Ivan Kurbskiy" claimed that a state TV company should stand up for the interests of the state; and since the state lives on tax-payers' money, it is serving the interests of the people. I asked him to clarify if he meant that state and people were the same thing. The respondent kept a long silence, and then began to improvise, trying to develop a non-contradictory concept (Interview 19). Obviously, he had not possessed this concept before (which demonstrates the lack of significance of such things for him). Similarly, "Mikhail Tarasyuk" constantly contrasted journalistic work with press-services and PR-departments that stood up for the corporate interests of particular institutions. At the same time he said that he was working in the "TV of oligarchs" who had a special vision of newsworthiness which they imposed on journalists.

While contradictions in identity building are typical for any social actors, in our case they were also grounded in deeper contradictions between, on the one hand, discourse on freedom of speech, generally regarded as legitimate by some part of society and urged on journalists, and, on the other hand, the rules of the game set by agents of power acting in the media's immediate environment. Several major ways of releasing the strain created by this contradiction were illustrated above. The first was taking the pragmatic/opportunistic position, as expressed by "Arseny Kuznetsov." Another way was to disregard contradictions in one's reasoning, as did "Mikhail Tarasyuk." A third way was to deny legitimacy to the classical discourse on press freedom, and to legitimize the existing order.

General societal disagreement on major values, so common in the 1990s, filled the public domain with very different ideas, the circulation of some of which is unthinkable in the West. This made it possible that the third of the positions mentioned could be declared quite openly, even in public, unless there were special restrictions imposed by owners on that. For example, Mikhail Ponomarev, the anchor of the major *RTR*'s news-cast "Vestiy," in his interview with *Obshchaya Gazeta* (Varshavchik 1998) tried to justify himself against criticism by Prime Minister Yevgeny Pri-makov in a way quite alien to the traditional discourse on press freedom. Primakov had rebuked *RTR* saying that this state-owned company did not defend the interests of the government in an appropriate way. Ponomarev gave several examples trying to prove that he had defended the govern-ment with diligence, professionally, and called Primakov "the master in the best sense of the word." Another journalist, "Vitaly Bogdanov" criti-cized a city TV company for being too politicized in favor of the governor, also on grounds far removed from ideas of press freedom. It was not such politicization he thought to be inadmissible – he claimed that the bias, when too obvious, was a sign of poor professionalism and was weakening trust in the channel.

A fourth way to release the strain in identity building may be called realistic normativism. The legitimacy of discourse on press freedom is not denied, and the structural constraints are also acknowledged, but compro-mises that emerge from this situation are accepted by a journalist not (only) out of his "egoistic" interest. Making news as close to the ideal as the external limitations allow is regarded as a normatively better option than being kicked out of the profession altogether. Thus, a *PTV* top manager said in his interview: "our task is to do our job so that it, first of all, could be accomplished, that is – so that we could stay on the air, keep on covering the government's activity, show it as it is, simultaneously not depriving the society of ourselves as a source of information, because if the government switches us off as a mass medium, the society will lose this information" (Interview 27).

Concluding remarks

Being closest to the final product of news making, rank-and-file journalists are, nevertheless, not the most powerful agents in this game and are exposed to numerous influences. This does not mean that rank-and-file journalists are passive recipients of power, they also are active players. Thus, in cases where there are no special instructions from superiors, their relationships with sources are constructed as bargaining combining coop-eration and struggle, of which these relationships can hardly be ever puri-fied. But what journalists control almost entirely is the format of news as a genre. They share this control with their bosses, but on this matter both sides have a general consensus, and no other actors are given access to arrangements related to format. Even when journalistic standards were rapidly changing in the early 1990s, and the sphere of consensus narrowed significantly, media professionals tried to solve contradictions among themselves, and very little audience research was carried out at that time.

9 Center and periphery of power

Media top managers as power mediators

No-one is as interested in preserving media organizations as their heads: if an outlet ceases to exist, external agents keep their places, rank-and-file journalists, though they also become losers, have a good chance to find an equivalent position, but chief editors and directors can count on that less frequently. However, this is not the only reason why top media executives may really be recognized as the centre of the universe called "media production." It is with them that multiple social influences, both from within and from outside media organizations, come together, and it is they who constantly have to strike a balance between all of them. They stand at the boundary of their media organization with the external world as a two-way filter and conductor. Their own resource is also double-faced: for the outside world, they appear as holders of journalistic resource (skills, access to media production etc); for their subordinates in the organization they represent power to create and enforce rules, very much like that of owners or state agents. Sometimes top executives themselves own shares in their company, and quite often they are among its founders. Therefore, practices of media heads can be divided into two big groups: those directed within media organizations and those oriented to the outside world. Proceeding with the topic of the previous chapter, I shall start with the first group and consider media executives' relationships with rank-and-file journalists.

Media executives and journalists

In relations between media executives and rank-and-file journalists the balance of power is obviously shifted in favor of the former. Most of the time their interaction takes the form of direct orders; as in any formal organization, superiors' instructions to their subordinates are taken as a natural state of things – at least that is what my observation has shown. Thus at *PTV*, the St. Petersburg bureau of a Moscow TV company, it was numerous phone calls from Moscow, about twenty calls a day. Most of the calls were about journalistic routine (assignments, schedules, agendas etc). But this does not mean that other elements are never included in these seemingly routine instructions: managers' professional ideas, their personal tastes and preferences and the demands of various external agents are conveyed by them. Illegitimate instructions are sometimes (though not always) disguised as legitimate ones, so the motives behind managers' instructions are often hidden from direct executors. Once the respondent "Vitaly Bogdanov" tried to interpret the reasons why his story about the fifty-fifth anniversary of the lifting of the siege of Leningrad[1] had been killed. He said that "perhaps they have their own higher reasons, they do not want to arouse 'sympathy to Petersburg' when the Minister of Interior has come to 'the criminal capital'[2] to fight crime" (Field notes 2: 19.01.1999).

Another journalist explained why he was sent to shoot the Minister of Interior, why he had been told to ask a particular question about President Yeltsin's health and why other companies were not interested in it. He said that their TV company "is a TV of oligarchs," and the problem with Yeltsin's health is significant for them, while state-owned TV would rather ignore this delicate topic. Such type of reasoning was easily combined with explanations based on the interests of the audience.

At *STV*, where I could see the complete cycle of city news production, all questions and problems were solved on the local level. After each broadcast either the head of the information service or the head of the city bureau of the TV company went downstairs to the news-room and made his/her comments. The relations between the journalists and their superiors were quite open.

Information about hidden advertising, as I mentioned in Chapter 6, was written in the newsroom on the assignment board. Managers paid special attention to ordered materials and controlled their production. Once "Menshikov," *STV*'s top executive responsible for news, having read a news story script, told the journalist "Huh, you've given them 150 bucks-worth of praise here!" (the advertised company had paid less). As for the reporters, they showed their negative attitude to such tasks, but regarded them as their duty. During my study I saw only one case when a journalist refused to work over a *zakaz*, it was in *Vesti Starograda*. She left the newspaper soon after. There I also watched an episode when an already published story was discussed, and a journalist tried to convince the editor that hidden advertising deceives people. That happened when the newspaper was being transferred to a new owner, and it was the old team who tried to make protests, but the new editor was gradually pushing them away.

Several episodes involving transmission of influence from state agents by media executives could also be seen at different objects of observation. Once a top manager said to the stuff of the newsroom, "there is no Yeltsin for you! ... I mean as an object for negative comments." She referred to the fact that the TV company was owned by the state. One of the journalists said as a semi-joke, "No freedom at all" – "Yes, you do have freedom!," the manager began to object energetically, but was interrupted with everybody's burst of laughter. Another case was when the same executive killed a story about a press-conference by the St. Petersburg leader of the Chechen diaspora, though the shot material had not even been assembled into the final product, and the top editors had not yet seen it. As the journalist said, they were afraid of critical notes addressed to the authorities.

Later "Menshikov" unintentionally shed some light on this episode in his interview with me. He was saying that stories he usually selected for preliminary reading/watching (and editing) were the most important political events where "the accents had to be put in the right way." I asked him what would happen if something "wrong" were to be broadcast by any chance. He gave an example of another press-conference of the Chechen diaspora leader that had taken place before my observation started:

> [T]he leader of the Chechen diaspora gave a critical comment on Mister Putin ... The state television must not afford such things ... We've got very good guys, the journalists eh – and I hope that all of them can look at events from the point of view of their federal significance, and all feel themselves to be workers of state television, but sometimes there happen some faults in brains ... sometimes when a person goes, for instance, to the press-conference of the Chechen diaspora leader, absolutely – pro-Dudayev[3] [conference], he must understand that it should be presented in the course of state policy – and then I, you see, did not read it [beforehand], and there was a big scandal about it, and when I watched the story – you see, sometimes we are attacked, somebody would call, say something, I always defend [the journalists], but in this case the story was – really strange.
>
> (Interview 26, January 2000)

And this is how the *Vesti Starograda* chief editor enforced obedience in the coverage of a conflict between the mayor of Starograd and the *Starogradian* bank, both of whom were the paper's founders:

March 28, planning meeting

NIKOLAYEV (CHIEF EDITOR): We must give, maybe, a short news item...

GOLUBEV (head of department of politics and economics): But you don't allow us to cover things honestly. Everybody is terribly disappointed – Yaroslav, Alexei and others.

NIKOLAYEV: Disappointed with whom?

GOLUBEV: With you.

NIKOLAYEV (losing control): I am not interested in that! Let's go back to planning. Staff in your department, by the way, haven't submitted their plan.

GOLUBEV: With their salary they may ignore submission of plans.

NIKOLAYEV: If so, soon they won't have any salary!

(Field notes 1: 28.03.1997)

This episode leads us to consider sanctions that are used by top executives in media organizations in order to enforce their decisions. As in any corporation, media managers have access to a vast range of various positive and negative sanctions that can motivate their subordinates to submit to their will. Thus, GDF monitoring reflects a lot of cases when journalists' works were killed, including well-known TV programs, such as "Sovershenno Sekretno" (Top Secret) by an investigative celebrity Artiom Borovik, suspended not long before the 1999 parliamentary elections (GDF 24.06.1999), or an interview with the widow of one of Chechen separatists' leaders, that was broadcast to the Far East but cut out of the European version of Leonid Parfyonov's famous Sunday analytical program "Namedni" (Recently) at *NTV* in 2004. The connection between suppression of these pieces and their content which was contradictory to external agents' interests can be easily traced. Sometimes anchors and hosts, especially well-known ones, report such a link publicly; however, Parfyonov, *NTV*'s highest-rated anchor, paid for such a statement with his dismissal. Similarly, the *Vesti Starograda* chief editor, besides forbidding coverage of the bank-mayor conflict, killed the story about Nikitin (see Chapter 3). In that case the story's author explained it by the pressure of the FSB, although no immediate sanctions against him followed.

Another method TV managers use to control news production is forbidding journalists to participate in a particular broadcast, while the program itself is kept on air. As a rule, this course is taken after certain material was published, as a punishment or an attempt to prevent mistakes/disobedience in future. For example, a news anchor of Leningrad Region TV Anna Kulikova was suspended from air in September 1998 (GDF 23.09.1998). According to GDF data, the reason was her statement that Valery Serdukov who had just been appointed acting Governor of Leningrad Region was actually not supported by the regional elite.

A tougher measure is a dismissal of a journalist. As shown above, this may affect even the most outstanding anchors, to say nothing of rank-and-file journalists. The difference is that famous cases, including Parfyonov's, are usually high-profile, while ordinary cases go unnoticed by the public except, perhaps, the GDF monitoring audience. Thus, as GDF reports, in August 1998 the chief editor of the news program "Mestnoye Vremya" (Local Time), Irina Shulekina, was dismissed by the General Director of the respective TV company *Vladivostok* (the Far East region) for "permanently neglecting duties at work." It happened after a live broadcast in which she criticized the company management for setting up political censorship during the election campaign of the Vladivostok mayor (GDF 28.08.1998). However, as my observations show, dismissal is an infrequent practice. More common is either pushing a journalist off step by step, creating unsuitable working conditions, or dismissal of whole teams after top management has changed (in this case the motivation is "the company's new concept and policy"). A tricky measure that concerns show hosts and authors is suspension of the program without formally firing its leader. Being perfectly legal, this procedure actually makes the unwanted journalist redundant. A number of events on St. Petersburg TV channels in 1998–9 can serve an illustration.

According to GDF, in November 1998 the administration of *Channel 11* closed down a TV news program "Sobytiye" (Event). According to its anchor Sergei Chernyadev, six weeks before that, a *Yabloko*[4] party official Mikhail Amosov had suggested to Chernyadev that he start a pro-*Yabloko* propaganda campaign for the elections to the St. Petersburg Legislative Assembly. Otherwise Amosov threatened to close the program using his contacts with *NTV*, which was a shareholder of *Channel 11*, Chernyadev said. But according to the version of a respondent from *Channel 11*, there was a different reason for closing: its air time was given to the newly started program, *Segodnyachko-Piter*, which had good prospects for becoming popular at that time, but not at the time slot it had been previously scheduled for (it had coincided with "Vremya," the main national night newscast). Besides, Chernyadev's "Sobytiye" had been broadcast by two channels – 11 and 40 – and broadcasts by the latter were not stopped (Field notes 2); so it is not quite correct to say that the program was really closed down. It is also worth mentioning that respondents characterized "Sobyitie" as an "aggressive," "quarrelsome" and "low-quality" show, that had been repeatedly traveling from channel to channel.

After some time "Sobytie" appeared at *TRK Peterburg* (the former *Peterburg – 5 Kanal*), and in October 1999 Chernyadev was appointed head of the news department of the company. Making sense of this appointment is possible in the context of the changes that took place at the Channel after federal transmitting networks had been taken away from it (see Chapter 11). Shrinking from national to local broadcaster, the channel was renamed *TRK Peterburg* and made a joint stock company in early August 1998, with the controlling share belonging to the city and the regional administrations, and the rest – to a number of private banks. The staff was reduced by two-thirds, because a local channel needed much less human resources than a countrywide TV. Mid-August 1998 was the time of the national financial crisis that ruined a large proportion of Russian banks. In November, as private shareholders left the company, another personnel reduction took place. Payments of salaries, amounting to $70–$200, were delayed for months, total broadcasting time was reduced and vacant premises were let.

Chernyadev was appointed in October 1999, about half a year before the elections for governor. Just after his appointment he made a statement at a staff meeting which immediately became famous through Petersburg mass media: "It is Yakovlev[5] who is our governor, and *Yabloko* should be done away with" (confirmed in Interview 34). After that a group of the most popular journalists left the company; it was a rather uncommon case of collective protest. The anchors of a well-known news program

Inform-TV, Svetlana Agapitova and Innokenti Ivanov, gave a special press-conference, where they explained that they refused to work in the news program after the appointment of Chernyadev (GDF 13.10.1999). Soon Agapitova's host program was closed down because, according to the official explanation, the technical equipment was required for the election campaign. Respondent "Valentina Latypova" who was made to leave *TRK Peterburg* at the same period told me how other journalists were being involved in the campaign:

> The journalists before the elections were just given money openly, they went to Chernyadev's office, for example, and he just gave them cash, well, let's say, a month's salary, for example.... Well, for people who had to take care of their families – to get a premium for – for the job they were already doing just for their [regular] salary – it was of course really great. So very few people refused to take the money. The most principled ones – well, that's the fact I know, for example, "Nina" left for "*LTV*," and Chernyadev was just running after her along the corridor and shouting, "take a hundred dollars!" She said, "I won't do such things, won't work with you." And she left.
>
> (Interview 34, November 2000)

This example shows that media top managers widely used positive sanctions along with negative ones. Besides direct payments for political campaigns, they could include proceeds from hidden commercial advertisements, cooptation and promotion, and various non-monetary motivations. Thus, the *Vesti Starograda* chief editor, besides suppressing discussions on the permissibility of hidden advertising, at other meetings was quite peacefully persuading his subordinates to take part in it using the inclusive pronoun "we": "Each one of us should do it, should look for advertising. Otherwise we all will be ruined." (Field notes 1: 17.02.1997). This attempt to create a feeling of commonality of interests, although it did not give immediate results, worked in the long run. Similarly, "Menshikov" referred to the well developed identity of his subordinates as "workers of state television," who had internalized "the course of state policy" and did not need to be pressured.

Generally, sharp conflicts between journalists and top media managers were exceptional; much more often I used to observe not conflicts and confrontation, but subordination and agreement. In the flow of routine activity superiors' decisions were not discussed at all, and rank-and-file journalists were not interested in their political motives. When the story about the St. Petersburg leader of the Chechen diaspora was killed, I asked the responsible journalist why they just did not tell him to make his text "positive"; he said that "a superior's decisions are not to be discussed." Indeed, no organization would be able sustain itself if the relationships of its members were predominantly conflictual. In general, journalists' strategies toward superiors coincide with the four types of attitudes to external influences described in the previous chapter, varying from moderate to strong conformism. At the same time, conflicts have their significance even for those who are not engaged in them: they become known to communities of journalists in the form of gossip, which demonstrates to them the risks and boundaries of their possibilities.

Media executives and owners

Actions of media executives directed outside most often represent communication with owners; when directed toward other external agents, they are usually either coordinated with owners, or mediated by or even delegated to them. This, of course, applies to those media organizations where owners and top managers are clearly different persons or groups of persons, and it is their interaction that I will consider in this section.

While dominating their relations with rank-and-file journalists, media managers are obviously junior partners in their contacts with media owners. Even when media managers possess considerable authority, it is typically because it has been delegated to them by the owners, and its amount wholly depends on the will of the latter. As already mentioned, owners usually prefer to delegate internal interactions to top managers. It is top executives who are obliged to subject all subordinates to the will of the owner, who by and large does not interfere in journalistic activity on a day-to-day basis. However, sometimes owners, especially state ones, demand proof-reading or other close control of all or some pieces, killing certain stories or ruling out certain journalists. Respondent "Valentina Latypova" described for me the changes that took place at *Peterburg – 5 Kanal* after its controlling share was transferred to the city administration:

> [I]n '98, when there were the elections to the [city] legislative assembly, those famous Petersburg lists[6] and so on ... *glasnost* was exterminated from Petersburg television forever ... we don't know if the [governor's] wife was calling [television], but they say that yes. And not only calling, but even coming there, administrating, nearly making personnel appointments, eh. But before the elections in December '98 there appeared, let's say, several people from Smolny[7] at the television who started, so to say, to pressure the department heads and carry out the policy of Smolny.... There appeared those stupid programs about how everything is so good in Smolny, and how everything is so good in our city.

> (Interview 34, November 2000)

Although "Latypova" dated the "extermination" of *glasnost* at Petersburg TV to 1998, "Vitaly Bogdanov" described very similar practices of people from the election team of the previous governor (Interview 12). He also mentioned similar methods of management practiced by a private owner, referring to his acquaintances from the respective channel.

There is little evidence about methods of settling disagreements between owners and heads of media organizations, whether these disagreements are shaped as negotiation or conflict. GDF data is scarce: its monitoring reports a few such conflicts at the moment of the dismissal of media heads when the latter protest against the new appointments. Furthermore, the monitoring displays cases only with participation of state owners. However, various sources, including general media themselves and academic literature (e.g. Zassoursky 1999; E. Mickiewicz 1997), contain data on "voluntary" resignations of media top managers and about their public statements in which they hint at "political" causes for their decisions. But no reliable information about the essence of such conflicts usually surfaces, although several examples may be given. Thus, *Peterburg – 5 Kanal* director Oleg Rudnov explained his resignation in 1997 by his disagreement with the decision to transfer the channel's relay transmitting network to the control of *RTR* in Moscow (GDF 15–16.07.1997). A well-known fight was the long-term conflict of *NTV* with one of its owners (see Chapter 12). Nearly complete absence of data on conflicts with private owners does not mean that they do not have a power component or conflict of interest; rather it means that these conflicts are solved in a more concealed way than those involving state owners.

Cooperation of owners and media heads seems more common, but there were very few respondents who agreed to talk about that. The majority limited their talk on this topic to general statements saying that owners usually did not carry out detailed control over daily actions of all employees, and as a rule outlined general direction for work ("company's policy"), sometimes making key appointments. Touching on his relations with the owner, respondent "Vladislav Menshikov," the head of the department of news and socio-political commentary at *STV*, said the following:

> I do not get any direct instructions, with rare exceptions, but I know that today it is necessary to talk on this and this, today we should give the floor to that person. I even know to whom we should *not* give the floor under any conditions at our channel.... I can't just dial the number of Mister, say, "Semyonov," the head of the company,[8] and ask "And what do you think on this matter: shall we give it or not?" First, I might be not able to reach him. I must make decisions myself.
>
> (Interview 26, January 2000)

Menshikov's statements are in general confirmed by other sources, including my own observation. Owners were not seen in newsrooms on a daily basis – moreover, rank-and-file employees seldom had access to them at all. Heads were said to go to instruction meetings from time to time.

Various sources suggest that such meetings can be straightforward; this refers especially to state owners in the regions with relatively authoritarian elites. But Boris Berezovsky was also referred to by one respondent as a person inclined to straightforward instructions which, furthermore, could be changed several times a day if it concerned such important questions as his own image.

However, often instructions are given indirectly, and meetings take the form of "press-lunches," "media parties" or other high-society events where guidelines are hinted at. Commenting on the basis for making decisions, "Vladislav Menshikov" also underlined the importance of intuition and professional experience developed through continual work with multiple sources of information. Sketchily, they may be divided into three groups:

First, regular, but not daily talks of media top managers with owners who give general guidelines:

> [N]ow there came the chair of the company, we had talks with him, yes – for me a half an hour talk is enough to understand where our company is going, whose interests it is now going or wants to defend, what a situation there is and so on.... Who is Dorenko? He is the favorite boy of Berezovsky, everybody knows it, that is they just have personal contacts, so it is not eh ... some influence through somebody – good heavens, what a nonsense! He just can call him anytime and say something. The same about Svanidze – the best friend of Chubais.[9] They communicate personally, you see ... when guys are having a drink together – say, Berezovsky with Dorenko, or Svanidze with Chubais – what is it, an instruction? No. Maybe, a request, maybe, just such an informal talk. And ... naturally, after such a talk certain conclusions are made. Even if this talk is about something, well, abstract. Nevertheless, naturally, I think the main questions of politics [are solved like this].
>
> (Interview 26, January 2000)

These and other data suggest that both media top managers and their owners belong to the single political and business elite, at the federal or regional level. They are not only connected with partnerships and cooperative relations, mutual obligations and various "friendships" resulting from it, but also share a common habitus, in Bourdieu's sense. That is why it would be misleading to regard them always as opposing sides; on the contrary, they form alliances in the struggle against other media and their strategic partners.

For example, in an information war known as the "Battle for *Svyazinvest*," the groups of Berezovsky and Gussinsky, who lost the privatization auction for *Svyazinvest*, a giant telephone company embracing seventy-six of eighty-nine Russian regions, stood out on one side against the winner, though unsuccessfully (for more details see Zassoursky 1999: 242–71). One of the *NTV* top managers told me in interview that *Media-MOST*, Gussinsky's media holding of which *NTV* was the core, was very much interested in buying a share in *Svyazinvest* in terms of the organization of its business. Indeed, a share in this giant telecommunications company could be of use for anyone involved in neighboring business. So it seems plausible that participation of *NTV* top managers in this war was hardly forced.

A second source of information mentioned by "Menshikov" is media: his own TV channel, "friendly" and "hostile" media whose messages may indicate the change in the balance of power.

Finally, "Menshikov" pointed out the vital importance of personal sources of information; he called them political "friends," providing otherwise inaccessible information about changes in the list of friends and enemies and other details of the political situation:

> It is just acquaintances, politicians, well, I don't know, in other spheres who hold certain positions and have certain contacts and who, correspondingly, have certain information ... So this is purely our friendly relations, and they know that well ... I am not the person who will disseminate this information well – who will do with it something that from their point of view should not be done with information. And that's all. That's why on mutual trust.
>
> (Interview 26)

Communication with such sources takes place in a number of ways: by phone, at the location of an event for a news story, at "high-society gatherings," the correct choice of which is also very important:

> There are, of course, certain places to hang around ... and it is not a secret: both at federal level and at local level much politics is done at gatherings of this kind. They may be called differently, say, well, a meeting at a marketing-club or ... a friendly lunch or something, – well, differently ... I am very much afraid to show up at an unnecessary gathering or at a low-grade gathering.
>
> (Interview 26)

Some data are available concerning strategies of top media managers in the situations of conflict between different owners/sponsors/backers. "Nikolai Bazarov," the chief editor of one of Moscow newspapers, did not see it as a problem:

INTERVIEWER: What happens to a newspaper if it has two or three backers, and they have quarreled with each other?

RESPONDENT: Well, one of them will eat the others. Here you are, the situation of *Izvestiya*. There are *ONEXIM* [bank] and *Lukoil*... The already non-existent *ONEXIM* and *Lukoil*, but *ONEXIM* had at some point taken a little more [shares], and that's all, in fact *ONEXIM* is sitting there, *Lukoil* does not manage *Izvestiya*. What do you want? It's our market, it's a wild market. Russian market – is a wild market. Just to bite your head off, and that's it.

INTERVIEWER: Well, what should the chief editor do? If a contradiction of their interests has appeared, what shall he publish?

RESPONDENT: The chief editor is appointed – lobbied by the one who has more. Therefore, he works for this owner.

INTERVIEWER: I see. So he does not have any difficulties?

RESPONDENT: Not at all, absolutely. He knows well that the board of directors has, say, seven persons, and that four of them are from, well, a company X, which holds the controlling share. So, I will work for these four, I don't give a damn about all the rest, because if these four vote, I shall stay the chief editor, and that's all. It's all easy.

(Interview 36, January 2001)

In *Vesti Starograda*, however, I came about a problematic situation, mentioned in the last section: in spring 1997 the newspaper owned by the *Starogradian* bank and the city government found itself witnessing a conflict between the bank and the Starograd mayor. The latter had tried to relocate all the municipal accounts, moving them from the *Starogradian* bank and a few other banks to *Omnio* bank, which was said to have helped the mayor in his electoral campaign. The editor-in-chief, Nikolayev, suggested publishing a small news item, but had a conflict with the head of the political department who demanded "honest" coverage. As a result, nothing was published at all, and the head of the political department commented on the situation for me:

A newspaper is always among multiple fires. On the one hand – and I told Nikolayev about it – it is impossible not to stand up for the bank that feeds us. Especially because it has suffered from this situation most of all. But on the other hand, to quarrel with the mayor – that's not playing into our hands either. We are getting printed for free thanks to him – we owe the printing house more than two million. And he – not personally, of course – has to call there and urge them to print us. Shall we sling mud at him after that? In short, Nikolayev's position is understandable. But to me he seems too cautious. As a result we haven't said anything on this topic, and others have beaten us to it.

(Field notes 1: 29.03.1997)

The available data, thus, suggest that relations of top media executives with their owners is a complex that includes everything from conflict to negotiation to cooperation to "friendship," among which cooperation and strategic partnership seem to prevail. As in other industries, owners and executives manage to come to agreement on the division of labor and power, reserving internal questions and routine external contacts to executives, and leaving external problem-solving for owners. But unlike many other industries, decision making by top media managers is considered to be more legitimate than that by media owners, which encourages both to conceal the dominance of the latter in their relationships.

Media executives and audience: an excluded actor

The outlined structure of managers–owners' relations does not apply to all media, a large portion of which are managed in a slightly different way. First, there are media where top executives own a substantial share or, as happened with the famous "yellow" newspaper *Moskovski Komsomolets*, own a media organization entirely. Second, during the 1990s there were the media owned by journalistic collectives and managed by their elected representatives. In the early 1990s such media organizations were not uncommon, since such was the order of privatization of formerly state media and, furthermore, the press freedom "euphoria" encouraged journalists to form teams and to establish new media with similar structure. Both these organizational types differ from those with a clear owners–managers distinction by their mode of communication with the external environment: in these organizations top administrators negotiate all questions with external agents themselves. Possible types of relations that media representatives may initiate with various outside actors, such as advertisers, sources or state agents are touched on in respective chapters, while here I would like to consider some aspects of general strategies that top executives adopt in their relations with the extra-organizational environment as a whole, defining clients, choosing partners and making alliances. In particular, I will address the role of audiences in this process.

Media top managers about whom I managed to collect data paid much attention to finding a clientele to which their media organization may offer its service as an essential constituent of its success. It is now acknowledged that audiences, as media's "official" clients, often arouse only the transitory interest of media professionals, while their true and final clients are advertisers, as real sources of profit. While, to some extent, Russia in the 1990s was no exception from this situation, in the last decade of the twentieth century it witnessed some specific circumstances which developed this trend much further.

First, I would like to repeat that I do not regard audiences as "real" actors because in Russia, like everywhere, the structure of the media industry does not give the possibility of establishing direct contacts between the audience and media professionals. Thus the latter build their strategies upon audiences' images constructed by various methods, in particular, on the basis of actions of special intermediaries, such as audience research organizations. The practice of this mediation throughout the 1990s was, as everything else, loosely institutionalized, and varied greatly from periphery to Moscow, where it resembled the situation in the advertising and PR-services market. Several leading agencies that emerged in the first half of the 1990s measured audiences differently, so that their results, including ratings of particular shows, were strikingly divergent. In addition to that, the trust in ratings was in general very low, especially when a research company serviced only one media organization. This caused constant dissatisfaction in an advertisers' community waiting to allocate their commercials in the most efficient way, that is on the basis of "objective" ratings. Under the pressure of advertisers, in 1996 the heads of the leading national TV channels agreed to use the services of a single firm, and chose *Gallup Media*[10] which was the first to introduce people meter technology. Having thus got an advantage in the audience research market, *Gallup Media* soon achieved a nearly monopolistic position in it, much like *Video International* in the advertising market.

Few of my respondents showed satisfaction with the work of *Gallup*, and no-one failed to point out the arbitrary character of ratings as an indicator of the audience's interests. In particular, respondent "Pavel Yakutovich" (Interview 29) said that *Gallup*'s sample is far from being enough, especially when it is necessary to analyze a certain target group within the general population represented by this sample. He also said that the results of polls and focus-groups are not comparable. Nevertheless, all respondents agreed that since this method of monitoring is accepted by the market, as Yakutovich put it, and no other is available, it is the one they have to use. Thus, with introduction of audience polls in the countrywide channels, the Russian national TV audience has quickly acquired the status of a commodity sold to advertisers at the price appropriate to its volume at the current moment. "Pavel Yakutovich" expressed the idea exactly in these economic terms: "our commodity is people. It is they whom we sell."

Answering the question how ratings transform into decision-making inside a media organization, a *PTV* top-manager described two practices (Interview 27). First, efforts are made to adjust the content of the program to the supposed interests of the social group which is assumed to dominate among viewers in the current period of time. Second, editors try to shift the program in the schedule so that it can reach the maximum of its target audience, or so that it will not coincide in time with popular programs of other channels. Finally, if neither of these measures helps to raise the rating of the program, the latter is closed down. However, this is not applicable to news. Companies try to avoid shifting news within the schedule, except in cases of counter-programming, which was not widely known in the 1990s. Usually if the news rating is lower than that of other channels, companies try to adopt the style of work of more successful competitors. This scheme of rating-based action is generally confirmed by other studies (e.g. Pekurny 1982), that also point at the indirect character of the connection between media managers and audiences, and at the plasticity of audiences' images constructed by the former.

However, audience plasticity based on ratings will seem not as considerable if one looks at relations between audiences and media in Russian regions of the same period. Unlike in Moscow, there audience polls were poorly developed: ratings were measured irregularly, as a rule – by media organizations themselves on the basis of telephone polls – and advertisers' trust in them was even lower than in the capital. Often audiences were not studied at all because of lack of funds for such surveys. In such cases advertising was usually sold at fixed rates that were post factum adjusted to the demand expressed by advertisers. Or rank-and-file columnists and anchors themselves sought funding that could support their columns and shows, but this strategy seldom applied to news. At the *Vesti Starograda* editorial board the journalists were constantly discussing who their target readers finally were, and what information they needed. As a rule, each editor insisted that it was the production of his/her department the reader wanted most. The editor-in-chief, as mentioned in Chapter 8, tried to target simultaneously the local elite and common people seeking for family reading, which provoked even more confusion and diverging criteria of newsworthiness. It was a *Vesti Starograda* reporter who called the audience "a myth that a journalist invents for himself" (Interview 5).

Media executives defining their clients: media as means of intra-elite communication

A key question that arises from this description of the media–audience relation is: if in the 1990s a reader, a viewer or a listener was such a mythical character who hardly existed at all, then why there were actors ready to invest money in media? Indeed, even if an external agent decides to use media not as a source of profit or a means of commercial promotion of goods, but as a propaganda resource – even in such a case the main aim of using this resource must be to influence public opinion. The point is that the last statement is only partly applicable to Russia. Different sources, including my respondents, confirmed that news and socio-political media were to a great extent a channel of intra-elite communication, not mass communication. Most sources/advertisers/backers addressed their messages to those who were able to make decisions, including decisions on the problems of these particular sources, advertisers or backers. Among these decisions, the ones concerning distribution of enormous portions of the state property that was being privatized during the 1990s, were of special importance for all key players. In other words, mass media were regarded by external agents as a means of solving their personal problems, so they did not care much about "official" media audiences. Thus, the *Starogradian* bank must have regarded the attention of the mayor to *Vesti Starograda* newspaper much more important than the attention of the thousands looking for family reading. PR professional "Galina Mirskaya" vividly described the same idea:

> [B]lack PR, it, of course, is intended not for a wide audience, not for the public – the public doesn't care a damn who has fallen out with whom, who's fighting against whom; this is not the information that can capture people . . . in most cases it is just like a kick for the rival . . . the thing is, that this money, enormous money, that is circulating in that black PR, in most cases is spent, well, to avoid a real war, with bloodshed, shooting rivals in the streets, and this is just, well, a precaution. When one says, "well, I know this and that . . . well, my actions will be that and this." And the other answers, "you bastard, and I also know something about ya" [laughs]. And so they'll butt each other a bit, and then they'll dine out somewhere, have a good drink together, and make peace.
>
> (Interview 33, November 2000)

To attract such clients, an adequate strategy of a media head is not to meet the interests of "officially declared" wider audiences, but to make clients think that the media outlet is consumed by decision-makers and other elite members. For this purpose, newspapers, for example, were freely distributed in places where VIPs typically gathered, as well as sent to press offices of private corporations and state bodies. The pervasiveness of this practice, however, poses two further questions. First, why would intra-elite media mask as mass editions instead of openly positioning themselves as targeted at the elite? And, second, taking this reasoning even further, why would this narrow community choose to communicate through such an expensive channel as mass media at all, instead of, for example, writing letters or just engaging in interpersonal communication? The second question is the one I asked different types of my respondents, who, strange as it may seem, were particularly uncertain answering it. Thus, "Nikolai Bazarov," editor-in-chief of a Moscow newspaper, while calling attention to the lack of connection between media and wide audiences, was quite laconic and not very convincing commenting on the problem:

RESPONDENT: [Communication through media] is a private correspondence between one another. Here is one oligarch, another oligarch, a third oligarch. And a means of correspondence is a newspaper, for example. Each writes a letter to another in his paper: you are a scum, swine, son of a bitch. That one writes back: hey you, rascal, villain. A third one writes: you are both bastards, and I am white and fluffy. And that's all. This is a private talk, that's why the reader does not buy it. A most important indicator is the circulation, look at it, it's ridiculous [looks over newspapers at his table]: eight thousand, ten thousand subscribers. What's that? It all has closed, withdrawn into itself. [This is a means] of an intra-corporate struggle. It's a means of communication of press-services of banks and companies among each other.

INTERVIEWER: Yes. I have already asked other respondents this question: why then not choose a cheaper means of intra-elite communication?

RESPONDENT: They are hoping to urge the public about something.

(Interview 36, January 2001)

Another respondent, with vast work experience in PR and political consulting, admitted that he was asking himself the same question all the time, but could not find an answer. A clue to this question was given by still another political and commercial PR professional "Dmitri Gorski," who pointed out that by phone or in a private talk one can agree about a personal deal or alliance, but if one wants to promote one's information to the whole community, one can not do without mass media. Respondent "Alexander Gurevich," from the PR department of an oil company, noted that among people able to make decisions of a certain importance, there could appear such characters as rank-and-file policemen or tax inspectors who could not be reached through interpersonal communication. Similarly, although for different reasons, VIPs are also not always available in person, even to their elite "fellows."

This reasoning, however, does not shed light on the first question – why would not all these media openly present themselves as elite? My observations suggest several possible reasons. First, as noted by some respondents, media's clients, in order to maintain their positive image in the eyes of their target audience, however narrow it is, needed the information to "circulate," so that, existing as a background, it would not give the impression of something manufactured by the interested party, and gradually become an uncritically taken common-sense belief. The effect of such circulation could better be reached through non-elite mass media. Second, the size of the media outlet where a client published his promotional pieces was usually perceived as an indicator of the amount of his resources. Thus, a message ordered for and communicated through a national TV channel pointed to a source of much greater power than one published in a local newspaper. Third, though probably less important, what media heads seemed to find valuable for their professional identity is the possibility of creating "genuine" media products within time or space remaining free from any kind of *zakaz*.

Finally, what looks like the weightiest reason is that media top managers, besides leasing their media for intra-elite communication, usually tried to cater for other types of clients, of whom "regular" commercial advertisers were of less significance, while those who ordered for electoral campaigns were more crucial. To attract both those groups of clients media executives needed to make an impression that their edition had a relatively wide audience – *impression* here is a key word. Thus, "intra-elite" newspapers, besides engaging in the widespread practice of overstating data about their circulation, used to pay news stands for "lying" in them in order to make an impression of being popular. Since street press traders usually refused periodicals with poor sales, presence in their stands was meant to be a sign of the newspaper's success. Also, such editions often shrank in intra-election periods and increased pagination and circulations shortly before and during political campaigns. Similarly, TV and radio stations, besides overstating their reach, rating and share, also expanded, or offered to expand their broadcasting before the elections.

Thus, obscuring the data about media organization's real resources, goals, and clientele turned to be a part of media executives' conscious strategies aimed at survival and development of their organizations. Summarizing numerous details about these strategies scattered across various chapters, in terms of their relation to clients, media executives' practices may be conventionally divided into four groups. First is attachment, through sale or other kind of entire subordination to a single client who becomes an external owner. Second is "jumping" from one big backer to another, depending on the situation. Third is "retail" sale of time and space as a hidden advertising-propaganda resource to anyone who would pay. These three types loosely correspond to forms of influence on media organizations exercised by those external agents who fall into the advertisers–owners continuum (see Table 6.2 in Chapter 6). A fourth type differs radically from the first three by the choice of clientele and presents a classical normatively "right" strategy of catering for the interests of audiences whose attention is then sold to legal advertisers. Among all these strategies, the first has shown it grants socio-political media organizations maximum sustainability in the long run, while the last has proven to make media vulnerable and exposed to various risks (this does not apply to entertainment media). Many media have passed through some or all of these strategies of their managers. A typical trajectory began from the fourth, "right" strategy, quite usual for early 1990s, then slipping to the second or third, or both in turn, and ending up either with the disappearance of the publication or with the first strategy. The latter, thus, being normatively "wrong," was very "right" in terms of organizational success.

Concluding remarks

As I have hopefully shown in the previous chapters, the universe called news production has a quite complex structure of power relations: not only are power resources distributed unevenly, but also practices of power are very asymmetric. This asymmetry creates zones that can be called center and periphery of power. Audiences, having no direct access to other participants of the game, are thus deprived of the possibility to elaborate their own strategies – at least in the same sense as all the other participants – and are, therefore, systematically excluded from the process of news production. Media top managers, on the contrary, are very central in this game – although not because they have the biggest resources, but because of this unique structural position. All other players, bound by intricate and contradictory relations, need a coordinating center, a mediator of external and internal influences, and a social buffer.

Taking these roles, media top managers also become collectors of diverse information about the distribution of power in their environment, and such data collection is a very delicate process. Different influences reach the heads of mass media most of all in the form of information on agents' interests and possible sanctions, and this information is often presented as hints and indirect indications. On this basis top media managers make their decisions, trying to avoid sanctions before they are imposed, and thus having to engage in complicated manipulative strategies. The result is that most power relations are shifted from the sphere of open, clearly observed conflicts or deals to the sphere of concealed interactions. Moreover, since information about power distribution and potential sanctions is a resource, and is used to media managers' advantage, but sometimes can also be dangerous to reveal, it is very seldom betrayed either "outside" or "inside" a media organization, or at least is carefully measured. Thus the heads of mass media play the role not only of a buffer, but of an informational filter: a filter that is placed in the very centre of power agents' inter-relations and that makes this sphere so "informationally opaque."

Another important reason for this opacity, and of additional audience exclusion, is the specific choice of clients that top managers of the Russian media have made most often throughout the 1990s. In public discussions both within and outside the Russian journalistic community, media have been frequently accused of unwillingness to comply with the laws of the market – that is, to shrink to the number able to support themselves on revenues from legal advertising and sales. The irony is that Russian media did comply with market laws, responding to the existing demand – only the service demanded, as well as the sources of demand were, from a normative point of view, "wrong." Media's main clients were not audiences, and not even legal advertisers, but hidden promoters, propagandists and external owners. They, in turn, have been very busy solving their own problems: bargaining for new rules of the political game, arranging privatization auctions and distributing oil fields. The Russian audience has been silently watching this show. When the first post-transformation dust settles down, it will be the time to see if this situation is going to last or to change.

Part III
Special studies

10 Regional media landscapes
Diversity of power configurations

"Take as much autonomy as you can swallow": these famous words said by Yeltsin to leaders of the Russian regions after the collapse of the Soviet Union may become an epigraph to this chapter. So far I have been considering the institutional, or quasi-institutional dimension of power distribution in the sphere of news production, but it is equally important to look at its geographical distribution. Throughout the 1990s the political situation in the eighty-nine subjects of the Russian Federation were so dramatically different that, both in public discussion and in scholarly discourse (Gelman 2000), Russia was said to have eighty-nine political regimes rather than one.

Spatial decomposition of the Russian state: historical context

The diversity of Russian regions is far more than political. Russia is an extremely vast country with eleven time zones and about ten climatic zones: from depopulated permafrost-covered tundra and taiga, embracing almost the whole of Siberia and the north of the European part, to the subtropics of the Black Sea coast and the northern Caucasus, with a huge population density and birth-rate. Industrial and post-industrial enclaves, centered around big megalopolizes, are scattered all over the country, along with other rich regions whose prosperity is based on raw materials. They include such cities as St. Petersburg (Baltic coast), Yekaterinburg (Urals), Krasnoyarsk (mid-Siberia) and Vladivostok (Pacific Coast). These zones of wealth alternate with depressed rural areas, suffering from high unemployment and outflow of manpower that leaves half-idle the remnants of gigantic Soviet farms and heavy industries. Urban Christian (or rather post-Christian) post-modern lifestyle of Russian-populated cities, traditional agricultural Muslim society in the northern Caucasus and nomadic reindeer breeder culture in the tundra – all this coexists within one state.

The eighty-nine heterogeneous "subjects of Federation" were inherited by Russia from the intricate Soviet system of administrative division. As a result Russia has forty-nine *oblasts* (regions), twenty-one *respublika* (republics), six *krai* (federal territories), eleven units called "*avtonomny okrug*" (autonomous districts) that are situated *inside* federal territories or republics, and two "cities of Federal significance" – Moscow and St. Petersburg – that in 1993 were separated from their regions and granted the status of subjects of Federation. The Russian Constitution (1993) gives equal rights to all subjects of the Federation, simultaneously providing some of them with additional rights (thus, republics can have two official languages – Russian and the local one – while regions cannot). In practice, the relations of subjects of Federation among each other and with the "Center" are unclear.

Moreover, their predecessors, the Soviet administrative units, had often been set up quite arbitrarily. Some of them, mostly monoethnic regions of European Russia, as well as a number of Siberian areas, were based on even earlier pre-revolutionary provinces; they are usually called *oblast* or *krai* and have the name of their principal town in their titles. Others were created as a realization of the Bolshevik idea of the right of every "nation" (ethnic group) to a certain degree of political autonomy within a new Soviet state (these are usually called *respublika* or *avtonomny okrug* and have the name of the indigenous ethnic group in their titles). In some cases such units were established in the areas inhabited by peoples with strong cultural traditions and identities; in other cases the idea of a "national" (ethnic) autonomy was introduced rather artificially. The first group is first of all represented by the Muslim peoples speaking languages of the Turkic family, some of which populate central and east-European Russia, and others, the most resistant to assimilation, dwell in the northern Caucasus. Having been conquered by the Russian empire at different times, these ethnic groups have preserved many of their traditions and/or, together with their colonizers, have formed unique cultural patterns in their regions. On the other hand, many now assimilated peoples of Siberia and some other non-literate peoples, by the advent of Soviet power, had hardly had any ethnic or national identity. On the contrary, these identities emerged as a result of the activity of Soviet authorities who supplied local languages with alphabets based on Cyrillic script, introduced compulsory schooling, established media both in Russian and in local languages and set quotas for representatives of indigenous peoples in State and party organs.

About seventy years later mobilization of local ethnic identities along with economic resources became a basis of the struggle of regional elites with the "Federal Center" of post-Soviet Russia for political autonomy of those elites. At that time many regions, especially those having ethnonyms in their titles, even declared their sovereignty (the so-called "parade of sovereignties"), although none of them, except Chechnya, ever went much further than declarations. However, the disastrous Chechen example, on the one hand made the Federal elite take all such declarations quite seriously and, on the other, "vaccinated" other regional elites against radical separatism. The object of bargaining, then, became limited to distribution of power within the boundaries of the Russian state. Richer regions, especially when their elites could legitimize their quasi-separatism with the ethnic/national trump card, were more successful in retaining their independence from the Center. Simultaneously, in some poor regions, that possessed no actors powerful enough to compete with local governors, the latter took advantage to accumulate all power in their hands, turning into local "barons." As long as they continued to declare their vassal loyalty to the "Center," the Federal elite often tolerated them saving its time and resources to fight for control over richer regions. It is not surprising that these processes often became referred to as the "feudalization" of Russia.

It is this feudalization, nourished by the partial decomposition of the State on the federal level, that allowed the very uneven political development of the regions and led them to form "89 political regimes" within formally one country. In fact, it is difficult to consider all of them regimes because a regime presupposes relatively stable order and institutions, but in the unsteady 1990s this was applicable only to some regions. First, those were the provinces, usually economically poor, where little had changed since Soviet times – there the "State" on its local level had never dissolved. Second, some regions had lived through intensive change in a couple of years and come to something that looked like a new stability. But there were many that were rapidly changing, often through intense social conflict, and it was not clear whether this conflict served as a way of transformation into something else or whether it was going to become a long-lasting characteristic of the local order. Against this background local media landscapes could not remain uniform.

Toward a typology of regional media configurations

It must be admitted that the multiplicity of economico-political situations described is primarily responsible for the variety of regional media landscapes. Practices of media professionals and sources per se showed little diversity in different regions, while strategies of state and economic actors, and of CIGs, where applicable, varied greatly. As noted by the authors of the large comparative study of Russian regional media models, "Having come out from the single 'Soviet uniform' Russian regions have picked different ways. Traveling through contemporary Russia, one also travels in historical time: from the year 2000 one can enter the 1930s and 1950s. Within one state medieval khanates rub shoulders with Chicago of gangsters' times" (Yakovenko 2000: 107).

Studies of Russian regional media are very scarce, the one cited above being the only systematic research that, therefore, deserves some special attention. Entitled *Public Expertise: The anatomy of freedom of expression*, the study was carried out twice – in 1999 and 2000 – by a number of established Russian NGOs. It positioned itself outside the academic realm, declaring openly normative goals, and relied on a number of teleological presuppositions. The aim was to quantify and measure press freedom in all regions and draw a map of freedom of "mass information" in Russia. On the basis of research in eighty-seven regions (it excluded two northern Caucasus republics – Chechnya and Ingushetia) each subject of the Federation was ascribed an index of press freedom. This in its turn was formed from the three indexes of freedom of access to information, freedom of production of information and freedom of dissemination of information.

All indexes were calculated on the basis of very heterogeneous data,[1] and the authors acknowledge the conventional character of each individual region's rank, but claim the list of ranked regions as a whole reflect basic trends. Indeed, for a person generally acquainted with the situation in the Russian regions it is clear that Moscow or Yekaterinburg media organizations possess more resources and autonomy than those from Bashkortostan or Taimyr. Yet much of the quantitative data on media, despite the shortcomings of the methodology, gives material for further analysis.

After ascribing ranks to regions, the authors grouped all of them into the following seven categories, called regional media models (Yakovenko 2000: 106–18):

1   market model;
2   transitional to market model;
3   conflict model;
4   modernized Soviet model;
5   Paternalistic Soviet model;
6   Authoritarian Soviet model;
7   Depressed model.

These categories are scaled according to their proximity to the democratic ideal, the "market model" implicitly being the closest.[2] Assignment of a region to a certain model loosely corresponds to its rank in the general list: regions exemplifying more "democratic" models tend to have higher press freedom ratings. However, there are significant exceptions. Thus, Nizhni Novgorod region ascribed to the market model is only fifty-fourth in the list; regions of the "Transitional to market model" are scattered everywhere, from fourth to eighty-fifth positions (Yakovenko 2000: 16–17), which poses questions about the consistency of this category and points at its residual character. Generally, while the criteria of this classification are obviously multiple (they include such parameters as media density, share of private media or level of regional economic development), these criteria are not made explicit and, moreover, different media models are described by different sets of attributes.

Thus, the market model is characterized by high media density, high share of non-state sources of income in the regional media budget and dominance of non-state media. It also demonstrates the highest level of media conflicts and violence toward journalists. The most numerous "transitional to market" model (thirty-two regions with more than a third of the Russian population) is described in rather vague expressions, such as "media space is divided into approximately equal parts – state and non-state" (Yakovenko 2000: 115); "the main difference from the Soviet media model is that the authorities already cannot or do not want to create a unified system of commanding media" (page 116). The conflict media model is said to emerge on the basis of the Soviet or the market models from "the frontal clash of authoritarian policy of the regional authorities with powerful economically independent media" (page 117). The difference between the three Soviet models looks like a difference of scale determined by levels of local economies (the poorer the region – the more oppressive is the regime).[3] Last, the depressed model is described by the authors in one sentence:

It is hard to talk about press freedom, media policy or media market in the regions where for a thousand snow-bound kilometers there is only one settlement with a dozen reindeer-breeders, and the capital is a village whose information needs are well satisfied with two local papers and one radio channel.

(Yakovenko 2000: 118).

What seems to have led the authors to such a heterogeneous classification of media models, are some important presuppositions and intentions implied in their text implies. First, although the authors do not openly equate democracy with the market, just stating connection between them, in fact the classification suggests it.[4] Second, the typology is implicitly teleological, expecting all regions to move towards the market/democratic model. While the paternalistic model is said to be preserved untouched since Soviet times, the modernized model is characterized as the one that has experienced some positive changes; the transitional to market model is teleological in its very title, and within the market model the authorities "already cannot just give orders to media" (Yakovenko 2000: 116). The shortcomings of such teleologism are clearly seen in assignments of some regions to certain groups, as in the case of Vologda region discussed further below. Third, while a desire to establish a connection between local politico-economic situations and media models determined by them is clearly traced in the observed classification, the data collected in *Public Expertise* do not seem quite relevant for this goal.

What could help to reach it is, I venture to claim, the dynamic approach that allows a more informal analysis of local politico-economic situations, through characterizing the number and quality of power agents/groups, their resources and strategies. Although such an approach has not been applied to media research in Russia, it has been very successfully used for regionalism studies within political science, first of all in the works of the Russian political scientist Vladimir Gelman. Thus, he defines four independent variables that determine local political regimes by comparing them with elements of a chess game: actors/players, institutions/rules, resources/pieces, and strategies/moves (Gelman 2000: 19). Using very similar concepts, I believe them to be applicable not only to the sphere of the political, but to any power relations, including those in media production.

Building a typology of regional political regimes, Gelman acknowledges that all Russian regions in the 1990s were experiencing an intensive transformation, which is defined by him through the category of indeterminacy – a state when the future of current rules and elites is indeterminate (that is, both may equally change or persist). As opposed to indeterminacy, a consolidated regime is characterized by low probability of elite replacement and rule change. While indeterminacy itself is hard to capture for analysis, what can be accounted for are, according to Gelman, scenarios of entry into and exit out of this unsteady state. A typology of entry-scenarios is assembled by Gelman of two classifications borrowed from the studies of Karl and Schmitter (1991), and Munck and Leff (1997), and includes such scenarios as conservative reform, elite pact, reform from below, social revolution and forced transition (Gelman 2000: 39). While detailed description of all three classifications would be superfluous here, I shall only explain the category of conservative reform that I am going to use later. It refers to situations where no change in the composition of actors takes place and the dominant position of the ruling elite is preserved thanks to its adjustment to new institutions.

Of much more relevance is Gelman's typology of exit-scenarios based on two criteria: type of strategies (compromise or force), and composition of actors. Cross-section of these criteria gives four scenarios (see Table 10.1).

As a typology of scenarios of *exit* from indeterminacy, this classification has certain problems. Gelman acknowledges that war of all against all is

Table 10.1 Gelman's scenarios of exit from indeterminacy

Composition of actors	Strategies	
	Compromise	Force
Domination of one actor	"Elite settlement"	"Winner takes all"
Absence of dominant actor	"Struggle according to the rules"	"War of all against all"

Source: Gelman 2000: 45.

not an exit at all, since it conserves indeterminacy instead of reducing it; he also admits that struggle according to the rules is a very fragile type and easily slips into elite settlement, while the latter may quite fast resettle into another configuration of actors or into an entirely different scenario. Thus, instead of leading to consolidated regimes, these scenarios often turn out to be temporary configurations. But understood precisely in this way, and supplemented with the category of conservative reform, the four scenarios describe very well the whole variety of situations in the Russian regions in the 1990s, embracing "never changed" provinces, "temporarily" or "forever changed" ones, and those going through intensive trans-formation. The resulting typology of regional media situations with examples is presented in Table 10.2.[5]

Like political regimes, media landscapes are regarded here as depend-ent on the composition of major actors, their resources, and strategies; however, to account for media production, the analysis should include not only political actors, but all those relevant to the sphere under study. The relevance of major economic actors has proved unproblematic during the research, but inclusion of autonomous media organizations, ironically, aroused some doubts. It turned to be debatable whether separate media, unsupported by any external agents, could grow powerful enough to take part in shaping local media "models."

In my sample of respondents, opinions on this matter have divided into two groups. Group A, that included Moscow media analysts and represen-tatives of journalistic and non-government journalistic organizations, held a position that autonomous regional media were not an exception and that they played significant roles in local media situations. Among such media those TV channels were named that usually took prizes at competitions of regional media. However, most regional journalists and experts who took part in regional electoral campaigns (group B) were inclined to think that all or nearly all media were to a significant extent dependent on various external actors. They disproved some major examples given by group A by naming backers of respective media organizations. Indeed, from various studies it is known that journalists' vision of their professionalism has little to do with objectivity and press freedom, so, instead of inquiring about each other's backers, they would be inclined to give prizes to those media organizations which have shown ability to produce dramatic and well for-matted products.

One of the "middle" opinions that seems quite plausible was expressed by an expert in regional elections Mikhail Malyutin. He claimed that, of course, small autonomous media did exist in many regions, but he had never met any autonomous media organization comparable in influence to what "a governor, a mayor or a big corporation could possess" (Interview 40). Most evidence I could find supports this vision, with one significant addition. In regional markets the media that could be (but not always were) relatively independent from local agents of power have been the

Table 10.2 Regional media-political configurations

Actors' major strategy	Holder(s) of major resources	Media-political configuration	Media pluralism and autonomy	Examples in Russia
Compromise	One	Pact configuration ("Elite settlement")	Very limited	Federal regime 1996, St. Petersburg Nizhny Novgorod region Vologda region
Compromise	Many	Competitive elitism configuration ("Struggle according to the rules")	Significant	Sverdlovsk region (Yekaterinburg)
Conflict	One	Monocentric configuration a) "Winner takes all" b) conservative reform	No	Republic of Kalmykiya
Conflict	Many	Conflict configuration	"Pluralism of dependent media"	Krasnoyarsk territory Voronezh region Federal regime 1997–2000

ones connected to big non-local media corporations, usually Moscow-based or (seldom) based in neighboring regions. Thus, major actors able to define local media climates are the biggest state agents, economic agents or CIGs big enough to play a political role, and some media organizations as junior players. Local media situations are, as seen from the above description, determined by the same set of "variables" as Gelman's regional political regimes and, therefore, could be termed media-political regimes or, as *Public Expertise* calls them, regional media models or, in Jonathan Becker's terms, mass political media systems (Becker 2004). However, given the extremely fluid character of local media situations in Russia, I have adopted a milder term "media-political configurations."

Monocentric configuration

Monocentric configuration, also called an authoritarian situation by Gelman, and closely correlating with the authoritarian media model of *Public Expertise*, is a situation where all the media are managed from a single center and reflect its interests. This configuration may emerge when one dominant media actor defeats others by force, and this may only happen when this actor is the local governor, with or without his CIG. No other group – whether centered around a relatively legal busi-nessman or a "criminal," to say nothing of separate media organizations – can completely erase all its competitors from the local landscape. It may happen only at the cost of this group itself transforming into the local government, but I know no such cases in Russia. Monocentric con-figuration may also emerge through conservative reform, when an old Soviet leader retains his power while meeting nearly no resistance. In this case not even a brief decomposition of the state, characteristic of the "winner takes all" scenario, takes place. The result of both scenarios is very similar. Indeed, "never-changed" monocentric regions had much more in common with those ruled by newcomers than with, for example, Voronezh region where the Soviet elite kept all the major positions, but became fractured, which gave a completely different media configura-tion. Monocentric configuration is very well exemplified in the republic of Kalmykiya: both Gelman and *Public Expertise*, despite some import-ant divergences, name Kalmykiya as a paradigmatic example of an authoritarian situation.

Situated in the steppe zone between the lower Volga and the northern Caucasus, Kalmykiya (pop. 318,500 in 1997) is a predominantly rural and extremely poor republic dependent on Federal subsidies. Like most "ethnically entitled" regions, Kalmykiya was founded shortly after the Bolshevik revolution. The foundation of its present principal town Elista, one of the three urban settlements in the republic, dates back to 1930. Kalmyks, formerly steppe Lamaistic nomads, speaking a language of the Mongolian group, comprise 45 percent of the republic's population against

37 percent Russians, and are involved mainly in cattle breeding (Petrov and Tyukov 1998).

The early 1990s in Kalmykiya were marked by a sharp conflict between old Soviet leaders representing different branches of power. This ended in 1993 when an adventurous and successful businessman Kirsan Ilyumzhinov, then thirty-one, won the local presidential elections. Although the personal involvement of Ilyumzhinov in violent entrepreneurship has not been proved, at the very least in all his activities he closely cooperated with representatives in this area. The changes in legislation that followed the 1993 elections led to numerous contradictions between local and Federal laws. To name only the major ones, the formation of all State bodies became dependent on the Kalmyk president's decisions and nearly all political organizations found themselves illegal. Extending the presidential term to seven years, Ilyumzhinov held special elections in 1995 and won them as the only candidate. Simultaneously Ilyumzhinov gained monopolistic control over the few Kalmyk enterprises, ousting all competitors from the republic. Throughout the 1990s Ilyumzhinov managed to combine promises of imminent Kalmyk sovereignty for local consumption with demonstrations of loyalty to the "Center" at the Federal level. Numerous financial scandals associated with him produced almost no reaction in Moscow.

The emergent media system was, first of all, as poor as the region itself: it contained a dozen newspapers, two TV channels and a radio station. Top executives of the largest newspaper *Izvestiya Kalmykii* (with circulation between 25,000 and 30,000 copies) were explicitly proud of "making Kirsan" during his electoral campaign (Makarov 1998: 9). Since big commercial TV networks and Moscow-based newspapers were not interested in the poor local market, the republic found itself in informational isolation, broken only by the *ORT* channel (the signal of *RTR* was, when necessary, blocked at the local transmitting center).

By 1998 the only newspaper not controlled by Ilyumzhinov was *Sovetskaya Kalmykiya segodnya* ("Soviet Kalmykiya today"). Its editor, Larisa Yudina, was the co-president of the local chamber of the *Yabloko* party – at that time the leading "right," democrat party in Russia. During financial crises the paper became funded by the party, although on *Yabloko*'s part it resembled a charity: it could not count on serious political influence in the region anyway. The position of the paper became especially difficult after a series of publications about commercial enterprises controlled by Ilyumzhinov. In early 1997 the editorial board of the newspaper was forced out of its office; this happened six more times during the same year. Local printing houses stopped printing the edition, and it had to be printed outside Kalmykiya. It led to a dramatic decrease of circulation to around 4, 000 copies: an amount that could be placed in the trunk of a *Zhiguli* car. Local distribution services refused to sell the paper. The editorial board could only find enough money to employ youths and retired people who stood near the central marketplace, but these were regularly beaten by unknown assailants or dispersed by police, the circulation being confiscated.

In June 1998 an unidentified person contacted Larisa Yudina on her home phone saying that he had interesting information about misappropriation of state funds. Yudina wearing her slippers went downstairs to the yard to meet the caller's car and never came back. Some time later her stabbed body was found in a pool in the distant district of Elista.

The case got national coverage. *Yabloko*'s leader Grigory Yavlinski publicly demanded an investigation to be carried out by federal bodies and personally called the vice-minister of Interior. FSB, Ministry of Interior and the General Procuracy formed a joint committee and, in contrast to many other murders of journalists, the case was carried to completion. Moreover, the person who was found guilty and imprisoned was not a rank-and-file killer, but Ilyumzhinov's advisor. However, the Kalmyk media-political situation did not change in the slightest.

Many analysts agree that Yudina's murder was an excessive measure: Ilyumzhinov had effectively controlled the local situation without it. The sentencing of Ilyumzhinov's advisor points to the negative attitude of the federal elite towards this event, but the combination of this sentence with Ilyumzhinov's staying in power indicates that the major goal of the federal reaction here was no more than to set certain limits to his activity. The federal elite clearly showed that actions, making the merger of violent entrepreneurship and statehood too obvious, were not welcome. Otherwise full control over local media was quite permissible.

This is confirmed by the story of radio *Titan* in Bashkortostan (see Chapter 4) which also got no reaction from Moscow. Bashkortostan itself, often given as another example of monocentric media configuration, is at the same time different from all other regions with its, albeit brief, story of popular mobilization, and thus deserves special consideration.

Situated in the south-east Urals, the Bashkir republic (as it was then called), like Kalmykiya, was founded soon after the Bolshevik revolution, but in some respects Bashkortostan is a contrast to Kalmykiya: its predominantly urban population, with incomes close to Russia's average level, exceeds 4 million people. Bashkirs, nomadic cattle-breeders, had borrowed Islam and Arabic script from their western neighbors, the Tatars, who spoke a very similar language. The proximity of Tatarstan has had an important effect on the political situation within Bashkortostan. On the one hand, in the early 1990s Tatarstan and Bashkortostan were the leaders of the "parade of sovereignties." On the other, the division of Bashkortostan's population into three big ethnic groups (Russians – 40 percent, Tatars – 28 percent and Bashkirs – 22 percent) gave rise to political parties based on ethnic affiliation. The dominance of the Bashkirs, provided by the monocentric rule of Murtaza Rakhimov, led parties representing the two other ethnicities into opposition. Two such organizations – the Tatar

Public Center and the *Rus*[6] movement – created a joint movement "For civil rights and social justice," chaired by Altaf Galeyev, the head of radio *Titan* (Titkov and Zapekly 1998).

This circumstance sheds much light on the story of radio *Titan*. First, it explains why an oppositional media outlet could endure for a relatively long period of time in a regime that had quickly succeeded in eliminating all other opposition media. Like the case of *Sovietskaya Kalmykiya Segodnya*, the example of *Titan* shows that this was possible only when such media were backed by relatively influential political parties. Thus the struggle that took place both in Kalmykiya and Bashkortostan was rather a fight between political actors than between the State and the autonomous (i.e. impartial and objective) media units, as GDF and *Public Expertise* tend to present it.

Second, the existence of real ethno-political cleavages within the population, reflected in *Titan*'s case, helps us partially understand its popular support, observed in no other cases except the story of *NTV*. This support also poses a difficulty in conceptualizing the Bashkir media-political configuration and in ascribing it to any of the categories considered above. Absence of popular participation in regional political life in the 1990s was so manifest that it gave reason to Vladimir Gelman to disregard "masses" as political actors and build his typology of regional regimes solely on the basis of a balance of power between elite actors (Gelman 2000: 22–3). Any typology of media-political configurations, based on Gelman's classification, including the one offered here is, thus, unable to give an account of cases involving popular participation. Karl and Schmitter's and Munck and Leff's typologies do regard masses as actors, naming the results of their actions "revolution" and "social revolution" respectively (Gelman 2000: 38). This suggests that masses are included in the analysis only when their actions have been successful – i.e. have led to regime change. Should masses be excluded from consideration in the case of failed revolutions, or failed media configuration changes? On the one hand, since both failed popular protest and its absence lead to the same result – monocentric configuration – exclusion of the masses looks legitimate. On the other, it is not obvious that the social situation in regions that experienced a failed protest movement and in those that have been stably monocentric, is the same. The case of Bashkortostan is, therefore, waiting for a more detailed study.

Pact configuration

Pact configuration emerges when one media player, or its backer, dominates the situation but decides to compromise with others – either because of lack of resources to suppress the competitors, or for normative reasons. This term best of all describes the media landscape at the federal level after the 1996 presidential elections: the dominant actor, the *ORT-*

Berezovsky CIG was definitely the main winner, but since it could not have won alone, it had chosen to coopt the main "opponent" – the *NTV-Gussinsky* CIG, as well as some other groups. Therefore the latter got their share of resources. A classical example of pact configuration at the regional level is the already mentioned Vologda region,[7] assigned by *Public Expertise* to "transitional to market model."

Such assignment must be determined by the politico-economic bicentrism observed in the region, with Volodga, the official principal city, and the second center – Cherepovets, that not only exceeds Vologda by population, but is also the location of the region's two biggest chemical plants and Russia's third metallurgic giant *Severstal*, the principal taxpayer into the regional budget. Although this might give good prospects for political competition (or struggle), and therefore space for media wars and some diversity in media content, instead the two power groups have to a significant extent merged. In 1996 elections for governor were won by Vyacheslav Pozgalyov – formerly *Severstal*'s vice-director and Cherepovets mayor. When I asked "Anton Sereda," my Vologda respondent, how many major agents of power there were in fact in the Vologda region, one or two, he said "one and a half" (Interview 42). To some extent the interests of the governor and those of the *Severstal* would always diverge, but in major affairs they would coincide and, in Sereda's opinion, there was little chance of them to quarreling in the near future. According to the data in *Public Expertise*, all the printing houses and nearly all print media in the region were private by the year 2000, and the region could boast a relatively high share of private radio transmitters. All this brought the region a high score for freedom of production of information. However, as Sereda said, nearly all media, except a few small newspapers, either belonged to *Severstal* or were funded by it. "As for the opposition newspaper," Sereda noted mysteriously, "*Severstal* is smart enough to understand that if there is no opposition, you should create it." When asked to comment on these words, *Severstal*'s press-secretary said nothing to contradict them. It is also significant that the *Public Expertise* authors for their section "Media conflicts in Vologda region" picked up the following example from GDF monitoring:

> Cherepovets: police officers were fulfilling the resolution of the regional arbitration court against the Free Trade Union of the *Severstal* joint stock company. They confiscated a computer that belonged to the *Fakel* newspaper situated in the Trade Union's office; the computer contained a lay-out of the newspaper issue with an article critical of *Severstal*'s top management. When *Fakel* editor-in-chief, Liudmila Ivanova, tried to oppose the withdrawal of the computer, she was handcuffed and severely beaten.
>
> (GDF 19.05.2000)

Juxtaposition of all these data suggests that what on the surface may look like moderate pluralism may in fact be the result of a concealed pact between major players. This demonstrates the vulnerability of the *Public Expertise* teleological methodology, since it looks highly doubtful that a movement from Soviet state-owned to "Severstalian" media can be called a transition to the market model. The Vologda case also shows that the very existence of two power groups, although it prevents the emergence of a monocentric regime, does not automatically lead either to democracy, or even to competitive elitism. The economic dominance of *Severstal*, coupled with its inability to erase such actors as the governor and mayors, is the best base for an elite pact.

This term also greatly helps explain the paradox of the Nizhni Novgorod[8] (NN) region, ascribed to the "market model," but ranked very low in the general press freedom rating by *Public Expertise*. Producing the fourth largest industrial output in the country (1997), in the early 1990s NN region also gained a reputation of the cradle of the market reforms, which it owes to its leader, young and highly educated Boris Nemtsov who ruled NN in 1991–7. Having invited economist Grigori Yavlinski, the leader of the democratic *Yabloko* party, then well known for his reformist programs, as an adviser, Nemtsov managed to give his region an international profile. He himself was one of the most interviewed politicians in Russia; no one could get to him as easily as journalists, and this strategy of positive information management contrasted sharply to the old Soviet style based on negative practices.

All this, probably, led *Public Expertise* to place NN into the category of "market" and, therefore, of the most democracy-friendly regions. However, a deeper analysis of the local political situation demonstrates that Nemtsov, unique among representatives of the old Soviet elite in the region, showed himself as master of compromise and engaged in a complicated resource exchange with all the major actors. As a result, most Soviet administrators kept their positions, and one of them, Ivan Sklyarov, former communist party leader, became Nemtsov's vice-governor. Maintaining the image of market reforms also did not equate to real market reforms, and the "friendly" attitude to journalists as a part of positive information management did not mean the democratization of media, which is reflected in "harder" *Public Expertise*'s indexes, such as the absence of private printing houses in the region. The bubble of the market reforms cradle collapsed when in 1997 Ivan Sklyarov was elected the new governor.

Conflict configuration

Pact configuration is possible when resources available in the region are enough to be distributed among several, or at least among two, actors. Therefore such configurations are not found in the poorest regions. If resources are distributed relatively evenly, and no one can dominate, actors may choose either to elaborate common rules of the game, or to fight uncompromisingly, in which case a conflict configuration emerges. Most Russian regions experienced brief periods of such wars, but in some of them this situation persisted for years.

Perhaps, the best known of such areas is the Krasnoyarsk territory[9] which I shall consider here. Although not the richest in terms of people's incomes, this huge Siberian region contains a large number of big industrial enterprises that became an object of fierce struggle in the 1990s. Among them, enterprises of heavy industry, especially non-ferrous metallurgy, prevail, including the well-known Krasnoyarsk aluminum plant (*KrAZ*) and Achinsk alumina complex, both of which found themselves in the very center of local media life throughout the 1990s.

Since 1991 Krasnoyarsk has been constantly experiencing various conflicts. First, because one of its leaders became a member of the anti-Gorbachev putchist group in 1991, the territory suffered an almost entire replacement of its old elite, and the new one appeared to be very fragmented. Second, the first half of 1990s was marked by constant conflicts of the territory's administration with both autonomous districts whose status was unclear. Third is the already mentioned severe struggle for rich local enterprises. As one of the respondents joked, "During the last three months four directors of *KrAZ* have been discharged, and all of them are still alive. Doesn't look an aluminum-style situation" (Interview 40). The *KrAZ* leader in the second half of the 1990s, Anatoly Bykov, a man with the reputation of the local godfather, followed the entire trajectory of a violent entrepreneur: from racketeer to the established businessman who was approaching the position of the absolute master of the region when he brought to governorship General Alexander Lebed, formerly Yeltsin's dummy competitor for the Russian presidency.[10]

Contrary to Bykov's hopes for a puppet governor, Lebed's entry into the game in 1998 became a fourth circumstance that deepened the conflict. The first events that happened after his election were several arrests of members of the former administration, and conflicts both with the mayor of Krasnoyarsk, Pyotr Pimashkov, and the major commercial leaders, including Bykov himself. Running forward slightly, I should mention that Bykov was finally jailed and Lebed perished in a helicopter crush.

All this directly determined the local media situation. By 1998 Krasnoyarsk possessed three big TV channels: private – *TVK* and *Afontovo* – and *GTRK*, the local branch of the second national channel *RTR*. The first two were regular winners of competitions of regional media and had a good reputation among their colleagues throughout Russia. At the same time, *TVK*, whose blocking share was held by Bykov, was well known as an "aluminum television," which could be easily seen from its pro-Lebed coverage in the 1998 elections. Before Lebed's accession to power, *Afontovo* and *GTRK* were getting subsidies from the territory budget and were considered supporters of Valeri Zubov, then the territory governor, and, naturally, supported him at the elections. After Lebed's victory both channels found themselves in a difficult position (Chigishev 1998). A revealing characteristic of *Afontovo* was described to me by Mikhail Malyutin:

> Kim – he's the *Afontovo* head – used to be a deputy of the territory parliament, but has stopped now, because this body is now stalemated, it has no power. Pimashkov – the Krasnoyarsk mayor – has persuaded him to lead his party block in Krasnoyarsk. Formally, leaving the territory parliament for the city parliament, Kim has been demoted. But, as I say, the budget there is very small, and as the territory [parliament] gives nothing to *Afontovo*, now Mister Kim will most probably become a head of a committee of something like information policy or broadcasting and so on, and *Afontovo* will de facto turn into the city's channel.
>
> (Interview 40, January 2001)

Thus, instead of offering his conditions to *Afontovo*, Lebed yielded it to a powerful competitor. Moreover, having all the resources to subordinate the local branch of *RTR*, he failed to do it immediately. Several years into his governorship Lebed still did not enjoy full control. His overall strategy towards media turned out to be ineffective. For instance, one of his vice-governors, the leader of a pro-Lebed youth movement that used to beat up "wrong" journalists, once became especially known for trying to disperse a legal demonstration of human rights activists in the central square of Krasnoyarsk. For that purpose, he brought a few hundreds of his young supporters and proclaimed the square the place for a discotheque. While such an action could be successful in a monocentric Bashkortostan, in Krasnoyarsk the opposition channels were more than happy to show the drunken mob of Lebed's supporters chasing scattered HR activists. All these mistakes finally resulted in a weakening of Lebed's position and spoiling his image with the local audience. In 1999, Valeri Zubov, the former governor and Lebed's opponent, became the deputy in the State Duma representing one of the two electoral districts of Krasnoyarsk city; the other became represented by Alexander Klyukin – the key figure of Bykov's *TVK*. Both based their campaigns on anti-Lebed slogans.

However, soon after that Lebed managed to beat his main enemy, Bykov, having united with his numerous powerful rivals – CIGs that possessed huge economic capital, connections in Moscow and media resources. By 2002 Bykov, although released with a suspended sentence, lost control over most of his enterprises, including *KraZ*, Achinsk alumina complex and the *TVK* channel. The methods employed in this anti-Bykov war are illustrated by the story of the armed takeover of the Achinsk complex in Chapter 4, including throwing a *TVK* reporter out of the window as one of the milder measures. Victory over Bykov gave Lebed a good chance to lead the region to a pact configuration, but he perished the same year Bykov was released.

The story of the Krasnoyarsk territory, first of all, shows that, like monocentric regions, conflict provinces are better described not as clash between the oppressive state and the independent media, as *Public Expertise* suggests, but as a struggle of power groups using media as weapons. The difference is that in conflict regions no actor manages to dominate, which also has a different effect on the local media landscape. Fighting for their backers, media find themselves in a competitive environment and, no matter what the nature of this competition is, it leads to greater diversity of media, and to a necessity to better justify the defended positions in the presence of the rival (dis)information. In richer regions, like Krasnoyarsk, the fight of big players also creates some space for the emergence of small autonomous, or quasi-autonomous media as separate actors. Thus, the Krasnoyarsk print media-holding *Komok*, that grew around the respective newspaper, throughout the 1990s tended to play its own game, leasing its pages to various candidates during elections, and catering for mass audiences in the inter-elections periods.

Conflicts akin to Krasnoyarsk's situation demand the presence of a powerful non-state actor opposing either the governor or the mayor of the principal city, or both. However, most Russian regions are not rich enough for that, and the main opposition occurs *between* the governor and the mayor. Compared to the Krasnoyarsk type, this produces a poorer media landscape – as, for example, in the Voronezh region,[11] whose media situation was described to me by respondent "Samuel Petrenko":

> In the region and in the city [of Voronezh] a fight is going on now. The mayor – he cannot be called a democrat,[12] of course, because all of them have come out from the same partocracy, and he used to be in one company with the governor. But the mayor is a pragmatist, he is "beyond politics," as he claims, and in fact he is – I worked in his electoral headquarters, and I can say: no political ideals at all, only the ruble. So, naturally, he can be conventionally called a democrat. And the governor is red.[13] Two years ago they were competitors in the local [governor] elections. Unfortunately – I worked in the headquarters of the present mayor – he lost.... Why – because Voronezh is a "MICial" city, 70 percent of enterprises belong to the Military-Industrial Complex, and, correspondingly, they are not working.[14] ... Although, naturally, we have a relatively strong criminal mafia, none the less, as everybody says, our main mafia is FSB. Because Voronezh, to repeat, is a MICian city, and in the MICian cities FSB is stronger than any mafia....
>
> On regional supplements of Moscow papers.... Before we [regional bureau of *Komsomolskaya Pravda*] acquired our own

building, the local authorities tried to exercise some pressure. Naturally, everybody knows, it's not a secret, that the *Komsomolka*[15]
belongs to *ONEXIMbank*. At the Voronezh level it, naturally, affects
almost nothing, *ONEXIMbank* doesn't even have a representative
office in Voronezh. Naturally, as long as we did not have our own
building, we rented [an office], the risk existed all the time that if you
write something wrong, the red power will – and as *Komsomolka* is
naturally a paper if not strongly anticommunist, then at least right,
right-centrist, it is clear that we do not always write things they like.
The lefts. But as soon as we got our own building, as soon as they
understood that even if they offered us money – you know, the
[municipal] budget funding – we would refuse, and moreover would
make this public, so it would be even worse for them – they understood that they don't have any levers of influence....

But *Komsomolka*'s independent position is exceptional. No one
else has a similar one. All are to some extent dependent. Look at
Moskovski Komsomolets ... they would promote themselves well, but
there is one thing. They do not manage to cover the local political situation relatively objectively because they are sitting in the premises of
the *VorGTRK* – it is the local municipal television, which is entirely
under the governor's heel....

Local editions. There's the regional newspaper. It is the *Commune*
newspaper, you can judge it from the title. They are criticizing us,
openly naming ... and therefore we use the same [tactic] ... There is
... the so called *Voronezhski Kurier*, it is considered to be the first
Voronezh democratic newspaper, it still exists, but it is also in a subordinate position, only it's subordinate not to the governor, but to the
mayor. And it is considered a department of the city administration.
Its editor holds a position as a head of some department of the city
administration. And the newspaper is funded [by the local authori-
ties]. Naturally, if they write anything against the mayor, they will
have problems.

There are several papers that, like tender calves, suck two cows.
But the point is they don't suck out a lot, they are a little supported by
both sides, and they are swaying back and forth, yes, but they don't
influence local public opinion much.

(Interview 6, June 1998)

Yekaterinburg: democratic success or concealed pact?

Competitive elitism, or struggle according to the rules configuration,
emerges when none of the leading actors can dominate, and the leaders
choose to elaborate the rules of the common game. This leads to formal
institutionalization, manifested in the political realm by party building and
development of respective legislation. It creates prerequisites for the

future emergence of a democratic regime, though does not necessarily lead to it. In Gelman's view, this type is represented first of all by Sverdlovsk region (Yekaterinburg);[16] *Public Expertise* singles out this region as well. My own modest examination of the Yekaterinburg situation has brought me to equivocal conclusions.

Occupying the central part of the Ural Mountains, Sverdlovsk region, with Russia's third biggest population (4.7 million) and its third largest industrial output, is one of the richest in the country. Yekaterinburg, the principal regional town and the home city of Boris Yeltsin, is also considered the third in political significance after Moscow and St. Petersburg. In 1993 the regional elite, led by Yeltsin's former ally and appointee, Eduard Rossel, joined the so called parade of sovereignties declaring the region the "Ural republic" and announcing plans to extend it to neighboring regions. Yeltsin dismissed Rossel, but two years later he was elected governor (Petrov, Titkov and Mukhin 1998).

After that regional political life was dominated by antagonism between Rossel, with his party *Renovation of the Ural*, and the mayor of Yekaterinburg Arkadii Chernetski, with his party *Our home – our city*. Nearly all media became divided between these two leaders. Chernetskiy controlled three large Yekaterinburg newspapers, two TV channels and some other less important media. He also used to exercise some control over *SGTRK*, the regional affiliate of *RTR*. In general, Rossel's media army looked more powerful: within Yekaterinburg he controlled *Regional TV* channel and, though not without difficulties, *Channel 10* – the only private company broadcasting in the metric band – as well as two news agencies, and a few Yekaterinburg newspapers. Furthermore, what was very important for his influence outside the capital, he inherited from the Soviet media system an array of neighborhood papers, that comprised, according to different estimates, from thirty-eight (Mozolin 2003) to fifty-three (Markelova 1999) editions.

If this were the full picture, Sverdlovsk region would be similar to many bi-polar provinces of the country. But, as in Krasnoyarsk, Sverdlovsk's multiple enterprises aroused the competition of violent entrepreneurs who soon came to constitute the local business elite; unlike Krasnoyarsk, this competition did not lead to a monopoly, though a dominant group also emerged. Throughout the 1990s it was the so called *Uralmash* syndicate (the *Uralmashians*). Having started from standard criminal activities such as racketeering and illegal vodka production, the *Uralmashians* soon won over similar groups in Yekaterinburg and by the mid 1990s began successfully investing money into legal business. But to move further in this direction, they needed contacts with state actors and, therefore, supported Eduard Rossel, then dismissed by Yeltsin, at the elections for governor in 1995. *Uralmashians* did not start their own media empire, but used their (never proved) alliance with Rossel to get privileged access to all media controlled by the new governor. This alliance also became the basis for their further legalization. In 1999 they registered an NGO "*OPS 'Ural-mash'*": the Russian abbreviation *OPS* stands for both "public political union" and "organized criminal association" – the latter is how the *Ural-mashians* were described in official police documents. *OPS* as NGO included all the main *Uralmashian* leaders and employed one of the best journalists in Yekaterinburg as its press-secretary. Rossel himself used media to publicly declare that *Uralmashians* "no longer had problems with the law." All this, however, did not save one of the *Uralmash* founders, Alexander Khabarov, from four failures in Duma elections: either his reputation as local godfather was too strong to be easily overcome, or his use of media was ineffective, or both.

Ironically, his junior competitors were more successful. Several Yeka-terinburg businessmen established their newspapers before various elections, and some of them did win. It is interesting that two of *Uralmash*'s main competitors – Pavel Fedulev and Anton Bakov – managed to win elections without total control over certain media organizations. Part of the explanation is that both were lucky enough to possess a reputation of businessmen, not criminals, although Fedulev's biography is surprisingly similar to Khabarov's. In any case, both Fedulev and Bakov needed media coverage. While Bakov founded the political movement *May* whose actions were making news with professional constancy, Fedulev did not do even that. How was it possible for them to win?

An important factor here is the existence of a cluster of "independent" media – that is, as a Yekaterinburg expert put it, media independently "trading influence" (Trakhtenberg 2004). It is they who could be cooperated with when needed. A core of this group of media was *Channel 4* and later a media holding that grew around it; it included a news agency, an advertising agency and a number of other media. Of course, in the presence of powerful local agents the channel could not survive alone but, unlike many others, its leader Igor Mishin chose to seek support outside the region, but within media business. At first *Channel 4* became an affiliate of *Ren-TV*, a Moscow-based entertainment network, and then – of the much more popular *TNT* that, along with *NTV*, was a part of Gussinky's *Media-MOST* holding. Neither *Ren-TV* nor *TNT* had any interests in the region except profit, and since both made money selling media products, there was no sense taking sides. That, of course, does not mean that air time was never sold to any of them: what was not sold was the organization as a whole.

The described situation poses the question as to whether the Sverdlovsk media landscape is different enough from other regions to constitute a separate type of media-political configuration. A more permanent alliance of *Uralmash* and Rossel, as contrasted with the failed pact between Bykov and Lebed in Krasnoyarsk, does not indicate a stronger desire to elaborate rules of the game; rather, it resembles the pact configuration in Vologda. The fact that many Sverdlovsk players channeled their activities into party building may point at Sverdlovsk's uniqueness, but in the sphere of media the competition between those players did not look any more peaceful and rule-driven than in Krasnoyarsk. Thus, the 1999 gubernatorial elections were marked by a sharp increase in violent acts against media, registered by GDF. They included the bombing of an editorial car and of Igor Mishin's apartment, the arson of an editorial office, two physical assaults against journalists in the streets, the theft of editorial computers with layout and of printed circulation, and numerous acts of blackmailing (GDF 01.04, 06.04, 21.05, 03.08, 17.08, 17.09, 22.09, 27.09 1999). These acts were usually accompanied by demands to change editorial policy. Thus, Sverdlovsk does not seem much different from the conflict configuration of Krasnoyarsk type, but still its difference from bi-polar Voronezh looks important: the multiplicity of agents of power provides richness and diversity of media.

Concluding remarks

Coexistence of different media-political configurations within one fractured and rapidly changing society gives some theoretical insights. First, it reveals the limits of such concepts as a national media system, showing internal diversity and fluidity of the country's media landscape. Second, the absence of many background inter-regional dissimilarities, that often become an obstacle in international comparative analysis, allows the singling out of factors responsible for the difference between regional media configurations, and a closer investigation of these factors. In a loosely structured society media landscapes seem to be determined first of all by the number of major power groups, which may produce monocentric, bi-polar, or multi-polar situations. The number of agents, in turn, much depends on the richness of local resources and their "initial" distribution – the one that emerged shortly after the collapse of the monolithic Soviet regime. Actors' strategies also matter. Since compromise strategies tend to produce pact configurations – that is, a single group with some closely cooperating subdivisions – diverse media emerge where efforts of major agents to compromise are limited. Thus, paradoxically, the prevalence of conflict strategies leads to a competitive environment that pushes media to develop themselves as more and more attractive products. Where local resources can support more than two major agents, a space emerges for media as relatively autonomous, albeit junior agents, capable of carrying out their own policies, such as "independent trade with influence." Those of them who decide to unite with non-local non-political agents push themselves and, as a by-product, other media of the region, towards commercialization.

11   The story of *Peterburg – 5 Kanal*

Unlike the comparative description of regional media-political configurations, the story of *Peterburg – 5 Kanal*[1] is a small-scale case study.
However, it also has a certain significance for the national media history:
had it been noticed by the Russian journalistic community in time, it might
have become an indicator of future changes that unfolded full scale under
president Putin. While the collapse of *NTV* manifested the institutional
consolidation of the state, the failure of *Peterburg – 5 Kanal* anticipated
state consolidation along the spatial axis.

Although St. Petersburg in many senses rises above other regional
centers, its media situation has had more similarities with other provinces
than with the capital, and thus exemplifies a relatively developed regional
market. The city itself, with its population of a little less than five million
people, is the second largest in Russia after Moscow (nine million), and
the second in terms of development of various "post-industrial" attributes
(communications, science, culture and entertainment industries, etc.)
Founded as a new capital of the Russian Empire in 1703 and having
played this role in 1712–1918, St. Petersburg also has an image of the cultural capital and a "window to Europe." The expression itself was first
used by the city founder, Russian Emperor Peter I: the new capital was
then the only Russian port, both military and trading, on the Baltic Sea. It
was also modeled after European towns and was meant to become the
center of Russian modernization and westernization. Since 1993 St. Petersburg is the only city, except Moscow, that has the status of a separate
subject of the Russian Federation (other subjects are provinces, not
cities).[2] All this generates constant rivalry between the two capitals, where
St. Petersburg, however, is always the envious loser.

The main reason for this is the self-accelerating concentration of all
major resources in the capital; this, at least, was true for the whole period
of 1990s. Metaphorically, St. Petersburg's general position at that time can
be illustrated with its share in the Russian advertising market: while
Moscow, comprising some 6 percent of Russia's population, took about
three-quarters of advertising money in 1998, St. Petersburg shared about 5
percent of this money, leaving the remaining 20 percent to the rest of the

country (Grozny 1998: 16–18). Thus, being far behind Moscow, St. Petersburg was still ahead of others: it accumulated roughly one-fifth of non-Moscow advertising while comprising only roughly 3.5 percent of non-Moscow population. However, the difference between St. Petersburg and other regions was mostly a difference of scale, while the capital was different structurally. Moscow media were closely merged with the national. On the one hand, a large proportion of media founded as local either turned or had ambitions to turn into national with time. On the other hand, the news of national media carried predominantly Moscow content; often Russian national media were called "the press of the Sadovoye Ring," referring to the name of the ring road that circles the business and political center of Moscow. Furthermore, all national media were located in Moscow, with one exception: *Peterburg – 5 Kanal.*

The rise of *Peterburg – 5 Kanal*

In Soviet times St. Petersburg (Leningrad) State television, with its only channel, was a part of the local TV and radio complex funded and ruled by local authorities just as many other regional "teleradiocompanies." But during *perestroika* in the late 1980s it gradually received a whole system of about 400 relay transmitters that covered most of the European part of Russia. It therefore fell under the jurisdiction of the National "teleradiocomplex" with its four Moscow-based channels and became the only national channel whose production was generated outside Moscow. The official reason for giving a regional TV station such a privilege was that Leningrad TV had become extremely popular by that time. Indeed, its popularity was beyond doubt: the city's journalistic community was no less professional than their Moscow colleagues, but was farther from the controlling center, and thus sometimes enjoyed greater possibilities for innovation. St. Petersburg TV became famous with Alexander Nevzorov's "600 seconds" newscast that introduced a news format radically different from glossy Soviet journalism; Bella Kurkova's "Piatoye koleso" (Fifth Wheel) analytical program; Kirill Nabutov's "Adamovo yabloko" (Adam's Apple), a "men's show," one of the first to touch on questions of sex, and many others. But the main reason for St. Petersburg TV's popularity was criticism of the Soviet State and a strong appeal for more radical economic, political and cultural change. The "central power" certainly did not want the spread of such broadcasting, so the only agents who could promote this spread could be anti-Gorbachev forces who then were concentrated at the level of Russian Socialist Federative Republic authorities, Yeltsin among them.

Whether this is so is a matter for further study. It is known, however, that after a failed anti-reform coup d'état in August 1991 and Yeltsin's accession to power a new director of St. Petersburg TV was appointed: this was Viktor Yugin, the editor-in-chief of one of the most pro-reformist newspapers in the city. He took an active part in the August events on the side of the reformers headed by Yeltsin, and was in personal contact with the Russian president.

However, Yeltsin's supporters met strong opposition within the channel led by Alexander Nevzorov who had tacitly supported the coup in 1991. It was difficult to fire him primarily because he had become extremely popular in the previous years because of his vigorous and critical reporting. He himself was both the anchor and the reporter of his "600 Seconds," a program that for the first time introduced reporting perceived as "Western": scandal, drama, criminal details and elements of investigative journalism. Nevzorov's talent is still widely recognized by the journalistic community, while some of the methods he widely used – such as forgery and invented events – are considered inappropriate. In early 1990s, however, the wider public knew very little about his morally dubious deeds and found few alternatives to his vivid program.

Thus it is plausible that the dismissal of Yugin as soon as October 1992 was explained partly by the fact that he could not (or did not *want*?) to cope with Nevzorov's subversive activities within the company's collective. His successor was Bella Kurkova, a journalist and producer to whom *Peterburg – 5 Kanal* owed no less of its popularity than it did to Nevzorov. She was also a vigorous Yeltsin supporter; after his armed conflict with the Russian Parliament in October 1993 when Nevzorov was again in the anti-Yeltsin camp (this time together with Yugin), she did not hesitate any longer to take "600 Seconds" from the air, despite its popularity. The official reasoning was not connected with political events, and the journalist himself was not fired. Thus he kept the possibility of continuing with his subversive activity, launching numerous scandals against Kurkova. The channel itself broadcast openly pro-Yeltsin reporting, especially during the 1993 events. It may have been coincidence, but in late 1993 *Peterburg – 5 Kanal* got a subsidy of $2 million for buying new equipment. Earlier Yeltsin had signed a decree separating St. Petersburg TV from the Federal "teleradiocomplex" into an autonomous State organization *Peterburg – 5 Kanal* that retained all the property it had been using before. Federal funding, however, was secured.

The difficulties of *Peterburg – 5 Kanal*

The channel did not flourish for long, due to several factors. First, Kurkova's style of journalism – an intellectual critique of the State that made the channel popular in late 1980s – could not be applied full scale since she supported the new authorities; furthermore, the format itself was no longer in big demand with the public.

In economic terms – and this is a second factor – *Peterburg – 5 Kanal* had a clear disadvantage compared to Moscow-based national channels: it received even less funding (while being unable to get in direct contact with advertisers at the national level). By 1994, its budget was fifteen times less than that of its competitors. The mentioned $2 million did not help: Kurkova's new deputy director, a certain Syroyezhin took the money in early 1994 and soon disappeared somewhere in America. The scandal did not erupt until a year afterwards when this information leaked to the press, and in a few months, in mid-1995 Kurkova resigned.

Her reasons for resigning deserve special attention. She publicly called Syroyezhin a "smuggled-in spy" and always seemed sincere in regarding him a part of a secret Moscow plot whose aim was to gain control over the property of *Peterburg – 5 Kanal*. She claimed that *5 Kanal* was carrying out its own investigation, informing the Federal police about Syroyezhin's movements and asking them to prevent his escape abroad, but still the police took no action. Her first warnings about the plot date back to 1994 when they seemed a complete nonsense; later events, however, suggest that they might have had some foundation. Before describing them, I shall consider other factors that were weakening the channel.

A third factor was internal conflicts. Being stimulated by the Kurkova-Nevzorov struggle, they gradually involved more and more journalists. Rumors about Moscow conspirators willing to deprive the company of its property, and journalists of their jobs, led to severe internal competition. People started uniting in various trade unions fighting each other. Some journalists – the most popular and productive – fled to richer Moscow channels, often together with their shows (the legal possibility of registering any TV program as a separate media organization gave hosts and communicators the right to move their shows to any channel they wished).

Fourth, the reputation of the channel was undermined by various violations in which Kurkova's participation, unlike in the Syroyezhin story, was beyond doubt. For instance, in 1994 *5 Kanal* which by that time was already unable to fully fill its air time, illegally subleased five hours of it to a TV company named *Svezhy Veter* (Fresh Wind). Just a little later this fact caused big difficulties to *Peterburg – 5 Kanal* in its struggle for this very air time with a mysterious competitor named *TeleExpo*. This firm emerged from nowhere in Moscow and surprisingly quickly got a license for broadcasting through *5 Kanal*'s Moscow transmitter – which also contradicted the law, but did not cause problems for *TeleExpo*. Its backer revealed himself a little later, but this is the subject of the next section.

Here, it is interesting to point out a strange coincidence: the *Fresh Wind* TV company was said to be funded by the *Lis's* company of Sergei Lissovsky, one of the two leading entrepreneurs in the advertising business of that period. The same Lissovsky owned a 35 percent stake in the *Ekran-TV* media selling agency that had the exclusive rights to sell *5 Kanal*'s advertising time. He well might have had possibilities to press *5 Kanal* to give him part of their air time. This cannot be proved, but many analysts considered the conditions of the contract between *Ekran-TV* agency and *Peterburg – 5 Kanal* oppressive for the latter.

Since a bias in power in favor of media selling agencies is characteristic of Russia, the fault of *5 Kanal*'s top management in this case is questionable. However, many other counterproductive actions of *5 Kanal* managers are known, and this was a fifth factor in its weakness. For example, Kurkova's successors decided to imitate *CNN* and produce news every hour – a similar project had not long before failed in Moscow. For a *CNN* style to emerge, Russia lacked America's extremely rich media market where channels may work out specific formats. The result for *Peterburg – 5 Kanal* was also unsuccessful: it became unable to broadcast uninterrupted films, shows and many other items of its traditional programming. The news, at the same time, was unsuitable to become the channel's strongest product: unlike *CNN*, *Peterburg – 5 Kanal* could make mostly only local news having a shortage of reporters, time, and events themselves. Respondent "Vitaly Bogdanov" told me how journalists had to make fake live inserts, retell events they had no time to shoot and repeat the same stories many times (Interview 12).

Another disadvantage of *Peterburg – 5 Kanal* in terms of news production was the result of the structure of Russia's information flow: as mentioned earlier, nearly all events of national significance took place in Moscow. That is why it was difficult to make national news outside the capital. *5 Kanal* could not afford its bureau in Moscow, to say nothing of other regions, and had to rely on secondary sources retelling news from news agencies and buying pictures from other channels. Thus by late 1996 the channel had extremely low ratings, having lost most of its advertising, star journalists and popular shows. In fact, the already existing weakness of the channel did allow for the realization of the "Moscow plot" of which Kurkova had warned.

Struggle for transmitters

The culminating events happened in 1997 when the "Moscow plot" surfaced itself in the form of a fierce struggle over *Peterburg – 5 Kanal*'s network of relay transmitters. Actually, it was rather not a pre-planned plot but quite a messy fight that involved many agents of power. The key actor who remained silent most of the time was the president: in the absence of legislation on broadcasting, the distribution of State property in the sphere of media was de facto regulated by presidential decrees. Thus the aim of any other actor was to convince Boris Yeltsin or people who could influence him to make decisions in the actor's favor.

Some agents were predominantly economic. For instance, the then rising *NTV* was interested in broadening its audience. In its negotiations with the State Committee on Press, therefore, it justified its "right" to use the network by its popularity that allowed *NTV* to offer the Committee a fee for signal transmission 1.5 times higher than that of *Peterburg – 5 Kanal*. Because in late 1996 *NTV* had already received a gift from the president (the license for using the frequency of *Channel 4* throughout the whole country), it could hope for further donations.

A second player was the upper chamber of the Russian parliament, the Soviet of the Federation, which at that period was a gathering of governors of Russia's eighty-nine subjects of federation. The governors proposed that the president make *Peterburg – 5 Kanal* the "channel of regions" with its office in Moscow, thus hoping to make it a medium for voicing interests of regional elites. However, the governors' unity was undermined by the most powerful of them – Moscow mayor[3] Yuri Luzhkov who at that time had presidential ambitions: it was he who backed the fast release of the license for the previously mentioned *Tele-Expo* TV company that intended to use the Moscow part of *5 Kanal*'s transmitting network. When this project failed, Luzhkov started lobbying for a more compromising idea of creating a channel of the two capitals *Red Arrow*.[4]

A third (winning) group of players was the alliance of the top management of the second state channel *RTR* headed by Nikolai Svanidze, with the vice-minister of culture Mikhail Shvydkoi. Their project was use the *5 Kanal*'s network for the creation of a new educational channel *Kultura* (culture) as a branch of *RTR* with its production in Moscow. The St. Petersburg "piece" of the network was planned to be given to the northern capital (that is, to be at the disposal of its governor), and *5 Kanal*'s staff was to be offered participation in *Kultura* production on a temporary contract basis. In terms of formal logic, the project looked quite peculiar: approximately a year before that, a channel similar to *Kultura*, *Russian Universities*, had been shut down because of the "shortage of resources"; it was the frequency of that channel which *NTV* got by presidential decree.

The fourth group of actors was two-fold and included the management and the staff of *Peterburg – 5 Kanal*. Neither were interested in the projects listed above: the management was to lose part of its power and material resources, and the people – their jobs. Their number was inevitably going to shrink after the transformation of the national channel into the local. As for the participation in *Kultura* on a contract basis, journalists were inclined to doubt this promise because *RTR* already had its branch in St. Petersburg with a strong culture-oriented production (a propos: the position of head had been secured for herself by Bella Kurkova even before she left *Peterburg – 5 Kanal*).

Finally, the fifth participant of the game – the mayor, and later the governor, of St. Petersburg. The mayor Anatoly Sobchak who governed in 1991–6 was openly struggling for the national status of St. Petersburg TV. As for the strategy of his successor Vladimir Yakovlev, not much is known about it. Ideally, the governor should have been interested in keeping the national broadcasting in his city since he did have much influence on it. However, he may have regarded this as unrealistic and joined the *Kultura* project, especially because his accession to power is attributed to a number of Moscow backers that included Luzhkov himself. In any case, this project prevailed 1.5 years after Yakovlev's election to his post, and the only non-Moscow national channel ceased to exist.

Epilogue

After fall 1997, *Peterburg – 5 Kanal* lost its national audience. During 1998 it was liquidated and reopened as a new enterprise *Teleradiocompany Peterburg* (*TRK Peterburg*). Two-thirds of its personnel was cut. The controlling share passed to the local administration (both the city and the Leningrad region, 37 percent and 14 percent respectively), and 49 percent – to private banks. Banks at that time were the major investors and sponsors of media, but after the financial crisis in August 1998 some of the sponsors went bankrupt and others discontinued their funding. Another staff reduction took place; those who were left got no salary for approximately half a year. The share of the local administration in the company grew by 17 percent, and the unprofitable channel in fact came under full administration control.

The culmination of its dependency came in the appointment of the new news director Sergei Chernyadev in October 1999, about half a year before elections for governor. Chernyadev had been known as a scandalous and ruthless anchor of a secondary local channel; he achieved extra "popularity" in the city's journalistic community after his appointment by his words in the first personnel meeting: "It is Yakovlev who is our governor, and *Yabloko* should be done away with," whose representative was Yakovlev's main competitor in the coming elections. Three of the remaining popular news anchors left the channel after that. Two of them held a press-conference and openly connected their resignation with Chernyadev's appointment. Some other journalists had their shows taken off air; others, however, started getting envelopes with money that roughly equated to their monthly income. This, compared to other city channels, was extremely low, but still equivalent to the average income in Russia – approximately $100. Whether for all these reasons or not Yakovlev won the elections in 1996.

Later events brought even the local leadership of the channel to an end. In fall 1999, *RTR* launched its regional "window" in St. Petersburg – a period of time when local production, including news was shown on its local frequency. This had no relation to the *5 Kanal* story and was part of Mikhail Lesin's policy of gaining control over local news production. Facing this challenge, the private *NTV* also opened its regional window. Two network channels (*6* and *11*) that had started local news even earlier also became more active. Thus *TRK Peterburg* had to face competition for four big TV companies.

Finally, the radio part of *TRK Peterburg* (*Radio Peterburg*) was in fact destroyed in March 2001. With the Soviet tradition of wire radio, most homes in Russia are equipped with "one-button" receivers, while only some have "three-button" receivers. In St. Petersburg, the first (and for many – the only) button always carried local radio, while the third had the national *RTR*. By decision of the new Ministry of press, *RTR* was not only switched to the first button, but also took *Radio Petersburg*'s most popular programs into its schedule. Thus, "one-button listeners" were entirely captured by *RTR*, while people looking for the local radio on the "three-button" receivers missed the "true" *Radio Petersburg*, not only because it moved to another button, but also because they could not recognize it in what was left of it. Instead, they found their favorite programs on *RTR*.

As for *RTR*, the irony of its victory was that former vice-minister of culture Shvydkoy first became the head of *Kultura* and then replaced his ally Svanidze in the post of *RTR* director. According to available evidence, Svanidze had hoped that the unprofitable *Kultura* would be soon shut down and that *RTR* would acquire full use of its transmitter network. Instead, Svanidze lost his leading position at *RTR*.

12   The story of *NTV*

The story of *NTV* is an example of a complex campaign launched by the state agents and their non-state allies against a media company. While the story of *Titan* radio is much more dramatic in terms of people's sufferings, this is a story of a successful defeat of the national private TV that was considered the national leader according to many criteria. Of course, there is no direct evidence about the role the government and Putin personally played in this story, but the chain of events makes this role obvious. That is why from the very beginning I treat this story as an anti-*NTV* campaign.

The rise of *NTV*

NTV started in 1993 as a production TV company that rented a limited time slot from *Peterburg – 5 Kanal*, then broadcasting almost countrywide. The young company became rather popular – partly because of the popularity of the *5 Kanal*, partly because of its own features. Later, it became even more well known when in early 1994 President Yeltsin suddenly granted *NTV* prime-time in the national *Channel 4* which had been broadcasting low-rating educational and cultural programs. No tender or any other public procedure for allocation of this frequency was carried out. There is no evidence as to why it was *NTV* who got it. It is known, however, that in 1993 the *NTV* team had negotiated with Vladimir Gussinsky, the head of *MOST* bank, after which *NTV* started rapidly gaining popularity, accumulating power and connections and gradually growing into a large media holding – *Media-MOST*. Its office moved into the building of the Moscow city administration, which was one of the grounds for analysts to claim the existence of an alliance between Gussinsky and Moscow mayor Yuri Luzhkov. Paying high salaries, *NTV* attracted many popular journalists, including the former news anchor and then political commentator Yevgeni Kiselyov. He moved to *NTV* from *Channel 1* together with his popular Sunday political program "Itogi" (meaning sum total, summary, or major results). Unlike the slow-changing state-owned companies, with a huge bureaucracy and few stimuli for development, *NTV* was dynamic and quickly copied Western patterns of media production, which was especially true for the style of news presentation. In the absence of such a commodity as objective news *NTV* filled this empty niche in the market. In general, its concept was "news + films." It first started successfully scheduling Western films which dominated its air time, but later it was among the first to reintroduce the products of Soviet popular culture.

What really made *NTV* a sensation was the start of the first Chechen war in late 1994, when the channel showed many sides of this campaign that the federal government preferred not to be shown. The government itself had nothing to offer to the audience. While this topic is discussed in more detail in the next chapter, here it is enough to say that *NTV* got the reputation of an independent and objective media outlet which it continued to exploit later.

The conclusion that objectivity for *NTV* was rather a commodity than a normative ideal may be drawn from analysis of Gussinsky's other activities, whose CIG at that time was the second strongest after the alliance of another entrepreneur, Boris Berezovsky, and the "Family" of Boris Yeltsin. The role of the intermediary between Berezovsky and Yeltsin is usually ascribed to then very influential Alexander Korzhakov, Yeltsin's personal bodyguard in 1985–91 and the head of his Security office in 1991–6. It is not by chance that the information war between Berezovsky-Korzhakov-*ORT* and Gussinsky-Luzhkov-*NTV*, known as "Goose hunting," happened in winter 1994–5 and became the first significant media conflict of the 1990s. The expression is a play on Gussinsky's name (*gus* is Russian for "goose") once voiced in public by Korzhakov whose influence within Yelsin's "Family" was growing rapidly. Given the generally important role of the security services in Russian politico-economic life of that period, Korzhakov's increasing influence is not surprising. In the course of the information war the popular *NTV* show "Puppets" satirized the situation, after which a criminal prosecution was started against *NTV*. Other publications in this war also point to Berezovsky's and Korzhakov's common interests, and at contradictions between Berezovsky and Luzhkov on a vast number of questions – Luzhkov, among other things, stood out against a new increase of import tax on cars (Lilin 1998). It is also not a mere coincidence that this war coincided with privatization of *Channel 1*, which was meant to strengthen the information resource of the "Family," both in the future elections and as a part of the military campaign in Chechnya. Thus, the media component of this conflict was only the tip of the iceberg, while its other facets included an armed incident in the center of Moscow on 2 December 1994, lost by Gussinksy's CIG.

Volkov (2002) points out that the main cause of this incident was the public demonstration of power by the *MOST* security department headed by a former KGB officer. Besides accompanying Gussinsky in armored vehicles full of armed people, and other security activities, the department carried out political and commercial espionage, in particular, collecting *kompromat* involving the political and business elite (Volkov 2002: 178). Later Gussinsky was publicly accused of using these materials for "blackmailing" his rivals through his media outlets (Interview 35), which suggests that what was presented by *NTV* as "objectivity" and "independence from the government" might have been a method of economic and political competition. But at that time most details of the conflict stayed concealed. On 2 December 1994 Gussinsky's bodyguards were unexpectedly beaten up by "unknown masked people." Moscow FSB (KGB) chief, at Gussinksy's request, tried to "arrest" these "armed bandits," sending his own soldiers, but the "bandits" turned to be President's Security office members and themselves arrested the FSB people. For his intrusion the Moscow FSB chief immediately paid by his dismissal, while Gussinsky fled abroad for a while. However, in the longer term Gussinsky won: Korzhakov's enormous power finally frightened Yeltsin himself, and he dismissed his bodyguard shortly before the 1996 presidential elections.

Since then Gussinsky's business was developing rapidly; by the end of his "oligarchic" career he had an entire media holding, with newspapers, magazines, a radio station, a publishing house and the first commercial sputnik in Russia. Before the 1998 crisis, *NTV* was one of the few Russian TV companies that was about to become profitable. To launch its satellite, in summer 1998, just before the financial crisis, *Media-MOST* took a $211.6 million loan from *Vneshekonombank* for a term of two years, with annual extension. But when the time of extension came, that is in summer 1999, *Vneshekonombank* refused to extend the contract and demanded the repayment of the full amount: this was the first signal of *NTV*'s future problems.

The first problems

Of course, any bank may have financial reasons for breaking contracts with its clients; however, details of this story point to the existence of other causes. The contract was terminated after consultations with the head of President Yeltsin's administration, Alexander Voloshin (Varshavchik 2000a). The event also coincided with the foundation of the new Ministry of media, headed by the founder of the then monopolistic *Video International* advertising agency Mikhail Lesin. Finally, the event happened several weeks before the appointment of Putin as prime-minister, four months before the autumn 1999 parliamentary elections, and eight months before the spring 2000 presidential elections. As Anna Kachkayeva points out, "in summer 1999 it became clear that the creation of a business-political alliance of the 1996 type was not only unlikely, but just impossible. The Russian political elite could not come to an agreement on a candidate acceptable to all the clans competing in business and politics" (Kachkayeva 2001).

The reasons why Gussinsky refused this time to join the pre-electoral alliance headed again by Berezovsky are unclear. Some journalists from

NTV claimed that they did not want to repeat their mistake of 1996. Anyway, *Vneshekonombank*'s action was clearly a sanction that *Media-MOST* experienced after refusing to join the game. But *MOST's* debt was paid by one of its major shareholders, Russian giant gas monopolist *Gazprom*, which had bought a 30 percent share of *MOST* back in 1996. This purchase of shares of a private media group, which went unnoticed in the also "electoral" 1996, was pointed out by a few media analysts who noticed that it might lead to a decrease in *NTV*'s autonomy (Belin 1996: 63). The fact that *Gazprom* itself was a partly state-owned organization (Mukhin 2000: 135), and the appointment of its head depended on the Federal government, also played an important role in this story.

Why did *Gazprom* pay *MOST*'s debt? This may indicate different things. First, it may mean that *Gazprom* at that time was a relatively autonomous structure, and that its interest was not identical to that of the group promoting Putin – after all, *Gazprom* was interested in *NTV*'s profitability. A second version is that Vladimir Gussinsky, due to the good work of his intelligence service, had some leverage of influence on *Gazprom* or, to be precise, its head Rem Vyakhirev. Anyway, *Media-MOST* was either not attracted to the pro-government campaign or excluded from covering the parliamentary elections of 1999.

The elections, therefore, became dominated by two major competing groups. Moscow mayor Yuri Luzhkov, in an alliance with one of the former prime-ministers Yevgeni Primakov, formed the political block *Otechestvo – Vsya Rossiya* (*OVR*, Fatherland – All Russia) which became the main competitor of the newly created pro-Putin party *Yedinstvo* (Unity). The latter's media resources were obviously bigger, and included *ORT*, controlled by Boris Berezovsky, and the state owned *RTR*. Both channels had a larger reach than Gussinsky's *NTV* and much larger than *TV-Center*, a network TV company founded by Luzhkov. Despite Gussinsky being associated with Luzhkov, *NTV*'s coverage of the elections was considered by most analysts the most balanced. The main cause seems to be the fact that the Gussinsky-Luzhkov CIG, being a weaker partner and a debtor, could not attack *Yedinstvo* in the way *ORT* and *RTR* attacked *OVR*.

In particular, Luzhkov was accused of participation in the murder of an American businessman and in the assassination attempt on the Georgian president Eduard Shevardnadze; the elderly Primakov was mocked for having an artificial limb. Most such attacks were carried out in *ORT*'s "'Time' with Dorenko" political commentary program by its anchor Sergei Dorenko, young and handsome, with a very masculine voice, who made fun of both Luzhkov and Primakov at any suitable opportunity. When Luzhkov pursued a defamation suit against Dorenko and won it, Dorenko made a brilliant satire from taped passages of the trial. Besides stressing that Moscow judges were under Luzhkov's control, he quoted the most inept words of the judge, such as "I as a woman cannot understand how he [Dorenko] can behave like this." Commenting on this, Dorenko said that this strange woman "preferred the old to the young, the bald to the hairy, the round to the oblong."[1] Given the position of press minister Lesin, discussed in previous chapters, had *NTV* broadcast anything close to such mockery more than twice, it would have been liable to lose its license at once and absolutely legally.

After this campaign the Luzhkov-Primakov block still got a significant number of seats in the parliament, but not as many as both had counted on. Their hopes for the presidential post for either of them evaporated. Primakov left politics. The journalistic community split. *NTV* journalists, who had also been under attack all the time, said there were some things that could not be forgotten, while the rest admitted with regret that now it was obvious that the journalistic community could be manipulated.

However, before the presidential elections of 2000 big scandals in the media could play out against Putin, but he had covert sanctions at hand. From January 2000 *Video International* advertising agency (the one founded by the Minister of press) suddenly broke its contract with *NTV*, which ruined *NTV*'s plans for advertising revenues. It had to launch its own agency in haste. Another remarkable event of the same month was connected with the name of Oleg Dobrodeyev, the head of *NTV*'s news department, and the one whom the journalistic community regarded as one of the best professionals in news production. With other *NTV* people he also shared an image of a relatively "independent" journalist. By January, the conflict of *NTV* with Putin's team was obvious, and it looked like a battle between the "oppressor" and those who were struggling for freedom of the press. Many in the journalistic community watched the unfolding conflict with fear and hope, though, of course, realists were also numerous. But anyway, when Dobrodeyev suddenly resigned from his post at *NTV* and was immediately appointed to the same post at *RTR* (Varshavchik 2000b) this news had a shocking and sobering effect. After that, one by one, many *NTV* journalists started following his example. *RTR*, which had always been the poorest of the three national channels, by that time surpassed *NTV* in journalistic salaries – this was not only due to *NTV*'s financial difficulties, but also because funding for *RTR* was significantly raised in 2000.

Arrest of the oligarch

With time, the enforcement component in the anti-*NTV* campaign became stronger. In May 2000, after the presidential elections, people from the General Procuracy, assisted by Federal Security Bureau, searched the *MOST* offices. According to the official version, the activity of *MOST*'s security service was investigated, but in fact very different premises were examined. In early June the Presnya municipal court of Moscow brought in a verdict recognizing this search illegal and ordering the Procuracy to give back all the confiscated items. This shows that the control of the Presidential administration over the courts was at that time not at all total, and not everything was done at Putin's first order.

The next stage was the arrest of Gussinsky on June 13 – at that time, a rather unexpected event; before that few could have imagined that such a high-ranking "oligarch" could be arrested. He had been summoned to the Procuracy on quite a different pretext – to clarify some documents connected with his personal gun – but there he was taken under custody without official charge and put into one of the most dreadful prisons in Moscow, Butyrka – although he shared his cell with only two people. This event provoked a flood of protest statements of various high-status persons: famous politicians, NGO representatives, artists, and others. Among them, of special interest is a public letter of seventeen well-known businessmen: Gussinsky's "oligarchic colleagues" declared readiness to stand bail for Gussinsky. The list of those who signed the letter contained representatives of at least five of the nine national CIGs distinguished by Mukhin (see Chapter 2), including those whom he considers Gussinsky's opponents. His arrest was interpreted by them as "an attack of the authorities on oligarchs," which was explicitly stated in their letter. It is very interesting that Berezovsky was *not* among the signatories (in addition to Roman Abramovich who, unlike the two media barons still enjoys power). Commenting on his position, Berezovsky said: "Gussinsky became the victim of the machine which he had started himself." This indicates that Berezovsky at that time was still hoping to preserve his connection with the presidential administration.

Even the US President Bill Clinton and the USA Congress made public statements expressing concern about freedom of press in Russia. *NTV* had been making special efforts to construct an image of the main independent TV of the country, and after Gussinksy's arrest this campaign intensified. Gussinsky's first assistant, Igor Malashenko, was following president Putin in his first foreign tour to a number of European countries – a tour that "by accident" coincided with the arrest of the oligarch. In each place where Putin appeared, Malashenko organized press-conferences and made public statements on the alarming situation regarding press freedom and the law in Russia.

Gussinsky himself made a number of statements. The first was a handwritten notice he passed via his barrister from Butyrka prison; soon after his release he showed up in public on the *NTV* talk-show "Vox populi" devoted specially to this matter and anchored by Yevgeni Kiselyov, the *NTV* head. Gussinsky was extremely cautious in his speech; he only noted that he was not struggling against "oligarchs attached to the authorities. They *are* the authorities." At the same time Gussinsky refused Sergei Dorenko's invitation to take part in his "Time with Dorenko." In his next program the anchor cited Gussinsky's note addressed to him where the businessman politely explained his refusal. He wrote he was afraid that too little time had passed since his release, everybody's nerves were strained, and they both could say too much in a burst of anger.

Dorenko, in contrast, had come to the unscheduled live broadcast of "Vox populi" held during Gussinsky's imprisonment. It showed the studio full of popular journalists and public figures trying to guess if Dorenko would come. He was said to be on his way to the studio when Kiselyov cited Berezovsky's comment about Gussinsky's "machine" whose victim he himself had become. One of the guests then joked that Dorenko must now have turned back, but the anchor appeared in the studio soon after and even said a few words that became very popular. Though the former KGB officer Putin, he said, might have not been giving special orders to the enforcers, "they [were] hearing the music" and going forward.

It is very significant that precisely from 2000 both Gussinsky and Berezovsky started personally "working as newsmakers," which had seldom happened before. It was a good indicator of the weakening of their positions: "information resource," the weakest of all, is as a rule used as a last resort. Gussinsky's team was actively trying to apply other methods of information management, including the above-mentioned Malashenko's journey, *NTV*'s address to Yeltsin as the "guarantor of press freedom," and others. Though in general this method could not be very effective, it seems plausible that it was the international repercussions, organized by Gussinsky's media after his arrest, that led to his release in three days on condition of not leaving Moscow. The "large-scale fraud" of which Gussinsky was accused had been connected with privatization of some media outlets he had acquired several years before. Who made the decisions in the story of Gussinsky's arrest and release, and how, is of course not known for sure. Sergei Varshavchik, the investigative journalist, in one of his articles refers to Igor Malashenko:

> According to Malashenko, when his boss was thrown into Butyrka, just a couple of hours later he got a call from Mister Lesin who said that they'd meet. At the meeting the Minister of press, broadcasting and media brought out an ultimatum: *Media-MOST* is sold for $300 million, Gussinsky is released. Then – negotiations began in the course of which the minister was constantly taking phone advice either from the head of the presidential administration, or with the General prosecutor, coordinating details of the deal. So, if the *Media-MOST* head was getting too whimsical, General Procuracy investigators were quickly given an order to arrest somebody in his team, or to withdraw something from his estate in the course of another search.
>
> (Varshavchik 2000c)

The sum of $300 million appeared in other sources as well. The remainder of the cited text has indirect confirmation in Lesin's signature in the famous "Attachment 6" to the Agreement about the transfer and purchase of shares between JSC *Gazprom-Media*[2] and V.A. Gussinsky of July 20, 2000. According to the main text of the agreement, *Gazprom* had to obtain the *Media-MOST* holding and all its subsidiaries, including *NTV* channel, as a payment for the debt. Attachment 6 contains a number of interesting terms of the future deal:

> The criminal case of Mr. Gussinsky is to be closed ... he is to be transferred to the status of the case witness ... he is to be allowed to leave the country ... Mr. Gussinsky and top managers of the holding are to receive guarantees of their security and protection of their rights and freedoms, including the right to leave the Russian Federation without impediment and to return to the country.

The attachment also forbids all *MOST* media outlets to disseminate any information leading to "the discrediting of the institutions of state power of the Russian Federation," which is very close to official state censorship of the Soviet type. After the agreement was signed, persecution of Gussinsky was indeed stopped, and he went abroad where he immediately started looking for foreign buyers for the shares of *Media-MOST*.

The agreement itself was to be considered valid only under the terms of it being kept secret, but on September 18 *Gazprom-Media* accused Gussinsky of transferring assets to offshore zones abroad – which had not been planned by the agreement. After *Gazprom*'s claim the General Procuracy resumed legal proceedings against the *Media-MOST* management. At the same time media distributed a statement made by Gussinsky which betrayed the existence of the agreement of July 20; after this Gussinsky could never return to Russia, and he stayed mostly in Spain. In his statement he said that on July 18, two days before the agreement was signed, he had made another statement in presence of two American lawyers. In his July deposition for the lawyers he officially declared that he was under moral pressure and was being forced to sign the agreement. For that reason, Gussinsky said in September, his future signature under the agreement had to be considered null and void. Simultaneously, a scanned copy of Attachment 6 appeared on the Internet. The government took a silent pause – some were predicting Lesin's dismissal. Instead the prime minister Mikhail Kasyanov made a public speech where he just said that signatures of state officers were not to appear in agreements of private firms.

Search for foreign aid

Meanwhile Gussinsky's team was doing its best in using information resources, among other things trying to appeal in the name of press freedom and to the symbolic capital of certain celebrities, in particular, of Mikhail Gorbachev. The latter asked the president for a meeting, without result. Around the same time *NTV* became explicit in defending Gussin-sky, whether because the journalistic team changed its principles or because it just unmasked what had always existed. Anyway, before that any information had been presented as objective and impartial. Now journalists claimed they could not be impartial when they were under attack and everybody else was biased against them. For instance, another issue of "Vox populi," devoted to this conflict, experienced a change of decoration: a famous news anchor Svetlana Sorokina replaced Yevgeni Kiselyov as a host of the show, while he himself sat in one of the two armchairs for the main speakers. This gave him a legitimate opportunity to criticize his rival, *Gazprom-Media* head Alfred Kokh, who had also signed the July agreement and Attachment 6. This was a strange show: Sorokina constantly had difficulties when interrupting her superior, while most of the time she seemed unwilling to do so; her comments on speakers' arguments obviously favored Kiselyov. He himself looked nervous and appealed to moral order, while Kokh, calm and cold, used legal discourse. He referred to *Media-MOST*'s debts, "bad management" and "highly professional journalistic team," that, according to him, would by no means suffer after the selling of *NTV*. Here it is worth remembering that the other two national TV channels also had enormous debts. While reference to the discourse of law usually indicates that the existing rules fit the speaker's interests, the discourse of morality is the last shelter of weaker agents.

In October 2000 two other *Media-MOST* creditors demanded payment of their debts. Among them was *Vneshekonombank* again, with a $30 million claim, and it brought its suit to the court at a direct order of the Ministry of Finances. At the same time 63 percent of the shares of *Media-MOST*'s *Ekho Moskvy* radio station were seized in accordance with the decision of the Arbitrage court in respect of *Gazprom*'s claims. Vladimir Gussinsky was summoned twice to the General Procuracy to be interrogated as a witness. He replied from abroad that he was ready to give evidence but only outside the territory of Russia.

It is indicative that Gussinsky's former ally and rival Boris Berezovsky was also reportedly summoned to the Procuracy as a witness that autumn. Berezovsky, however, did not show up either and, moreover, made a sharp statement from London criticizing Putin's policy and saying he was not going to return to Russia. Approximately a month before that he had made a proposal to transfer the *ORT* shares belonging to him (49 percent) to a trust managed by a group of prominent men of art and culture. That is when the public learnt that, contrary to previous rumors, he did own so much, but the aim of the proposal stayed unclear. Later, in December, Berezovsky revoked it. In an interview to *Ekho Moskvy* radio station he said that the state would seize his shares even if this would lead to *ORT*'s bankruptcy.

On November 1, 2000 a settlement between *Media-MOST* and *Gazprom-Media* was signed. The same day the deputy General Prosecutor announced that if Gussinsky would not come to the interrogation scheduled for November 13, the search for him would be started worldwide via Interpol. As Gussinsky failed to turn up to the General Procuracy on November 13, he was charged with large-scale fraud again. Immediately after these charges were made, Alfred Kokh withdrew his signature from the agreement with the *Media-MOST* holding, which indicates that the settlement reached by the parties did not suit the major player of this game. A new agreement between the parties was executed on November 17: now *Media-MOST*'s shares were to be transferred to the new owner before the end of year. After that the story had clearly two parallel lines of development: one connected with criminal proceedings, and the other with economic negotiations.

The first line developed as a long series of summons of *NTV* journalists and executives to the Procuracy, some of them being arrested; more than a hundred searches were carried out in *Media-MOST*'s offices. Another feature was a constant "war of courts": some of them made decisions, others cancelled them, and often this process had many iterations. The final decisions in Russia were almost always in favor of *Gazprom*. On December 5 the Interpol National Bureau for Russia issued an international warrant for Gussinsky's arrest. A week later, on December 12, he was detained by the police in his villa at the Spanish resort of Sotogrande and transported to the Madrid prison *Soto del Real*. Later he was released on bail and kept locked in his villa. Soon after his arrest the Russian Procuracy demanded his extradition and the seizure of his assets in Spain. In late January Gussinsky rejected the formal proposal of a Spanish judge to be voluntarily extradited to Russia saying that he was subject to political persecution and that justice in Russia was not independent. In late April 2001 the National Court Board of Spain made a decision to refuse to extradite the businessman. The judges explained that they had doubts that the case did not contain a political component, and that the crime of which Gussinsky was accused was not a crime by Spanish law. Gussinsky was immediately charged with money laundering, but the events that happened in the "economic" line of this story made persecution of Gussinsky almost redundant.

The economic line was connected with search for the foreign investor that was announced in November 2000. At that time negotiations began between *Gazprom-Media*, *Media-MOST*, and *Deutsche Bank*. The agreement to be made stipulated that the *NTV* blocking share was to be sold with *Deutsche Bank* brokerage to a "renowned foreign investor." Had the deal been successful, *NTV* would have been owned by three legal entities: *Gazprom* (45.5 percent share), *Media-MOST* (29.4 percent share) and a Western investor (25.1 percent share). This news was followed by a long silence, until in mid January 2001 the information surfaced that Gussinsky had started negotiations with the American media magnate Ted Turner, and that Turner's representatives had met in the Kremlin with representatives of the Russian president to attempt to obtain guarantees that the Russian government would not interfere in *NTV*'s editorial policy. George Soros announced that he was ready to join a group of Western investors led by Turner that would purchase 25 percent of the shares of *NTV* and other *Media-MOST* branches. Soon after that negotiations between *Media-MOST*, *Gazprom-Media*, and *Deutsche Bank* failed, and so did Gussinsky-Turner negotiations.

On January 25, 2001 the Moscow Arbitration Court ruled to freeze *NTV* shares that were transferred to *Gazprom* as a collateral against loans. As a result, *Gazprom-Media* obtained a controlling stake of *NTV*. The same day, Alfred Kokh announced that a meeting of *NTV* shareholders would be convened to elect a new board of directors. At a press conference, Kokh said that *Gazprom-Media* was planning to revive an agreement with *Deutsche Bank* to search for a Western investor (this promise was never kept). Soon, however, *NTV* appealed against the court decision, and, since the court postponed the hearing of *NTV's* case for half a year, *Gazprom*'s ownership was put into question.

The pause that followed was marked by anxious waiting for the outcome. In March 2001 a number of political parties and NGOs organized rallies of protest against the anti-*NTV* campaign in Moscow and St. Petersburg. The Moscow rally attracted, according to different sources, from 5,000 to 15,000 people. It was much less than rallies in late 1980s, still it was the biggest rally since those times.

The fall of the fortress

The dénouement came in April 2001. *Gazprom-Media* scheduled its meeting of *NTV* shareholders for April 3, and publicly offered positions in the future board of directors to some acting *NTV* executives, including Yevgeni Kiselyov. This meeting was many times recognized both as legal and illegal by various courts, both before and after it was held. The then acting management of *NTV* and of *Media-MOST* recognized it as invalid and gathered the old board of directors which adopted changes to the company's statute according to which the editor-in-chief was to be elected by the creative team and could not be appointed by shareholders. Kiselyov (former *NTV* general director) became the company's editor-in-chief.

On April 3 the *Gazprom*-initiated meeting did happen and elected a new board of *Media-MOST* with Alfred Kokh as its chairperson. By that time *Gazprom-Media* got the full support of a *NTV* minor shareholder, a US citizen of Russian origin Boris Jordan, who held a 4 percent stake – just the number *Gazprom* had lacked to have a controlling share. Jordan was elected *NTV*'s general director; Yevgeny Kiselyov was also elected to the board of directors, but publicly refused this position. The position of the channel's editor-in-chief unexpectedly passed to an interesting character, Vladimir Kulistikov. Approximately a year before that, *NTV* executive Kulistikov had replaced "traitor" Oleg Dobrodeyev when the latter had left his post as head of the *NTV* news department for the same post at *RTR*. But next autumn Kulistikov himself left to head the state news agency *RIA-Novosti*. The April meeting brought him back to *NTV* already as a representative of *NTV*'s "enemy."

Next day, April 4, the *NTV* crew led by Kiselyov started a protest action. The channel aired only news programs and short reports from a meeting of *NTV* supporters, showing an empty and silent studio in between. The word 'Protest' in red was superimposed onto the *NTV* logo. Within less than a day *NTV* had to come back to its regular schedule to fulfill the terms of advertisement contracts, but the red "Protest" inscription stayed until the end of the battle.

On April 5 Vladimir Gussinsky met in Spain with ... Boris Berezovsky (!) to discuss the merging of *TV6* owned by Berezovsky and the *TNT* channel owned by Gussinsky. As the meeting of the reconciliatory committee of the "old" and the "new" *NTV* failed next day, Berezovsky gave an assurance that the "old" *NTV* would be able to broadcast on *TV6*. On April 7 some popular journalists left Kiselyov's team and accepted offers from the new management; at the same time rallies supporting freedom of expression and *NTV* were held in Moscow and St Petersburg.

On April 12 all the banks acting for *NTV* were officially notified that the authority to sign the company's financial documents was transferred from Kiselyov to Jordan. Kokh, Jordan and other representatives of the "new" *NTV* gave assurances that there would be no "storming" of the *NTV* office. Given the frequency of armed takeovers of enterprises in Russia, journalists had every reason to be doubtful about this promise. Kiselyov's team locked itself in the studio; the first night nothing happened, but the next night the office was taken. In the morning of April 14 the journalistic collective of *NTV* split up into two parts: some joined the new team, but forty-six journalists, including many popular anchors and reporters, headed by Kiselyov, left *NTV*. For some time they were hanging around the building. Later in the day Kiselyov got an offer from Boris Berezovsky to head *TV6* and accepted it: perhaps both parties forgot the attacks that *NTV* had suffered from Putin's team a year before that, when Berezovsky played a leading role in that team. Kiselyov's team joined him in the new channel and, moreover, took the jobs of the journalists who had been working at that channel before, and thus were thrown out of the company. The former *TV-6* workers publicly asked somebody to employ them, and most found a shelter in the new *NTV*.

Epilogue

In the next few months all *Media-MOST* media outlets experienced similar changes, though this attracted much less public attention. The holding ceased to exist. This is the end of story, but not the end of the adventures of the Kiselyov team, of which I will say a few words. The next year *TV6* repeated the fate of *NTV*: it was made bankrupt and liquidated, its frequency being put up to tender. Ten different CIGs, having united behind Kiselyov's team, managed to win the competition, but soon disagreed for financial reasons. The disgraced crew found a shelter at a low-rating network *Ren-TV*, but by late 2005, after a forced change of *Ren-TV*'s owner, it was completely dispersed.

The journalistic community stayed relatively indifferent to this story. Moreover, *ORT* and *RTR* benefitted by getting rid of a strong competitor. As mentioned in Chapter 5, two major interpretations dominated amongst the expert community: (1) the last fortress of press freedom was destroyed in Russia, and (2) *NTV* was just one of the political interest groups struggling for power that lost the fight. In my opinion, both extremes should be avoided. *Media-MOST* and Gussinsky might have been struggling for power, material resources and other personal interests, but a by-product of this activity was media diversity, since having a private national channel along with two state ones is definitely closer to the democratic ideals of press freedom. Simultaneously, the government might have been struggling for reconsolidation of the Russian state, against the "oligarchs" who privatized the state, and against Gussinsky personally, and the only way to this goal it could see lay through getting all national TV channels into the state hands.

13 Change in the coverage of the Chechen wars

Unlike other parts of the book, this chapter addresses not only practices of various agents trying to change the media product, but the product itself as well.[1] My main goal here is to show how the actual story of the two Chechen wars was transformed into a specific media discourse by deliberate actions of key players (especially of the state agents), as well as by the structural inclination of news as a media format to present wars as "an occasional series of unlinked reports about seemingly unrelated crises" (McNulty 1999: 270). A rigorous approach to such a goal would require the significant expansion of the theoretical approach used before, for which this final chapter is not a place – rather, it is written to illustrate a direction in which the research may be extended and in which, perhaps, new insights may be expected. Therefore, this text is closer to expert analysis: the terms "the actual story" and "the coverage" are problematic both conceptually and in terms of available sources. However, the conclusions presented here are not just a private opinion: they are based on long-term observation of the Russian media, and on multiple secondary sources. "The coverage" component is the most available and verifiable, and it has been most widely studied.

The concept of "the actual story," and the related concept of "truth," given the general constructivist predisposition of this book, would be quite illegitimate, if I wanted to take the constructivist argument to its extreme, but I do not. The situation of war, where people's lives may depend on the difference between "the actual story" and its "coverage" in media, clearly points at the limits of the constructivist approach. Because, as with many military conflicts, the full "actual story" of the Chechen wars is hardly known either by a single person or by all the people involved, here it is a reconstruction based on the comparative reading of different texts (Russian, Chechen and Western), including historical works and analytical articles in popular press. Thus, I do not claim my "actual story" to be the final truth; still, it shows how much a narrative of a war may differ from a TV news narrative if one carefully studies and compares multiple sources. Such a study, in particular, reveals that one of the main causes of both wars is the struggle of many countries for access to the oil fields in the

Caspian sea. Here Chechnya plays a crucial role since part of the pipeline that connects the Caspian and the Black seas runs through it. This chapter shows how the topic of oil was systematically silenced or at best marginalized in the media discourse and substituted with the rhetoric of "State integrity" (by the Russian officials) or "State independence" (by the Chechen leaders). It is shown how the structural orientation of the media towards unlinked stories finally helped the Russian government impose its discourse.

Historical context

Situated in the northern Caucasus, officially Chechnya is a subject of the Russian Federation, but throughout the 1990s it was either in a state of war or outside control of the Federal political elite. During the colonization of the Caucasus in eighteenth and nineteenth centuries, the population of Chechnya and neighboring Ingushetia demonstrated the most unyielding resistance to the Russian army. Before being annexed to Russia, Chechnya did not have its own nation state; no single clan (*teip*) controlled the whole territory. That is why in Chechnya, unlike the southern Caucasus, Russian colonizers could not rely on cooperation with the local political elite. This also became one of the major problems in Russian-Chechen relations in the 1990s.

During the Soviet period the Checheno-Ingush Republic was never absolutely pacified. During World War II a network of underground organizations in Chechnya established contacts with the Nazis and was preparing to support them with an armed rebellion. Because of that in 1944 *all* Chechens were deported to Kazakhstan and allowed to come back only after Joseph Stalin's death in 1957. People who remember the hardships of that deportation are still alive. Until the very 1990s most Chechens preserved traditional Islamic culture, peasant lifestyle and subsistence farming, while the urban minority was predominantly Russian. A century ago Chechnya had been an important oil producing region but, as its oil fields gradually became exhausted, its role changed to that of a transit territory, with some important roads, railways, power lines and pipelines (Titkov and Tyukov 1998).

As a pioneer in the "parade of sovereignties," Chechnya declared independence as early as 1990 (Ingushetia distanced itself from this action soon after that and stayed within Russia). From the very beginning the Chechen elite displayed multiple splits – initially between supporters and opponents of independence, and later between proliferating armed groups headed by so-called "field commanders." The federal political elite was rather inconsistent in its struggle against separatism, trying to use internal divisions and constantly shifting from enforcement to negotiations and back. As a result, during the last decade of the twentieth century Chechnya suffered two wars, the first lasting from late 1994 to early autumn

1996, and the second starting from autumn 1999 and never reaching a relatively clear end. Data about the losses vary greatly, but it is clear that they amount to a minimum of thousands killed and to dozens of thousands wounded. Many towns and villages, including Chechnya's capital Grozny, were completely destroyed.

No coverage: toward the first war

Thus the armed conflict in Chechnya did not start all of a sudden, but it attracted the significant attention of the media only after the failed storming of Grozny in November 1994. In the years 1990–3 public attention was engaged by the Yeltsin-Gorbachev conflict, the August 1991 putsch, the disintegration of the USSR, antagonism between Yeltsin and the parliament, Russia's economic difficulties, and crime. Against this background, the problems of a "distant" republic had few chances to get into the mainstream Russian media. This section speaks of events that found their way to the media years later.

Since the late 1990s, when a radical faction of the Chechen elite declared Chechnya a sovereign state, it was constantly gaining power in its struggle with the official Soviet leaders of Chechnya. In October 1991 – that is, between the August putsch and the decomposition of the USSR – radicals managed to hold alternative presidential elections that were won by General Dzhokhar Dudayev. Federal authorities refused to recognize his legitimacy and prepared a military operation, but by that time Dudayev's team had gathered its own informal army, and blocked Soviet planes at the airport where they landed. The federals retreated and later had to recognize Dudayev as de facto president. Moreover, by mid-1992 the Russian regular army had left Chechnya, abandoning its weapons (including tanks and aircrafts) which fell into Dudayev's hands. (Versions about secret support of separatists by some interest groups in Moscow surfaced for the first time in media during the first Chechen war, and have circulated ever since, however, without reliable evidence.) In mid-1993 Dudayev issued a number of laws bringing all power into his hands; in particular, the Chechen parliament lost its legislative function, and was driven from its building by military force (Myalo 2002). Chechen leaders of groups and *teips* opposing Dudayev settled in their home districts forming their own armed detachments; beginning military actions from late 1993, during the next year they took a significant part of lowland Chechnya.

After the events of October 1991 both the federal side and Dudayev's government initiated negotiations, but each time they came to nothing because neither side wanted to compromise on the major question – (in-)dependence of Chechnya. The new Russian Constitution adopted in late 1993 listed Chechnya as one of 89 subjects of Federation and contained no indication of Chechnya's special status. Furthermore, from mid-1992

Moscow blocked the banking system of Chechnya, and by 1994 had nearly stopped the delivery of oil to the Chechen oil processing plants which were the basis of Chechnya's economy. Much later Russian media would claim that this was done to prevent the rapid criminalization of Chechnya's economy, where proceeds from the illegal export of Russian oil and other goods were spent on weapons (Delyagin 1999). Although even the Chechen side recognized the facts of the theft of oil, the assessment of its scale is dramatically different; still, Dudayev's team undoubtedly viewed oil as an economic basis for Chechnya's independence (Abubakarov 1998).

None of the described events and problems was widely covered in the media before the war "officially" began; some of them, such as the economic blockade of Chechnya, were actually never covered. Most probably, journalists were themselves unaware of the complex situation in Chechnya, and it stayed on the periphery of the public attention until November 26, 1994. It was that day when the Chechen opposition to Dudayev secretly supported by federal troops attacked Grozny and was completely defeated (Abubakarov 1998; Kogan-Yansy 1999; Titkov and Tyukov 1998). Moscow's secret plan was revealed and aroused a scandal; nevertheless, the failed attack gave an impetus to a full-scale military operation against Dudayev's regime that lasted for almost 2 years with very limited success.

The first Chechen war: the media against the military

November 26, thus, cannot be called the first day of the war in Chechnya, as it might seem from media coverage: in fact, the war had been going there for months. Since before November 1994 it had not attracted public attention, the federal elite had little motive to make any information preparations for the storm. Moreover, it obviously did not expect the disclosure of its participation in Chechen events at all: the past Soviet experience of war coverage, in particular, in Afghanistan, gave no grounds for such expectations. However, the situation where the elite could afford to care little about late and implausible comments was back in the Soviet past. In the USSR, it could persist because it was supplemented by an effective mechanism of control over the distribution of messages – a mechanism which made official messages obligatory and the only ones available to the media. Criticism of important policies could appear in the media only when there were powerful opponents inside the elite, as happened with Afghanistan.

By 1994 the environment had changed dramatically; the elite had lost its old levers of control, but, not realizing this, it got "stuck in the previous media age" (Mickiewicz 1997: 244). Public denunciation of the war in Afghanistan by the elite itself, followed by withdrawal of the Soviet troops in 1989, created a precondition for the negative reception of any new military operation. This post-Afghanistan syndrome, coupled with low trust in official sources and Russian statehood in general, and the absence of the elite's monopolistic control over messages – all this led the account of the federal participation in the attack on Grozny to quickly mutate into the account of the federal invasion of Grozny.

The federal elite found itself totally unprepared for the negative reaction of the media. One of its most important problems was that it ceased to constitute a consolidated team and was represented by a number of competing groups and individuals. As a result, it had no clear policy on any matter, including the information management of the Chechen situation. A special press-centre was created a week into the operation; president Yeltsin addressed the nation after two weeks, and later silence continued to be a common strategy. At first the very fact of the military actions was denied. Many other accounts of the Russian officials contradicted the events, and the declared intentions contradicted their actions. To be fair, it is necessary to note that similar mistakes are known from other military campaigns, such as the Vietnam war and the British operation in the Falklands in 1982 (Baroody 1998: 9–10, 54–63): what unites them is that in all cases the availability of television was a relatively novel circumstance. Thus, the failure of the Russian federal propaganda has at least three causes: non-monopolistic control over news flow, presence of television and inconsistency in policy of the fractured elite.

Getting almost no information from the official sources, the State media who had voluntarily supported Yeltsin as a democratic reformer found it very difficult to ignore the real events and their alternative coverage by private media. Therefore, all three national channels, independently of their form of ownership, showed military actions and – inevitably – their failures. It was then that the problems of the Russian weapons left in Chechnya and its criminalized economy were picked up by all media. They were discussed in the context of asking who was responsible for the situation going so far. At the same time, all three channels underscored the importance of Russia's territorial integrity and the necessity to find a solution to the problem, opposing only the *methods*, not the *goal*.

Gussinksy's *NTV* more than others showed the sufferings of (supposedly) peaceful population, refugees, wounded people, destruction and the mistakes of the military. These scenes had a shocking effect, especially because this war was the first occasion in Russian history when violence was widely displayed on the screen. The reasons behind such *NTV*'s coverage are, however, not obviously pacifist. It is indicative that the start of the Chechen war coincided with the armed encounter between Gussinsky's *Media-MOST* security department and the President's security office in Moscow, and with the broader conflict of Gussinsky-Luzhkov-*NTV* and Berezovsky-Korzhakov-*ORT* CIGs (see Chapter 12). Negative coverage of the war, consequently, could be a part of *MOST*'s strategy of "media racketeering" of state agents – a method of struggle for state resources –

of which *NTV* was later accused. However, the activity of *NTV* – then a young growing business – was clearly directed not only to state agents, but to broader audiences as well. Its top management judged correctly that "truth" and "objectivity" were the goods most lacking in the Russian media market. General distrust on the part of the post-Soviet public to official messages helped *NTV* to quickly gain credibility and increase its ratings: in late 1994 *NTV*'s evening newscast "Segodnya" doubled its audience, catching up with *ORT*'s highly popular "Vremya." *RTR*'s "Vesti" also increased its audience by 1.5 times (Rikhter 1998): although *RTR*, as a state channel, was obliged to broadcast official statements and comments, it directly juxtaposed them with the completely contradictory reports from the scenes of battle; in contrast, Berezovksy's *ORT* stuck to the official line and more than others avoided showing violence.

The commercial or political motivation of *NTV* staff, however, did not mean that its journalists never based their actions on the values of press freedom – on the contrary, believers in press freedom saw *NTV* as an opportunity to combine "genuine" journalism, high salaries and professional promotion. Anyway, the first Chechen war was crucial for the formation of *NTV*, and *NTV*'s activity was crucial for the outcome of that war.

One of the most equivocal consequences of the authorities' strategy of silence was that their voice became lost among other points of view, despite the fidelity of the most popular channel. The military kept all journalists, including those from the state media, away from the areas they controlled; as a result, media, with *NTV* as a pioneer, turned to the alternative sources – the Chechens. Chechen separatist leaders were more than willing to present their version of the situation and demonstrated a much more effective information policy, actively cooperating with the Russian media: giving interviews, transporting journalists to sites of events, providing video- and audio-materials, etc. The developer of this policy, Chechnya's Minister for information and press, Movladi Udugov, even got the nickname of the Chechen Goebbels among Russian officials. Besides Russian media, separatists successfully used Western media, which was not difficult given the negative attitude of Western political elites to the Russian policy in Chechnya. Some Western media, for example Russian language radio *Liberty*, was listened to in Russia, especially by intellectuals, and thus brought separatists' voice back into the country.[2]

Finally, separatists tried to control media within Chechnya, in which they were less effective. In the early 1990s the numerous internal conflicts did not allow for complete suppression of press belonging to rival *teips* or armed groups. After mid-1993 all opposition newspapers were gradually closed, some journalists being arrested, but this period of full control did not last long. As long as the joint anti-Dudayev opposition was moving across Chechnya, it was establishing its media in settlements coming under its control. Heavy battles in early 1995 destroyed all the major printing houses, as well as the Chechen TV center that throughout the decade was several times stormed and taken by competing armed groups. Udugov's ministry, now illegal and chased by the federal troops, organized a mobile TV transmitting station and mastered a technique of intrusion into frequencies used by legal TV companies. Several newspapers also started publishing illegally in neighboring Ingushetia and Dagestan (Panfilov and Simonov 1995). Since by that time for security reasons top-executives of the Dudayev administration preferred to contact only journalists of their own media, the latter shared materials with their Russian colleagues; this was still another way for pro-Dudayev points of view to get into federal media.

As a result, coverage of the war in the federal media, albeit relatively diverse, became much shifted in a direction that played into the hands of separatists. Thus, although at the beginning most media gave space to both supporters and opponents of the military operation, the Russian side looked the initiator, which greatly delegitimized its position. The current sufferings of the local population and the horrors of war were shown naturalistically, while the past crimes of Dudayev's regime were simply retold. Victimization concerned not only the Chechen population, but also Russian rank-and-file conscripts who were shown as forced to take part in the war and unable to understand its goals. In general, the Russian army was portrayed as ineffective, corrupt and miserable; *NTV* paid particular attention to Russian military mistakes and failures (Rikhter 1998). On the contrary, separatists looked like true believers, willing and capable of defending their land. Since, contrary to federals, they gave many interviews, they were consequently presented as individual human beings, while the federal army looked like an anonymous grey mass (Liberman 1999a: 9–14).

Trying to overcome their negative image, the military officials launched a smear campaign against critical media, especially *NTV*, publicly accusing them of being paid by the "Chechen bandits." Since *NTV* had already gained public trust, the campaign did not achieve its aim. The military also looked for a legal way to close *NTV*, such as withdrawing its license for "giving deliberately false information." This made *NTV* more accurate and precise.

The ineffectiveness of control over the flow of information was the striking difference between the first Chechen armed conflict and the Gulf war, whose experience would play an important role in the second Chechen campaign. Back in 1991 Saudi Arabia and the USA fully controlled access to the area and almost entirely controlled the movements of journalists. Those journalists who were not included in the pool (a privileged group) just did not get visas. No effective protest took place because the most powerful media who could lead such a protest (e.g. *CNN*) were *in* the pool. For them, the pool was a great advantage because it effectively removed their competitors. In addition to restricted access, pool members were required to submit all reports for military review in English (Winseck 1992: 67). This rule worked because anyone who refused to obey could be threatened with exclusion from the pool.

This scenario did not work in Chechnya for several reasons. First, Chechnya was a part of Russia with no visa regime, so journalists could get there relatively easily. Second, the already mentioned army's lack of experience in handling war coverage in the new conditions was also important. Despite the introduction of prohibitive rules of accreditation (Panfilov 1999), threats to and arrests of journalists, and confiscations of cassettes/cameras by the military, media people found many breaches in this system of control arising from the impossibility of eliminating all contacts with alternative sources and all cases of independent travel. Finally, of big importance was the opportunistic behavior of people within the army which, along with other social institutions, had partly disintegrated. In fact, in the case of the army, disintegration had begun long before the collapse of the Soviet Union. Based on obligatory universal conscription, the huge army of eighteen to twenty year old youths had been used mostly as cheap labor force, poorly fed, humiliated and physically tortured by superiors, often involved in fraud and theft. Evasion of military service became not only permissible, but quite approved of in public opinion, and so common that even regular police-assisted conscription campaigns could not stop the annual decrease in the size of the army. It is not surprising, then, that poorly supported rank-and-file soldiers in Chechnya often let media people into restricted zones for bread, sausages, vodka, a call home from a journalist's mobile telephone, or even for an issue of the *Playboy* magazine (Zinchuk 1998). Sometimes soldiers cooperated with journalists just because they found it the right thing to do. Called up to military service against their will, they had very little identification with the army – unlike their professional colleagues in the USA.

Later, the negative coverage of the war gave the military a reason to blame the media for the failure of the first Chechen campaign. This situation is in some respect similar to the Vietnam war: it is widely believed that it was the media who helped to stop it. This interpretation has been questioned in some studies (Hallin 1986), but it is persistent because it meets the interests of the three major actors: the journalists (who look very heroic), the military (who release themselves from the responsibility for their mistakes) and the government (who thus demonstrates democracy at work). The real causes for the end of the Vietnam war seem multiple and complex, and resemble those in the Chechen war. Among them are the failure of the Johnson administration to mobilize the USA for all-out war, the contradictions in strategy for the war and inconsistencies in public statements.

This latest pattern of course could not have existed without the media which provide the very necessity to make public statements. However, the media can only turn public opinion against the national political elite, they cannot make the latter take this opinion into consideration in its decisions. Journalists had already complained about this during the first war in Chechnya. The situation in which the elite is most inclined to recollect public opinion is the elections: in Russia, the presidential elections came in May–June 1996; on April 1 the decision to stop military action in Chechnya was announced by Yeltsin.

The reasons why all major CIGs, including those of Berezovsky and Gussinksy, united behind the sick and extremely unpopular Yeltsin, were much discussed in the previous chapters. Here it is enough to mention that this alliance was a landmark in the coverage of the Chechen war that put an end to the sharp criticism of the federal policy in Chechnya. Suspension of large-scale military actions in April made it easier for *NTV* to justify an abrupt twist in its reporting: it looked as though the government had finally accepted the policy of negotiation for which *NTV* had always stood. Still, it was difficult to maintain the image of the end of the war since journalists in Chechnya witnessed the bombings and the new wounded continually brought in to hospitals (Panfilov and Simonov 1999). State media had another difficulty: unlike *NTV*, they had often used the label "bandits" and other accusatory terms for separatists (Rikhter 1998). Now, the former "bandit" Aslan Maskhadov, Dudayev's closest ally was recognized by the federal elite as Chechnya's leader and became the main partner in negotiations. For this role Maskhadov, as a fresh face, was slightly better than Dudayev, who was killed during the bombardment in May (coincidence?), still the official media hesitated as to how to present the situation. Even more difficult was reporting the inclusion of the Chechen "terrorist number 1" Shamil Basayev into Maskhadov's government. Basayev had been known for taking over a thousand hostages in a hospital in the southern town of Budyonnovsk in summer 1995. Despite this, the words "bandits" and "terrorists" disappeared very quickly after the end of the military actions in April 1996. For a while, the media would call Maskhadov and his team cautiously "Chechen leaders," "representatives of the Chechen side" or "the government of the self-proclaimed republic of Ichkeria." By autumn 1996, the terms confirming the fully legitimate status of the former terrorists ("president," "minister") were widely used (Koltsova 2000b: 94).

When the electoral dust settled down, Russia had a new media-political configuration. Major CIGs, including their media departments "not only kept power, that is political power ... all these fighters gained significant economic results: publicity, state loans, TV and radio channels, informational power" (Kachkaeva 2001). It is then that *NTV* was granted the whole time at *Channel 4* where it had before broadcast only in prime time. From late July the media and especially *NTV* returned to criticism of Yeltsin and the renewed fighting in Chechnya, but this criticism could never be as radical as before. To repeat the words of an *NTV* top executive cited in the previous chapter, "with our own hands we've created a monstrous system that's gonna eat us" (Interview 27).

Between the wars: unlinked stories about "unrelated" events

From late 1996 when the fighting finally stopped, Chechnya was no longer covered on a daily basis. Though it was never completely silenced, the reports were occasional and scattered; they did not provide a big picture of the situation. Most information about events between the wars appeared in the media not earlier than 1999.

Meanwhile, splits in the Chechen elite never disappeared: after a while a group of Maskhadov's most radical allies lead by the influential Shamil Basayev refused to cooperate with the federal elite and insisted on the full independence of Chechnya and the introduction of Shariat law.[3] While accepting Basayev's policy would have inevitably meant Maskhadov's dismissal, opposition to him would have led him to lose control over the situation in Chechnya; therefore, Maskhadov tried to maneuver between the two incompatible lines and play his own game: he simultaneously initiated separate negotiations with Western countries, showed loyalty to Moscow and tolerated Basayev's Wahhabist activity within Chechnya. Thus, to mention only some relatively mild consequences of this activity for media, by 1998 all female TV anchors were obliged to cover their heads and necks with kerchiefs; scenes looking even remotely erotic were blacked out (Khatuyev 1998). Federal media reported on public corporal punishments in Chechnya, but without any following official comment and without much response.

Maneuvering did not save Maskhadov from conflict with Basayev and from gradually losing of control, while "terrorist number 1" kept seizing various economic resources. Opposition to Maskhadov was also represented by less powerful field commanders with their own interests (thus, Maskhadov's TV was often attacked by various armed groups unhappy with its reporting, and had to change its location many times). According to available data, all these diverse groups of power had several main sources of income. One was the illegal processing and export of oil which went not only abroad, but also back to Russia, in particular, to the neighboring Stavropol region. Another significant source was money from the federal budget transferred for the restoration of the ruined republic. While people received no salaries or pensions, Basayev was forming a professional army. In 1998–9 he publicly demonstrated the skills of his fighters who graduated from his newly established military school. A third source, which became widely discussed only a few years after the start of the second war, was aid from abroad, especially from Muslim countries. Its real amount and significance is unknown, but it is widely acknowledged that a person named Hattab, native of one of the Arab countries, has been Basayev's closest partner and an influential field commander.

These major sources were supplemented by other criminal activities: robbery, cattle rustling (again, from the Stavropol region), kidnapping people and either selling them back or using them as slaves. It is hard to assess the scale of these activities, but officially 1094 people were registered as kidnapped between January 1997 and June 1999 (Delyagin 1999). Part of the impoverished and jobless "peaceful population" of Chechnya participated in it as well. Still, one should be cautious with all these data because since suddenly flooding the media in 1999 they have been actively used by the Russian government to legitimize its second military operation in Chechnya.

At the same time, what scarcely found its way into the mainstream Russian media in the interwar period, is information about the big game of "access to Caspian oil." This game may be understood better when taking into account Chechnya's geographical position and the interests of various countries in connection with this oil (for a detailed account see Collon 2002; Myalo 2002; a general overview is given in note 4). Since the United States, the most powerful player, showed interest in the demonopolization of Russian control of access to Caspian oil, in the early 1990s it started lobbying for the project of building a pipeline from Azerbaidjan through Georgia to Turkey, USA's major partner in the region. Having failed to guarantee the stable functioning of the Chechen part of its pipeline, since mid-1997 Russia was considering an idea to build a pipe line around Chechnya, which was still cheaper than the Turkey project. But in early 1998 Aslan Maskhadov signed a contract with Britain to extend the Dagestan–Chechnya–Russia line with a pipeline going through Ukraine and Poland. This project got a positive reaction from Moscow under the condition of Chechnya being refused its independence. Being also cheaper than the Turkey option, it had a good chance of being adopted by the consortium of oil companies working in Caspian oil. At that very moment "unknown bandits" carried out a series of terrorist acts in Chechnya; among other actions, they kidnapped the representative of the Russian president in Chechnya, General Vlasov, and beheaded four British engineers. The Turkey variant got priority in late 1998, and was finally approved at the OSCE (Organization for Security and Cooperation in Europe) Summit in Istanbul a year later.

The only "unknown bandits" capable of such large-scale provocation against Moscow was Basayev's armed opposition. While Michel Collon openly accuses the USA of supporting Chechen terrorists (Collon 2002: 186–7), there were some other players interested in helping them, which does not mean they did so: e.g. Turkey, as Russia's competitor; Saudi Arabia which is interested in blocking any access to Caspian oil; and bin Laden whose attempts to expand his influence to various Moslem countries are well known. Finally, Basayev definitely played his own game aimed at building an independent Islamic state on the territory of Chechnya, neighboring Dagestan, and probably some other regions. This is confirmed by his policy towards Dagestan – a republic separating Chechnya from the Caspian Sea. After Moscow had announced the idea of the

pipeline around Chechnya through Dagestan in mid-1997, Chechen separatists initiated negotiations with Dagestan about "friendship and cooperation." The negotiations failed, and in five days, in December 1997 Chechen
separatists carried out a series of terrorist acts in Dagestan. In May 1998,
at the time of the provocation against the Russian-British pipeline project,
they captured the parliament building in Dagestan's capital (around that
time Basayev demanded Maskhadov's resignation). In early 1999, when
Basayev actually got control over the Chechen government and defeated
Maskhadov, Chechnya was proclaimed a Muslim state ("Chechenskiye
khroniki 1998/1999" 1999). Its unification with other Muslim regions of the
Caucasus, primarily with Dagestan, was announced as an official strategic
goal. From this moment of the merging of the armed separatist opposition
with the formerly pro-Moscow government, Chechnya was actually out of
control of the Federal elite.

What part of this complicated story could a common Russian viewer see
in the mainstream TV news? Right after the end of the first war there were
mostly optimistic reports about the restoration of Chechnya, which soon
gave way to relatively disconnected stories. Moscow's announcement
about the pipeline around Chechnya was reported in mid-1997 (with no
emphasis on the importance of Dagestan); for a few months terrorist acts
in Dagestan were covered (pipeline not mentioned); still in a few months
there were stories about the kidnapped Vlasov, beheaded British engineers and the Dagestan parliament. After a long pause, it was reported
that Basayev had got a leading position in the Chechen parliament; this
was mentioned without reference to his past activities, including the
hostage seizure in Budyonnovsk.

In a series of disconnected reports the separatists' actions in Dagestan
could not be discerned as part of a meaningful policy. Rather, they looked
like just some more acts of unmotivated violence. The link of the separatists' persistence in Dagestan to its access to the Caspian Sea could be
traced, probably, only by experts who monitored all possible sources of
information. Neither the separatists themselves nor the federal authorities
were interested in stressing this link because it would inevitably point to
the major interest of the two political elites – the oil: the oil that meant not
only more profit but also greater political power. And indicating this
would in turn make it clear that the common people, both Russians and
Chechens, were just being used as instruments in this big game.

Thus, neither side talked about the oil in its official discourse. Separatists underscored the right of the Chechen nation to have its own
independent state, and later – its right to unite with other Moslems. The
federal elite stressed the importance of the integrity of the federation. It
talked about oil mostly in the context of other criminal activities in Chechnya, presenting them as a justification for its special policy towards Chechnya: for instance, the decision to build a pipeline around Chechnya was
explained by the instability in this region. As a result, the oil question

appeared as one of the consequences of the conflict rather than one of its major causes. The relative ease with which the authorities managed to voice their interpretation through the media between the wars is to a great extent explained by the dramatic decline of the media's interest in Chechnya in that period. Journalists believed that their audience was tired of the daily coverage of this ever-lasting conflict and, as the "compassion fatigue" concept tells us, this is not impossible.

The second war: the government dominates the media

Like the first war, the second Chechen campaign started from separatists' "sudden" and "unmotivated" invasion of Dagestan – at least as far as could be judged from the mainstream Russian media. An alternative belief is that this "invasion," like many events in the first war, was organized by the Russian secret police. Given the chain of events preceding the war, both versions seem simplistic. Concerning the FSB-organized invasion, if its goal was the maintenance of instability in the region, then the FSB's motivations are unclear; if it was to serve as a legitimization of a new war, it is doubtful that Russian authorities needed any special arrangements. A series of terrorist acts as listed in the previous section was followed in 1999 by small-scale but regular attacks by Basayev's fighters on Dagestan. So all that the federal authorities had to do was to present one of these attacks as "invasion" or, at best, to refuse to prevent a larger attack. One day in summer 1999 began with a sensation: the Russian prime minister announced that he had to send federal troops to repel the aggression of the Chechen bandits against Dagestan. The prime-minister who took the responsibility for such an important decision looked very heroic.

What was not reported at that time, is that these attacks by separatists were paralleled by similar acts of the federal forces. The actions were preceded by threats from both sides, especially after the merging of Basayev's opposition with Maskhadov's government in early 1999. Thus the second war, like the first, did not have a clear-cut beginning. The "invasion" was to a great extent a media-event. On the one hand, it looked probable because it fitted well with the separatists' previous actions reported in the media. On the other hand, taken out of the context of the separatists' oil-based policy, it also seemed odd. So it was not difficult to present it as a reckless action by a group of bandits who, gradually becoming criminalized and never having faced "an adequate reaction" from the federal center, finally "lost the plot" and decided they could fight the huge country of Russia.

Another version about the second Chechen conflict closely connected with the FSB plot version is that the war was designed exclusively as a major part of the election campaign for Vladimir Putin, whom president Yeltsin had recommended as his successor. It is interesting that a similar accusation existed during the first war, but reversed: then the decision to *end* the war was claimed to be exclusively a part of the presidential campaign. Though in both cases the link with the elections is obvious, it is hardly so straightforward. First, given the disastrous coverage of the first war, it would seem very risky to count on the positive reaction of the media in the second war. Furthermore, when after the "invasion" Putin became prime minister, the media unanimously ridiculed him claiming that one could hardly invent a worse recommendation than that of Yeltsin. Second, the conflict did exist and, as the analysis above has shown, the federal elite had many reasons to start military actions, with or without elections.

Third, it is not obvious that the government was going to start a large-scale war. At first it was announced that a "sanitary cordon" would be built around Chechnya – a kind of in-state border protected by the military. Indeed, the federal government seemed to take some steps in that direction: it asked the neighboring Caucasian state of Georgia to help in organizing a visa regime. The negotiations failed. When the federal troops, after pausing at the Chechen border, finally entered the republic, it became clear that a war had started. But this did not happen until October 1999; by that time the government might have been encouraged by the relatively positive reaction of the media.

So why was the coverage this time so different? First, of course, the "invasion" story made it much easier for the federal power to legitimize its military actions. Second, the reports from Chechnya gave a (well-grounded) feeling that the problem was still waiting for its solution. Tired of the passiveness of the sick Yeltsin, the people welcomed Putin who gave an impression of an active and decisive person. His policy on Chechnya was presented and taken as an indicator of his eagerness to find answers for a whole range of Russia's urgent questions. Third, each terrorist act between the wars gave the federal elite a chance to accuse Chechnya's president Maskhadov of inability to control the situation (which was also reported). This created the impression that any negotiations with the Chechens were in vain: when an agreement is made with one group, others immediately refuse to recognize it. All this gradually pushed public opinion towards a view that enforcement was the only way to solve the problem. The resemblance of the inter-war situation in Chechnya to its situation before the first war (growing criminal regime, no reaction from Moscow) allowed the government to declare the peace treaty of 1996 a mistake. To what extent the government itself believed in the problem-solving capacity of a war is, of course, unknown.

Anyway, from August to October, before the federal troops entered the uncontrolled part of Chechnya, the media were unanimous in their positive coverage. The divisions on this topic emerged in November and were still much less than in all other questions. In general, all the divisions were generated by parliamentary elections campaign that was taking place in autumn 1999 – a campaign that was called "a rehearsal" for the presidential campaign scheduled for the following spring. The fierce fights of that media war, in which Gussinsky's media joined a weaker, anti-Putin team, are described in Chapter 12.

Against this background, splits in the media concerning Chechnya looked really modest. As before, *NTV* was more critical. According to Semyon Liberman's monitoring (Liberman 1999b), it was more inclined to broadcast stories of refugees leaving Chechnya, while *ORT* and *RTR* (the main weapons of the pro-Putin team headed by Berezovsky) claimed that Chechens were coming back home. *NTV* showed frustrated Chechens dreaming of revenge against the Russians; *ORT* and *RTR* showed Chechens expressing their wish for peace. *NTV* assumed that the military were hiding the losses, *ORT* and *RTR* presented operations as successful.

Still, there were three basic items on which all the channels had a consensus. First, the necessity of military action (openly called "the war") was never questioned. At first, the government tried to exclude this word from the media discourse, but dropped the attempts, since the word turned out not to be dangerous for its policy. Second, the attitude to the Maskhadov-Basayev regime in Chechnya was unanimously negative; the armed separatists on all channels were mostly called "bandits" and "terrorists." Such words as "rebels" or "guerillas" were never applied. The media suddenly became full of reports of criminal activities in Chechnya, former and present, especially of heart-breaking stories of kidnapping and other acts of violence.

A third point of consensus was the predominantly negative coverage of the attitude of the West to Chechnya. It developed in the context of a general growth of an anti-Western mood amongst the Russian public which was gradually giving up a widespread belief that the West was going to help a weakened Russia build democracy and develop a market economy. The war in Kosovo contributed much to the growth of the negative attitude to the West: this campaign was taken as a ruthless intrusion into the domestic affairs of a sovereign (and Slavic) state. It is hard to say to what extent this attitude was shaped by the political elite or emerged independently, bringing a more nationalistic elite to power. Anyway, after Kosovo declarations by the West about violations of human rights in Chechnya looked hypocritical to many Russians, and the government did not hesitate to accuse the West of double standards. Journalists seemed to agree with this point of view. All this actually blocked any activity on human rights protection in Chechnya.

Besides some pre-existing public support, there was one more important reason for the smaller amount of criticism in the second war: this time the government managed to organize an effective control over the flow of information. It is not by chance that I now apply the word "government": since Putin had become prime minister, and then president, a group of people surrounding him demonstrated an ability to carry out a much more consistent policy than under Yeltsin. Furthermore, Putin seemed to make use of his experience in foreign intelligence, as well as the lessons of the first Chechen campaign, Afghanistan, and the Gulf war.

The first and the most striking change was that instead of hiding from journalists, the officials and the military regularly supplied them with information and public declarations. Putin himself was tireless in voicing the official interpretation of the situation, which can be summarized in the following statements:

1   we cannot leave Chechnya untouched, either inside or outside Russia, because the bandit regime is a regime that would inevitably want to expand;
2   since no-one controls the whole territory of Chechnya, negotiations have proven ineffective;
3   that is why a war is an awful, but sole available solution to the problem;
4   the separatists are supported mostly from abroad, primarily by Arab terrorists;
5   the bandits should be clearly distinguished from the peaceful population which does not want to fight and welcomes federal troops as a guarantor of stability.

All this is in fact very close to Soviet doctrine on Afghanistan which also declared the strategic importance of Afghanistan to the USSR, overwhelming internal support for the pro-Moscow regime, and only external support of the guerrillas (Downing 1988: 23).

Thus in autumn 1999 it seemed that the government moved from concealing unfavorable information to the active production of favorable information. Some journalists looked more satisfied than in the first war, saying that the military were more cooperative (Interview 21). But approximately in the middle of the winter 2000 it became clear that the new strategy was an addition to the old one rather than a substitute.

By that time the situation in Chechnya had changed. The quick victories promised in the beginning had not come about, and it was clear that the war was not going to be short. Whether this happened because of unexpected obstacles or, as some analysts claim, because certain interest groups in Moscow were deliberately protracting the war – the absence of an observable result was not likely to add to Putin's popularity. Although at that time the version about the deliberate character of the war was not widely circulated, media transmitted some other opinions, unfavorable to officials: the military are hiding the losses, the war split the Chechen population and provoked at least a part of it to support the separatists which may lead to an endless partisan war. This coincided in time with the shift of information policy in Chechnya to more radical measures.

From January 2000 the government actually introduced the pool system in Chechnya. Gradually, it became almost impossible to travel there without the military. Some differences from the Gulf war also existed: the list of pool members was not fixed from the very beginning, and the journalists were not formally obliged to give their texts to the military for editing, however the autonomy of media was extremely limited. According to new rules ("Rules of accreditation..." 2000), journalists had to get special accreditation at the Apparatus of the President's assistant Sergei Yastrzhembski and could cover the Chechen events "if they [were] included in a corresponding group formed by the Apparatus of the assistant in coordination with the leadership of the force structures ... and of the United military group in the Northern Caucasus" (clause 11). They were also obliged to "obey the internal regulations of the United military group in the Northern Caucasus and to fulfill orders of the responsible persons from the Apparatus of the assistant and from the force structures, accompanying journalists" (clause 12). In practice this meant that journalists could now enter the cordoned Chechnya only with accreditation and only together with the military (Dorsheva 2000). Therefore, journalists were usually found waiting in a special tent outside the basic press-center of the United military group in the Northern Caucasus in Mozdok, a town outside Chechnya, not far from its north-west border. The military would regularly pick up those whose stories they liked and take them to those places in Chechnya they found possible to show (Fedorov 2001). Otherwise media people could enter Chechnya as private persons, hiding their cameras and journalistic documents, but if they encountered the military inside the republic, they were detained and deported. This applied to reporters from all kinds of media: "pro-bandit," "pro-Western" and "pro-federal"; the more persistent were particular journalists, the more coordinated were the sanctions of various state agents. One of the most significant stories concerning a radio *Liberty* reporter Andrey Babitsky is described in a book by Oleg Panfilov (Panfilov 2004); Anne Nivat, a French free-lancer, also mentions her detention by the Russian "special services" in her book (Nivat 2000); more cases may be found in the GDF monitoring.

As a result, by spring 2000 the media were unable to provide vivid pictures of fighting. Instead, they used maps and even computer simulation of the battles, which obviously did not contain any shooting, destruction, or Chechen "bandits," alive or dead. In most reports media referred to official sources which stressed that nearly all the separatists were foreign mercenaries. Sometimes journalists expressed doubts about official statements, but seldom supported them with alternative information.

Why did the system of control of access that had failed in the first war work in the second war? There are several causes. First, this time the military commanders attracted more professional soldiers who were paid and identified more strongly with the army. Second, restricted access to data and places was combined with a well organized supply of official information. While in the information vacuum of the first war journalists *had* to seek for alternative sources, this time the need for that was not as strong. It was mostly correspondents of foreign media who violated the restrictions of the military and traveled on their own. As a result, they were most often the objects of various sanctions. A third component of the government's strategy was that the separatists were effectively cut off from the media; in fact, this was a consequence of the first two. Although separatists' media continued their illegal activity within Chechnya, their audience was limited, and functioning – irregular. Movladi Udugov concentrated his efforts on the Internet: at the famous site *Kavkaz Center*, initially available at the address www.kavkaz.org, and at the site of the *Chechenpress* news agency. To imagine their general style, it is enough to say that both sites persistently called the federals "occupiers" and "bandits," thus inversely mirroring the official federal discourse about themselves. Although these media were the most available to journalists and other users within Russia, the policy of the Russian authorities forced them to constantly change their addresses and names and wander from one server to another, and during crises (such as large-scale terrorist acts in Russia) they immediately went down. Furthermore, the total Internet audience in Russia is quite modest.

A fourth cause of success of the federal information policy in the second war is that, understanding the impossibility of controlling all stages of news production, the government gained effective control over the stage of dissemination of reports in the mainstream media (see Chapters 5 and 12). Consequently, it became quite useless to put effort into and take risks in collecting data in a dangerous region, since there was no opportunity to circulate them to wide audiences.

Finally, an important factor was the change of journalists' attitude to their work: the time of idealism about press freedom was left far behind. Some took the position that, covering a war, media inevitably participated in it on one side or the other, and they preferred to take the side of the government (Interview 21). Others just did not want their lives to be endangered: numerous stories about killed and kidnapped journalists also contributed to these fears.

This is how the situation looked by the start of the new decade and the new millennium. Although further development of the Chechen conflict is beyond the scope of my study, the recent events in Beslan[5] lead me to give a brief comment on it. From the year 2000 and afterwards any change in the coverage of the war by the mainstream media occurred only as a result of a corresponding change in the government's policy. For approximately a year media reported about the constant, albeit slow, advance of the federal troops in Chechnya. Then, when it was announced that the whole territory of Chechnya had been taken under the federal control and that there were only separate gangs left, media became dominated by two types of reports. The first was accounts about Chechnya returning to a peaceful life, various things being restored, and refugees coming back home. The second type of news, intended to illustrate the end of the major battles, were routine reports about small-scale skirmishes and explosions, provided with data on correspondingly small-scale losses for each accident and never – with general statistics for longer periods. Scenes of violence were nearly eliminated from the screen. The picture of the gradual normalization of the situation in Chechnya created by these reports is being completely disproved by very different alternative sources, from Udugov's sites to Anne Nivat (Nivat 2000), radio *Liberty*, reports of human rights organizations (*Memorial* and others), numerous stories by a *Novaya gazeta* war correspondent Anna Politkovskaya (2004), and others. Moreover, the discourse of the mainstream media was self-denying since it included reports of all the big terrorist acts that, one after another, occurred in Chechnya and outside it, and thus questioned the major idea of the official discourse. Only the most significant acts already form a relatively long list: explosion in a pedestrian subway in Moscow (August 2000), capture of an aircraft flying from Istanbul to Moscow (March 2001), explosion in the procession celebrating Victory Day in Dagestan (May 2002), capture of hostages in a theatre in Moscow (October 2002), explosion and complete destruction of the government building in Grozny (December 2002), blasts made by two female suicide bombers at a rock-concert in Moscow (July 2003), murder of pro-federal president of Chechnya Ahmad Kadyrov on Victory Day in Chechnya (May 2004), explosions of two jets in one day (August 2004) and, finally, capture of about 1,000 children in a school of a town of Beslan in the Caucasian republic of Northern Ossetia (September 2004). While fuller lists of terrorist acts may be found elsewhere (Dmitrieva 2004), this list is enough to envisage the background against which the idea of the gradual normalization of Chechnya was being promoted.

Even when two planes crashed the same day in August 2004, in the first hours officials tried to avoid an account involving terrorist acts. The coverage of the Beslan events was the culmination that changed the government policy and discourse. The government seemed to have no clear policy either towards the crisis itself or to its presentation or, rather, nobody, including the president, wanted to take responsibility and make decisions. President Putin did not address the nation until the crisis was over – that is, on its fourth day, having been absolutely silent before that. None of the officials ever contacted the terrorists during the entire three days, although officials claimed that the building would not be stormed and that negotiations were taking place. Although officials managed to block dissemination of the terrorists' major demand to withdraw federal troops from Chechnya, and – during the first days – of a realistic assessment of the number of hostages (around one thousand), there were many other things that got out of their control. Thus, media showed numerous armed representatives of the "peaceful population" hanging around the school – many of them were said to be hostages' relatives – and nobody paid attention to that until the end of the crisis. The school itself was so poorly cordoned off, that when the spontaneous attack began it was freely broadcast live (which might have been very helpful for terrorists). People all over the country could see nearly naked blood-stained children running out of the school under fire; the whole scene betrayed confusion: military and civilian men with wounded children in their arms were rushing about, swearing, and looking for ambulances which were not available. In general, the Beslan events had a terrifying effect which must have corresponded well to the goals of the terrorists.

Putin's speech on the fourth day was in many respects an echo of George W. Bush's speech after September 11, and contained some statements particularly important for the future of Russia. First of all, like Bush, Putin said that a war had been declared on Russia. It might seem that what had been euphemistically called an "anti-terrorist operation" in Chechnya was finally admitted to be a war, but Putin did not connect the Beslan story to the Chechen situation. Although Basayev and Maskhadov were accused of the Beslan terrorist act in other official messages, Putin's speech contained no such indication. On the contrary, he claimed that the war had been announced by "the international terror" whose goal was to drag Russia apart. Foreign help to Chechen separatists, especially from Arab countries, had been persistently mentioned by the officials throughout the second war, but now the emphasis changed: the events in Beslan were proclaimed only as part of a larger "intervention" of an external enemy into Russia. The enemy itself was not named, but right after Putin's speech state media launched a big anti-American campaign – something that had never happened in Russia since *perestroika*. The consequences of these changes for coverage of Chechnya by Russian media, and for Russia's political development in general, are now hard to assess. The only thing that is clear at the moment is that the Chechen war is far from being over.

Concluding remarks

The way Russian media covered the two Chechen wars is not unique to Russia. The tendency to provide disconnected stories about seemingly unrelated events in the "peaceful" periods, and an even stronger tendency to concentrate on the details of separate battles in the war periods was a result of the structural traits of news as a specific genre. As in many other countries, this tendency was reinforced by deliberate actions of the officials who just did not provide the background information that could connect the events. In both wars military actions, reported apart from their true causes, appeared as the essence of the conflict rather than its indicator. Therefore the ceasefire, to which the media might have indeed contributed in the first war, could look like a solution, while in fact the conflict just passed into a latent form, unnoticed by or uninteresting to journalists. Thus, with little in-depth coverage, media – intentionally or not – could not pressure Russian officials to really resolve the ever-present tensions in Chechnya. Instead, the government learned to prepare military interventions more carefully – in the ideological sense. These preparations provided the initial support of the media, which in turn encouraged the government for larger military actions.

This capacity for learning to manipulate media discourses also has parallels in the West. For instance, failing to arrange effective control of the information in Vietnam, US officials learned the lesson and gradually improved their policy. The pool system, first introduced in the Grenada campaign in 1983, was then successfully used in the Gulf war. Although the Russian government could never completely exclude journalists from Chechnya (unlike the early stages of Grenada, Falklands and the Gulf wars), it succeeded in separation of journalists from the areas of real fighting in the second war. Thus, quite in accordance with Western declarations about the necessity for Russia to learn from Western democracies, the Russian government has demonstrated a good ability to use their accumulated experience.

Conclusion

The Russian media experience of the 1990s, presented as a collection of stories involving the imposition of will, may appear as a very pessimistic picture. However, first, any description in terms of power relations may lead to pessimism, since it inevitably unmasks illegitimate phenomena; but a good remedy against pessimism is to keep in mind that this is not a full description. Second, pessimism is usually possible within normative reasoning, while the category of power was introduced precisely to avoid such reasoning, and to look at media production from another perspective – a perspective that may reveal something unseen before, both in Russian media and, perhaps, in media production in general.

Thus, in nearly all cases that at first glance looked like a struggle of the oppressed media for freedom of speech against oppressive state agents, media professionals appeared to either represent external power groups, or to stand for their own interests. This observation turns journalists from "innocent" objects of "evil" external pressure to players who initiate relations with other actors to gain access to those resources which are controlled by the latter and which, without their mediation, are not available to journalists. In other words, media representatives show themselves no less power maximizers than anybody else. Within other approaches this would probably be an indicator of the "limited development of journalism as an autonomous profession" (Hallin and Papathanassopoulos 2002: 177), manifest in the Third World and at the "fringes" of the West itself. However, the well-registered reluctance of Western journalists to report the significance of external pressures may not necessarily indicate the insignificance of those pressures; equally, it may point at better (deliberately) concealed pacts with external partners or at the domination over journalists. Thus, Russian journalists, while obviously more controlled, seem less dominated, or, perhaps, more sincere in their statements than their western colleagues.

Given the role of media professionals as power maximizers, the question "does Russian government still pressure the media?" (see Chapter 1) must be not only reformulated, but in some cases even reversed, for sometimes it was the CIGs and their "media departments" that were pressuring state agents in the 1990s, and not at all from ideals of press freedom. To get an answer and to give a fuller account of media development of that period, the question should best be put up broadly as "who pressured whom in Russian media production of the 1990s, and with what result?" This will bring state agents back into the analysis as important, but not the only, and not the only "evil" agents. Their importance is determined by the manifestly uneven distribution of resources among various actors: the amount of these resources obviously decreases from state agents to owners to advertisers to sources of information. However, one can hardly name a society where the situation is radically different (except, perhaps, well-integrated etatist systems of the Soviet type in which the very plurality of agents is non-existent).

A conclusion from here is not only that the difference between post-socialist Russia and the West is a difference of scale, for this again is a comparison along a normative democracy-authoritarianism axis. Rather, my conclusion is that, to account for an important part of this difference, it makes sense to base the very typology of national media systems on a different set of categories. Conceptualized in terms of power agents, resources, strategies and rules, the Russian situation looks more understandable, and its development – more predictable. The Soviet media system was, obviously, characterized by the dominance of one agent, or a limited group of them, accumulating all major resources, using enforcement strategies and relatively clear informal rules. The last decade of the century was different almost in all respects: it witnessed the proliferation of agents, dispersion of resources, absence of rules, and decrease in consistency of strategies. Two first conditions are indeed prerequisites of what traditionally is referred to as democracy, but no less important for it are clear, non-selectively used formal rules, which was not observed in Russia. The new informal institutionalization and concentration of resources that began under Putin makes the system more predictable and stable, but this shift is only very loosely connected with movement towards or away from democracy.

Why then is the development of Russian media system, and of the Russian society as a whole, usually interpreted as democratization under Gorbachev and Yeltsin, and reverse "authoritarionization" under Putin? This vision, dominant both in the West and among Russian intellectuals, though, of course, not empirically groundless, has a much stronger motive to emerge than "empirical groundedness." Yeltsin's regime, unable to produce any consistent policies (including foreign policy), fracturing Russian society and weakening it as an "actor" on the international stage, was more than acceptable for Western political elites as its stronger competitors – so it deserved appreciation and legitimization as democratic, or nearly democratic. Putin's strategy, aimed at state consolidation, and more consistent and autonomous policies, is less favorable for the West and, therefore, has to be to a certain degree delegitimized as shifting towards authoritarianism. In practice, I see little difference in, for example, the role of the Russian media in covering Yeltsin's and Putin's elections; the difference in coverage of the Chechen wars is better explained by the redistribution of resources between major elite players, than by loss of "kratos" by "demos." The difference in the degree of determinacy and institutional consolidation between Yeltsin's and Putin's Russia is, however, apparent. Routinization of new journalistic practices, professionalization of sources, consolidation of resources by state agents, and development of "satellite" businesses, such as advertising and audience research – all these stabilizing tendencies are easily observable.

The low degree of both determinacy and institutional consolidation is a feature of the Russian media in the last decade of the twentieth century that seems characteristic of all societies undergoing intensive social change, and thus may be expected in any collapsed regimes. Other features, such as the transparency of institutional borders, look nearly universal and to a significant extent are present in any societies. Virtually everywhere news production appears to be a cross-institutional activity that may take any forms, from the most legitimate ones, such as sourcing, to the whole range of less legitimate forms deriving from propaganda-advertising interests of external agents. Still, formation of large-scale CIGs as quasi-state entities is an extreme case: this phenomenon may emerge only under the condition of indeterminacy and institutional disintegration, and would decline as soon as regular institutions and rules return – which is now clearly seen in Russia.

Some other important features of the Russian media in the 1990s, although at first they seemed specific for the period of transformation, persist into the Putin's Russia. Above all, they are the practice of the private use of institutions and the prevalence of informal rules, that has been gradually substituting the situation of the almost complete absence of rules, typical of the early 1990s. To some extent, both patterns did occur as a result of institutional decomposition, and of a crisis of legitimacy of old rules and values; furthermore, informal institutionalization was probably the only possible, since formal rules demand a much longer time to emerge. On the other hand, both phenomena had been known in the Soviet Union, as well as they may be observed in other stable countries, albeit usually in those situated outside the "Western core." Therefore, nothing prevents them from becoming permanent features of the new Russian media system.

Formal institutionalization, however, is also taking place, stiffening what before had been practiced informally: thus, the new government's project of the law on press formalizes control of the owners over editorial activities, which, as I hope to have shown, was not at all unknown in the 1990s. At the same time, one of the first "institutionalizing events" under Putin was the introduction of tender commissions for distribution of frequencies; under Yeltsin they had not existed even in their present decorative form, which shows the ambiguous character of the on-going institutionalization.

In general, however, everything indicates that the emerging formal rules will tend to conserve the existing balance of power, that is, the dominant position of the stronger (state) actors. A look at the media history of the 1990s in terms of struggle of different power agents for resources makes this development very understandable. Indeed, state agents as holders of the biggest resources, no matter how confused they had been, would have sooner or later mobilized all these resources and used the situation of absence of rules to impose rules favorable for them. The general fatigue of all the actors contributed to this process tremendously. By now, it is clear that the transformational indeterminacy is over, and the rush of the "post-socialist" 1990s is giving way to the moderate pace of a new epoch whose name we still have to learn.

An example of an annotated transcript of an interview

Interview 12: an extract

We have such control, as either <u>an inner censor,</u> my own (what I may say, and what may not); and <u>our anchor and editor.</u> That is, we discuss the matter with the anchor, and he says, "The accents should be put like this," and we say – <u>We work for the company's policy.</u> Eh, well, you have the principle idea, well, either you suggest it, and they agree or disagree; or it can be the anchor's idea: today we need this or that, we consider it to be the main news of the day, so we require – ask you to provide this or that material. How you are going to write it...

how you are going to construct it, what people invite – it's up to you. Now it's yours.
But as for the idea – either you suggest it, or you are given it.
<u>So there can't be a censor there.</u> Or people just refuse at once. I have a story about a cup with a cracked edge in a café in Nevsky prospect. But they say: no, we don't need it. You'd better make a report about today's situation at Lomonosov Porcelain [factory] ... But no extreme darkness ... "Hey, look at these poor children of the workers, they are waiting for their moms and dads to come back from the factory and give them a piece of bread. They haven't been paid for three months already" – no, please, not like this.

– the leading role of control by superiors compared with other agents' control

– legitimating of control of the owners and top managers
– control of genre/ format: news concept
– betrays some information about firm control of superiors

– boundaries of a reporter's autonomy.
– journalists usually do not refer to internal control as censorship, more often they use this term for preliminary external censorship, especially by state agents

Make <u>a well balanced material,</u> that is <u>avoid extremes</u>: don't say "everything is fine, look here, this is fine china, the factory has survived in hard economic conditions," no, not like this, but no gloomy stuff as well. That is, make it <u>objective</u>. How you'll do it – your own problems. And that's all; so <u>we don't feel any pressure at all.</u>

– attributes of concept of objectiveness, seldom used

<u>We feel pressure when we come to the place, and they don't let us shoot.</u> Somebody is going to hide something. Why?
Because <u>it may do some harm to him</u> . . .

– opposition of internal pressure to external
– reasons for hiding information by sources

I: What do you mean "do not allow to shoot"?
"Vitaly": That's simple: you are not allowed, and that's all. For example, yesterday a reservoir blew up, a gas reservoir at the *Admiralty Works*. Has this picture been shown? No, <u>and never would be.</u>

(A story about this accident at the *Admiralty Works* was made nevertheless. The works were shot at from the opposite bank of the Neva river. The reporter also managed to have a talk with women-cleaners who had witnessed the accident.)

Because it is a secret military enterprise . . .
where there are military and state secrets . . .
So there, even if you'd like to shoot a blown-up reservoir, for example, you won't show workshops, loading cranes, well . . . they won't let you shoot . . .

– one of the ways for concealing information: regulations referring to state secrets

<u>interests of the State, they would say</u>. But actually the thing is that the plant just does not want to show all their stuff. Well, that's only an example, you see.

which is identified with interests of the state

Or a <u>tank truck went up</u> at a motor depot . . .
if you show that and make a story, the <u>depot will suffer rather unpleasant consequences</u> . . .
do they need that? You come there, and they tell you frankly –

– similar example from private business

or, for example, . . . umm . . . *brothers* solve their problems, <u>had their "work-out," a dead body there,</u> a jeep with bullet holes – so you

– similar example about illegitimate agents of violence

come, and *brothers* are standing there: no
shooting, man. Then either they will...
pardon, not for the record, will kick your head   – a threat of direct
off, so that you don't shoot, or just ask, "look   violence
here, man, get out of here, or you'll have
problems."
So you'll first think twice: shall you do this or   – reaction and
that, or not.   appreciation of
                                                       possible costs and
                                                       benefits

Chronology

1917	Bolshevik revolution. Nationalization of press begins.
1922	Official state censorship is introduced by establishment of Chief Board of Literature and Publishing, later renamed Chief Board for Providing Security of State Secrets in Press.
Late 1960s	Emergence of national TV and introduction of magnetic tape, allowing preliminary censorship of TV products.
1968	"Vremya," first national and most popular official evening newscast, goes on air.
March 1985	Announcement of *perestroika* and later of *glasnost* by the new Soviet leader Mikhail Gorbachev.
May 1987	Jamming of "enemy" foreign radio stations ends.
October 1987	First secretary of Moscow City Party Committee Boris Yeltsin attacks one of the senior Party leaders at Party Central Committee meeting. Yeltsin–Gorbachev rivalry begins.
February 1988	Yeltsin is removed from all major positions.
February 1989	Last Soviet troops are withdrawn from Afghanistan.
March 1989	First multicandidate parliamentary elections.
May–July 1989	Baltic republics declare sovereignty.
June 1990	Boris Yeltsin is elected president of the Russian Federation (republic within USSR).
June 1990	Adoption of the first USSR Law on Press and other Mass Media: censorship is prohibited, establishment of non-state media is permitted. Rapid development of non-state media, especially press.
Autumn 1990	Chechnya declares its sovereignty.
August 1991	Anti-Gorbachev conservative putsch is

	suppressed by Yeltsin's team and widely opposed by the public.
October 1991	Separatist leader Dzokhar Dudayev is elected president of Chechnya.
December 1991	Leaders of Russia, Ukraine and Byelorussia announce that their countries quit the USSR and establish the Commonwealth of Independent States (CIS).
December 1991	Leaders of other Soviet republics, except Baltic states and Georgia, join CIS (Georgia joins CIS in 1994). President Gorbachev resigns.
December 1991	Law of the Russian Federation "On mass media" is adopted.
1992	"Liberalization of prices" and hyperinflation. Start of privatization of state property. Subscription-based press collapses.
1993	First wholly private television appears.
June 1993	Dudayev seizes full power in Chechnya and removes the parliament out of its building by military force.
October 1993	After attempt to overthrow Yeltsin by leaders of the Russian parliament and the vice-president, Yeltsin dismisses the parliament, driving it out of the building by military force, and schedules parliamentary elections for December 1993. Censorship declared for several weeks.
December 1993	Parliamentary elections. Adoption of the new constitution by referendum.
Early 1994	Private *NTV* gets morning time on national *Channel 4* by the president's decree. This time is taken away from *Rossiiyskie universitety* state educational TV company.
October 1994	First high-profile murder of a journalist: *Moskovski Komsomolets* investigative journalist Dmitri Kholodov is blown up.
26 November 1994	Chechen opposition to Dudayev, secretly supported by the Russian military tries to storm the Chechen capital Grozny, but fails.
December 1994	Start of the first Chechen war. *NTV* takes an anti-war position.
January–February 1995	Transformation of State *Channel 1* into *Public Russian Television* (*ORT*) with 51 percent share belonging to the State.
1 March 1995	Vladislav Listev, newly elected *ORT* director and popular anchor is killed.

Winter 1994–5	First "Information war" between Berezovsky–Korzhakov–*ORT* and Gussinsky–Luzhkov–*NTV*. The first group wins.
June 1995	Chechen field commander Shamil Basayev holds a thousand hostages at a hospital in Budyonnovsk. His negotiations with prime minister Chernomyrdin are covered live by television.
January 1996	Chechen separatists hold hostages in a maternity hospital in Dagestan. Access of journalists is highly restricted.
January 1996	Major "oligarchs" unite to support sick Yeltsin at the forthcoming presidential elections. *NTV* top manager Igor Malashenko joins his electoral headquarters.
Spring 1996	*Gazprom* gas monopoly, partly state-owned, buys about 30 percent of *NTV*.
April 1996	Ceasefire in Chechnya is announced by Yeltsin.
May 1996	Dudayev is killed during a bombardment.
June 1996	Yeltsin is elected president.
August 1996	A peace treaty is signed with Chechen separatists. Shamil Basayev becomes one of the ministers in the new Chechen government.
Autumn 1996	*NTV* gets the entire national *Channel 4* by presidential decree. *Rossiiskiye universitety* educational TV company ceases to exist.
Autumn 1997	National relay transmitters network is taken away from *Peterburg – 5 Kanal* and given to the newly established state non-commercial *Kultura* channel by presidential decree.
Spring 1998	Radio *Titan* is suppressed in Bashkortostan.
June 1998	An opposition newspaper editor-in-chief Larisa Yudina is killed in Kalmykiya.
July 1998	*NTV* takes out big loan to launch a first private TV satellite in Russia.
August 1998	Financial crisis.
Early 1999	*Video International* advertising agency gets control over advertising on all national TV channels.
July 1999	Mikhail Lesin, founder of *Video International*, becomes Minister of press.
August 1999	Chechen separatists carry out large-scale attack into Dagestan. Prime minister orders the military to fight them.
August 1999	Vladimir Putin is appointed prime minister. Soon Yeltsin declares him his "successor."

September 1999	Establishment of the Federal Tender Commission responsible for distribution of frequencies.
October 1999	Full-scale military operation in Chechnya begins: start of the second Chechen war.
Autumn 1999	Parliamentary elections fierce campaign. Luzhkov–Gussinsky–*NTV* group loses to Putin–Berezovsky–*ORT* group.
Winter 1999–2000	Large-scale bombardments in Chechnya. Grozny is completely destroyed.
March 2000	Vladimir Putin is elected president.
May 2000	*NTV* and *Media-MOST* offices are searched.
June 2000	Vladimir Gussinsky is arrested.
June 2000	Yuri Luzhkov meets Mikhail Lesin. Luzhkov's *TV-Center* wins tender and extends its license.
July 2000	A secret treaty between Gussinsky, *Gazprom* and Mikhail Lesin is signed guaranteeing freedom to Gussinsky under condition of selling *NTV* to *Gazprom*. Gussinsky flees abroad.
September 2000	The secret treaty is disclosed. Procuracy resumes persecution of *NTV*.
September 2000	Boris Berezovsky flees to London and declares himself a political emigrant. He offers his shares in *ORT* in trust to well-known people in Russia.
February 2001	*PROMACO* provocation.
April 2001	*Gazprom* holds an alternative meeting of *NTV* shareholders and elects new board of directors. Next week old *NTV* team is driven from its office by force.

List of interviews

This list includes interviews cited in the book. Nicknames of anonymous respondents are given in quotation marks; real names are italicized. Interviews are listed in chronological order.

1 "Semyon Starozhilov," m, 70, *Vesti Starograda* reporter, formerly – head of its news department, May 1997.
2 "Anna Soroka," f, 52, head of social problems department at *Vesti Starograda*, April 1997.
3 "Andrei Basov," m, 39, deputy editor-in-chief of *Vesti Starograda*, April 1997.
4 "Viktor Golubev," m, 45, head of department of politics and economics at *Vesti Starograda*, May 1997.
5 "Marina Savchenko," f, 25, *Vesti Starograda* reporter, May 1997.
6 "Samuel Petrenko," m, 32, newspaper investigative journalist from Voronezh, June 1998.
7 "Tatyana Smirnova," f, 66, former head of youth programs at Leningrad TV, June 1998.
8 "Antonina Sokolova," f, 76, former head of news and politics programs at Leningrad TV, July 1998.
9 "Leonid Voronets," m, 70, former TV producer in Leningrad, July 1998.
10 "Lev Tolstov," m, 64, a St. Petersburg radio top manager, August 1998.
11 "Inna Savitskaya," f, 58, TV producer and creator in St. Petersburg, August 1998.
12 "Vitali Bogdanov," m, 29, reporter at St. Petersburg bureau of a national TV company, September 1998.
13 "Viktoria Diakonova," f, 34, former employee of Leningrad branch of *Glavlit*, September 1998.
14 "Vyacheslav Gryadin," m, 30, newsroom head at a St. Petersburg TV company, September 1998.
15 "Vadim Shnurenko," m, 45, St. Petersburg newspaper investigative journalist, October 1998.

16 "Georgi Potapov," m, an official from St. Petersburg committee on press, December 1998.
17 "Arseny Kuznetsov," m, 27, St. Petersburg TV anchor, January 1999.
18 "Mikhail Tarasyuk," m, 30, head of St. Petersburg bureau of a national TV company, January 1999.
19 "Ivan Kurbski," m, 43, reporter for St. Petersburg newscast of a national TV company, October 1999.
20 "Pyotr Senichev," m, 30, anchor at St. Petersburg newscast of a national TV company, October 1999.
21 "Kirill Marchenko," m, 38, reporter for St. Petersburg newscast of a national TV company, November 1999.
22 "Yelena Ivanova," f, layout editor at St. Petersburg newscast of a national TV company, November 1999.
23 "Yelena Petrova," f, senior layout editor at St. Petersburg newscast of a national TV company, November 1999.
24 "Fyodor Ozersky," m, 29, employee of PR department of a big oil company in Moscow, November 1999.
25 "Farkhat Ramazanov," m, 40, newsroom head at St. Petersburg newscast of a national TV company, January 2000.
26 "Vladislav Menshikov," m, 35, head of department of news and socio-political programs at St. Petersburg newscast of a national TV company, January 2000.
27 "Denis Komarov," m, 35, head of international department of a national TV company, March 2000.
28 *Oleg Panfilov*, director of Center for journalism in extreme situations at Union of Journalists of Russia, June 2000.
29 "Pavel Yakutovich," m, 50, head of information-analytical department of a big advertising agency in Moscow, November 2000.
30 "Anatoly Ilyin," m, 47, former employee at the President's press-center and former political consultant at the Soviet of Federation, November 2000.
31 "Dmitri Gorski," m, 30, employee of PR department of a big metallurgic company in Moscow, formerly political PR-man, November 2000.
32 "Alexander Gurevich," m, 30, deputy head of PR department of a big oil company in Moscow, November 2000.
33 "Galina Minskaya," f, 36, head of department of work with clients at a Moscow PR agency, November 2000.
34 "Valentina Latypova," f, TV anchor at St. Petersburg, November 2000.
35 "Maria Murtazina," f, 42, radio reporter and journalism professor in Moscow, January 2001.
36 "Nikolai Bazarov," m, 47, editor-in-chief of a Moscow newspaper, January 2001.
37 "Yevgeni Bulkin," m, 30, political PR-man and philosophy lecturer in Moscow, January 2001.

38 "Svetlana Vasilieva," f, 36, press-secretary of a faction at the State Duma, January 2001.
39 *Igor Yakovenko*, general secretary of the Union of Journalists of Russia, February 2001.
40 *Mikhail Malyutin*, political expert from Moscow, January 2001.
41 *Alexei Pankin*, editor-in-chief of *Sreda* professional magazine on media, February 2001.
42 "Anton Sereda," m, 48, journalist from Vologda, April 2002.

Glossary

Analytical/publicist article or program   as opposed to both *information* and entertainment media products, in Russian journalistic jargon refers to products in which important social and political issues are discussed, analyzed and commented.

Avtonomny okrug (autonomous district)   subject of the Russian Federation, named after a local ethnic group and situated inside another subject of Federation; partly subordinate to its "host" subject of Federation, but partly autonomous from it and subordinate directly to the "Federal Center."

Black PR   journalistic slang for an illegal or otherwise illegitimate part of public relations (information management) activities.

Bound news/comment   here: news or comment that became restricted as a result of unrecognized exchange between internal and external agents. Bound news is opposed to *hidden advertisement*, as a deal, concealed from outsiders, but well recognized by the participants.

Brothers   (Russian slang) usually low-ranking members of criminal groups; a friendly address used by *brothers* themselves.

CIG   see *cross-institutional group*.

Conflict media-political configuration   here: a situation of "pluralism of dependent media" resulting from relatively even distribution of resources among the major actors, none of whom wishes to compromise, and each of whom uses media as a weapon against others. Along with "dependent" media, this configuration may include managements of media organizations as relatively autonomous actors pursuing their own interests. See also *media-political configuration*.

Cross-institutional group   here: a relatively well integrated team aimed at increase of its resources and/or resources of its participants, and including agents from different social institutions providing it with different kinds of resources. They are usually: economic agents; state agents with their access to public resources and rule-making; enforcement bodies of any nature; and, possibly, advertising-propaganda resource provided by media. The term is used to denote temporary structures that substituted the weakened Russian institutions during the 1990s.

Dzhinsa akin to *zakaz*, but usually referring to stories paid for to individual journalists, secretly from his/her media organization management.

Enforcing ministries, enforcing structures the aggregative name of Ministries of Interior and of Defense and of Federal Security Bureau, including all their departments.

Enforcers the closest English equivalent of the aggregative name of Ministries of Interior and of Defense and Federal Security Bureau, including all their departments (e.g. police, different troops, secret service) and all bodies into which both structures have been ever reorganized or renamed; also used to denote separate representatives of those bodies, esp. their heads.

External agent of power here: agent placed outside media organization and outside the community of media professionals. Cf. *internal agent of power.*

External ownership here: ownership exercised by an owner whose final goals lie beyond media industry while the owned media organization is used as an advertising-propaganda resource, that later is converted into other kinds of capital. Cf. *internal ownership.*

FSB Federal Security Bureau, successor of the Soviet KGB.

Genuine news here: a news product corresponding to the most typical normative rules (independence from sources' information management, compliance with observable evidence, and some other).

Glasnost (publicness) one of the main slogans of Gorbachev's *perestroika* policy, which led to rapid autonomization of media in late 1980s.

Hidden advertisement a media product paid for by an advertiser or other kind of client and covering something or somebody in a favorable way, while presented as *genuine news* or independent commentary. Cf. *bound news/comment.*

Information here: any signs/meanings that may be raw material for media (first of all for news) production; may include "disinformation" as well.

Information article or program in journalistic jargon, a media product aimed at "informing"; in Russian journalistic jargon is opposed to *analytical/publicist* and to entertainment products. Besides news, it includes "informing" of something that is not necessarily "new" (e.g. legal or health advice). Information and publicist production is often united in a single department inside media organizations, while entertainment exists separately. Similarly, media organizations themselves are often divided by journalists into *socio-political* (those producing information and publicist items) and entertainment ones.

Information management here: activity constitutive of the role of professional sources of information or of their representatives. Aims at production of favorable coverage of the source, and/or at production of absence of its unfavorable coverage, or at unfavorable coverage of third parties.

Information war   an expression widely used to mean an aggressive propagandistic campaign, primarily in media, as a rule with wide use of *kompromat*, and usually involving two parties or more.

Internal agent of power   here: agent placed within the community of media professionals. Cf. *external agent of power*.

Internal ownership   here: ownership exercised by an owner who uses the owned media organization solely as a source of profit within media industry and has no other goals outside it. Cf. *external ownership*.

Kompromat   a journalistic slang word used to denote any information, true or false, able to discredit a person or organization; usually refers to published data or those intended for publication.

Krai (territory)   subject of the Russian Federation similar to *oblast*.

Media killer   (journalistic slang) a journalist, usually commentator or anchor, serving as a main instrument to defeat competitors in *media wars*.

Media war   see *information war*.

Media-political configuration   term used to account for variation in degree of media pluralism and autonomy in different regions of the "feudalized" Russian society in the 1990s. The variation is seen as resulting from local composition of agents, distribution of their resources, and the strategies they apply. See also *conflict, monocentric, pact*, and *struggle according to rules media-political configurations*.

Monocentric media-political configuration   here: a situation of nearly absent media pluralism and autonomy resulting from dominance of the single agent of power who chooses to suppress all competitors by force. See also *media-political configuration*.

Negative practice of power   here: action in which environment is altered by direct agent's actions, while resistance of others is physically suppressed, or change is made via actions of others, threatened with negative sanctions. Cf. *positive practice of power*.

Oblast (region)   subject of the Russian Federation named after its principal city, headed by a governor, with no reference to local ethnonyms, but able to contain autonomous districts (*avtonomny okrug*).

Pact media-political configuration   here: a situation of limited media pluralism and autonomy resulting from decision of the single dominant media player, or its backer, to compromise with other major agents of power. In this case the composition of major actors is neither a single team, nor a set of separate groups, but a loose alliance of several sub-divisions. See also *media-political configuration*.

Perestroika (reconstruction)   a reformist policy announced by the Soviet leader Mikhail Gorbachev in 1985, and the corresponding period of history, whose end is usually dated to the collapse of the Soviet Union in late 1991.

Positive practice of power   here: action in which environment is altered by direct agent's actions, while no resistance of others occurs, or change is made via actions of others, when their obedience is reached through implementation of positive sanctions. Cf. *negative practice of power*.

Power   here: action of imposition of agent's will.

Practice   here: typical action.

Procuracy   powerful body inside the Russian Ministry of Interior, headed by a prosecutor of the respective level (General Prosecutor, regional prosecutor etc.); responsible for instituting criminal proceedings and conducting investigations on them.

Respublika (republic)   subject of the Russian Federation, named after a local ethnic group, headed by a president (as distinct from *oblasts* and *krais* headed by governors), and having some additional rights in comparison to *oblasts* and *krais*.

Roof   (Russian slang) a person, a group or an organization offering businessmen a service of informal protection from competitors, unconscientious partners, enforcement and other state bodies, and from other roofs. Having grown from racketeer business, roofs in the 1990s acquired a wide range of enforcement functions, substituting police and similar state bodies, but staying private in their goals and repressive in their methods.

Socio-political media   see explanation to *information article or program*.

State agents   here: individuals occupying positions within organizations, formally defined as state bodies, and having access to resources provided by these positions. Since such agents may act against the ability of the State, as social institution, to sustain, here they are opposed to the traditional concept of State.

Struggle according to the rules media-political configuration   here: a situation of significant media pluralism and autonomy resulting from relatively even distribution of resources among the major actors who choose to compromise and elaborate common rules of the game. This configuration more often than all others gives room for media organizations as relatively autonomous actors pursuing their own interests. See also *media-political configuration*.

Zakaz (order)   (journalistic slang) a media product paid for by the advertiser and covering something or somebody in a favorable way, while presented as *genuine* news or independent commentary.

Notes

1 Catching the wind

1 In the West the media of the post-Soviet bloc are usually referred to as "post-communist" which, for insiders, is incorrect. Even the official Soviet propaganda never claimed that communism – an ideally just society – had been reached. The most common self-naming was socialism.

2 Taking into account the conventional character of the concept of the "West" and its possible antonyms, I shall apply it to countries traditionally referred to as "developed" and "democratic," that is Western Europe and North America.

3 This term, in Glaser and Strauss, denotes words and expressions used by respondents that can be borrowed for labeling similar scientific categories; however, the latter, according to the authors, should be constructed by the scholar (Glaser and Strauss 1967).

4 Database 1996, sorted by dates, may be found in Panfilov, Simonov 1997; database 1997 – in Avdeev *et al.* 1998. Electronic databases are published at Glasnost Defense Foundation website (homepage: www.gdf.ru), section "Monitor" (http://www.gdf.ru/monitor/index.shtml). This section provides links to files each of which contains events registered during a particular month. Since these files are very numerous, in this book I make only short references (e.g. GDF 01.01.2000), where *GDF* refers to Glasnost Defense Foundation Monitoring, and the date is the date of the event I am considering. Thus, the original story may be easily found in the corresponding online file or section of the paper-published database.

2 Russian media system

1 Data from licenses of St. Petersburg branch of the Committee on Press, November 1998.

2 Privatization of the state – use of state resources by state agents for their private purposes, as a part of general disintegration of the Russian state – is addressed in detail in Chapter 3.

3 In the Russian political spectrum of the 1990s the major opposition was between democrats (the right) who acted as reformists promoting liberalization of economy and political life, and communists (the left), who mostly stood for partial return to the Soviet regime. Throughout the 1990s the democratic niche was occupied by Yeltsin and any pro-Yeltsin party that could be established by his supporters before new elections (this phenomenon became known as "the party of authorities"). The communist niche was dominated by the *Communist Party of the Russian Federation* (*CPRF* or, in Russian, *KPRF*) lead by Gennady Zuganov. An important (and constant) share of votes was held by the *LDPR*

nationalist party headed by Vladimir Zhirinovsky, while the small share of the "extreme" democratic vote was collected by Grigory Yavlinsky's *Yabloko*, very popular with Western political elites. By 1999 the configuration had changed: the new dominant players began a fierce struggle for "the center," using a broad rhetoric based on populist slogans and exploiting simultaneously Soviet nostalgia, growing nationalist moods, and hopes for more effective economic reforms (that is, playing with electorates of other major parties). What had been "the party of authorities" split into two major rival groups, one of which, led by Moscow mayor Yuri Luzhkov, former prime-minister Yevgeny Primakov, and supported by Vladimir Gussinksy's CIG, lost to the pro-Putin group supported by Boris Berezovsky. By 2003, after throwing both Gussinsky and Berezovsky out of the game, "the party of authorities" reunited again and, successfully continuing to appeal to a communist electorate, reduced *KPRF* to a minor parliamentary faction. While the "extreme democrats" were excluded from the parliament due to intense competition within their narrow niche, the second leading role passed to a number of nationalist parties, that, being supported by the "party of authorities," were primarily used to take votes away from real opposition forces. Therefore, nationalists preferred to support the "party of authorities" in all its legislative activities.

3 State agents

1 Procuracy is a very powerful body inside the Russian Ministry of Interior responsible for instituting criminal proceedings and conducting investigations on them.
2 The closest English equivalent of the inclusive name of Ministries of Interior and of Defense and Federal Security Bureau, including all their departments (e.g. police, different troops, secret service) and all bodies into which both structures have been ever reorganized or renamed; also used to denote separate representatives of those bodies, esp. their heads. *Enforcers* differs from English "forces," first of all, in this potential to mean persons, not only structures; when structures are meant, the terms *enforcing ministries* or *enforcing structures* are commonly used.
3 The exact reference to the GDF monitoring is not given so that the real title of *Vesti Starograda* and the identity of its workers is not disclosed.

4 State and non-state agents of violence

1 Leaders of subjects of the Russian Federation that have the status of republics are called presidents.
2 Novosibirsk (pop. 1,440.000) is a big educational center in south Siberia and a monument to attempted Soviet high-tech.
3 The name of the organized criminal group headed by Kumarin who originally came from the town of Tambov.
4 Slang for usually low-ranking members of criminal groups, used by outsiders; also, a friendly address used by *brothers* themselves.
5 A Moscow-based entertainment network

5 Owners

1 Sergei Dorenko, the leading anchor and political commentator at *ORT* (Berezovsky's) channel, who made the main "propaganda" contribution to the campaign against and the defeat of Luzhkov's anti-Putin coalition in the 1999 parliamentary and 2000 presidential elections.

2 Although this statement was made in a public lecture, later, in an informal talk, Kachkaeva stressed its hypothetical character, as well as of some other data on Berezovsky mentioned by her.

7 Sources of information

1 It was widely believed that an effective electoral campaign in Russia in the 1990s demanded $1–2 "per voter capita." Some experts, however, considered these estimates too simplified and therefore meaningless (Malkin and Suchkov 2000: 46).
2 A large collection of articles and documents, claimed to be truthful, can be found at the above mentioned www.compromat.ru website, in the section devoted to Skuratov's case (http://www.compromat.ru/main/skuratov/a.htm). However, the character of this site, and especially the composition and character of links and references in this particular section, suggest that these data should be treated with considerable caution.

8 Rank-and-file journalists

1 *Sinkhron, standup* and *inter-shum* are Russian journalistic slang words, but their English roots are easily seen.
2 For journalists this meant objects relevant to the subject of the story, acceptable to be shown (killer's weapon found at the scene of crime, voting-papers from polling stations, etc.)
3 Address by full first name followed by patronymic is extremely polite and respectful.
4 Zuganov is the leader of the major communist party in Russia that took up to 30 percent of the vote at most elections throughout the 1990s. Since Russian journalists are generally inclined to democratic voting, the journalist meant that working for a communist was an extreme case, unlike Gorbachev and Luzhkov mentioned next who, while not being democrats either, are not so strongly associated with the communists.
5 Paraphrase of Vladimir Lenin's famous expression about the possibility of building "communism in one country." This slogan was introduced when the bolsheviks' expectations of the Russian example serving as a catalyst for the world communist revolution failed, and Lenin's government had to reformulate the Marxian prophecy in accordance with the changed situation. Since, seen from the 1990s, the success of the separately built communism looked more than doubtful, the respondent used the expression to hint at the doubtful character of freedom of speech in one newspaper.
6 The details of ideal notions of different freedoms in mass media were studied in the comparative Russian-American research supervised by Zassoursky and Wayett in 1996. Journalists of both countries were asked the same questions. The study revealed that Americans qualified fewer phenomena as due subjects for regulation, though in general the opinions of Russian and American journalists were quite similar (Zassoursky *et al.* 1997).

9 Center and periphery of power

1 The subject of this story refers to World War II when St. Petersburg, then Leningrad, was cut off for 900 days from the rest of the country by fascist troops and lost about a third of its 2.5-million population through bombings, starvation and cold.

2 The label of the criminal capital, attached by federal media to St. Petersburg, emerged in late 1990s as suddenly as it disappeared a few years later.
3 Leader of Chechen separatists regarded as a terrorist by the Russian authorities.
4 See note 3 of Chapter 2.
5 Governor Vladimir Yakovlev, then running for his second term.
6 The respondent is referring to one of the numerous scandals of that time when the governor issued a list of candidates whom he approved and for whom he recommended voting.
7 Name of the mansion that houses the city administration.
8 Respondent means the chair of the board of directors elected by the owners.
9 Nikolai Svanidze was the leading anchor and the head of *RTR*, the wholly state-owned national TV channel, for some time in the 1990s. According to "Menshikov," at the same period Anatoly Chubais, head of the *Single Energy System* company, Russian natural monopoly in electricity supply, was one of the leading *RTR* backers. Although Chubais was indeed in charge of media in Yeltsin's government around 1997, I have not found any other confirmation of his strong influence at *RTR*, except Menshikov's anonymous evidence.
10 Russian *Gallup Media*, which became a choice of TV top executives partly because of being a recognized international brand, in reality has nothing to do with either American *Gallup*, or *Gallup International*. *Gallup Media* is an off-shoot of the Finnish company with the same name, which has rather tense relations with both original *Gallups*. It even led *Gallup International* to bring Gallup Media to court, but the choice by leading TV channels had been already made (Dmitrova 1999).

10 Regional and periphery of power

1 Among them the most important are:

1   regional media legislation,
2   media density (an index based on quantity of TV and radio companies and quantity of issues of printed editions distributed by subscription per capita in a given region),
3   development of the advertising market (shares of State subsidies and income revenues from non-State sources of income in aggregated regional media budgets),
4   ratio of "State" to private media in the region,
5   regional taxation and funding policy towards media organizations,
6   quantity and character of media conflicts (based on the data of GDF monitoring),
7   percentage and quality of replies of local authorities to test journalistic inquiries made during the research.

2 Here the conflict model has been arbitrarily put by me in the third position, while the authors' description of the models suggests that they are inclined to put it, together with "Transitional to market model" somewhere between models 1 and 4, but not one after the other.
3 Thus, authoritarian regions, being generally poor, have the small non-state money and few media outlets, all or almost all of which are controlled by the leader through prohibitory measures. Paternalistic regions have more media, and little share of non-state money is explained not by the poverty of the region, but by the local funding policy: not being able to prohibit, the local leader tries to "buy" as many media as he can. Modernized regions have both many media and a large share of non-state money, but the local political elite –

it is not quite clear how – still manages to exercise significant control over the media.

4 This follows first of all from the traditional understanding of press freedom as freedom from the State; this understanding leads authors to see non-state media – that is, private, commercial media living wholly within market economy – as freer and more independent. Admitting the imprecise character of such an approach, the authors argue that market limitations are far less severe and dangerous for press freedom than those of the State. For the Russian situation, however, this approach seems so imprecise that it leaves out too many important factors. For instance, the share of aggregated regional media budgets that is not formed from state subsidies in the *Public Expertise* project is considered to be formed from advertising revenues, although in other texts Yakovenko himself disproves this assumption. As has been already mentioned, according to his estimates, legal advertising revenues together with official state subsidies covered no more than 30 percent of media budgets in the late 1990s.

5 Although fully based on Gelman's classification, this typology substitutes some of his terms with more concise ones. Thus, "war of all against all" is termed "conflict configuration" (as in the *Public Expertise* classification). "Elite settlement" is called "pact," despite the fact that Gelman pays special attention in divorcing these terms in his book, and stresses that pact, as a means of dismantling the old regime, is not the same as elite settlement, as a means of exit from indeterminacy (Gelman 2000: 44). However, while this may be important for conceptualizing regime transformation, it hardly seems significant in the context of the present chapter, and a shorter term looks more appropriate.

6 Ancient name of Russia.

7 This region (pop. 1.3 million in 1997), centered around the ancient Russian town of Volodga (founded in 1147), is situated several hundred miles to the north of Moscow. Modestly economically developed, predominantly urban and populated almost exclusively by Russians, it is perceived as the heart of the "Russian north" (Petrov *et al.* 1998).

8 Situated in the middle of European Russia, NN region (pop. 3.7 million in 1997) is a highly urbanized and industrialized area. An ancient cultural center, Nizhni Novgorod was founded in 1221 at the confluence of two big rivers Volga and Oka. There the Volga, which connects the northern and southern parts of European Russia, is now crossed by railways connecting the country from east to west. By the 1990s the region possessed well developed engineering, machinery and metal-working industries, including one of the leading car plants; one-third of its output was produced by the Military Industrial Complex (MIC) enterprises.

9 The Siberian city of Krasnoyarsk was founded by Russian colonists in 1628. The territory itself, the geographical center of contemporary Russia, stretches almost from the country's southern boundary to the Arctic ocean along the river Yenisey. Its population numbers over three million people, almost exclusively Russians, while the northern part, embracing the Evenk and Taymyr autonomous districts, is scarcely populated. The majority of the region's huge industries are located in the south, around Krasnoyarsk, except the *Norilski Nickel* giant corporation situated in the polar town of Norilsk and producing about one-fifth of income of the territory's budget (Petrov and Zapekly 1998; Petrov, Titkov and Zapekly 1998).

10 As a political figure Lebed had been created by Yeltsin's team during the 1996 presidential elections. For his victory Yeltsin, opposed in the media to the communist leader Zuganov as a democrat to an authoritarian, needed to capture a share of the so-called "patriotic" (nationalist conservative) electorate who defi-

nitely would have preferred communists to democrats. An "honest soldier" Lebed, with his frightening voice and rough speech, was an ideal character to seize these votes in the first round of elections. Presented to the public with a mixture of patriotic slogans and market promises, he took as much as 15 percent of votes and came third after Yeltsin and Zuganov. Before the second round he asked his electorate to give their votes to Yeltsin and after his victory got a high position in his team. A few months later he was sacked after a sharp conflict, the details of which are unknown.

11 Voronezh region (pop. 2.5 million in 1997) is the heart of the so-called Black Soil area – a vast territory between Moscow and Ukraine known for its agricultural production and communist orientation of its voters. Such electoral behavior is typical for either rural or poor areas and is the reason for the large proportion of old Soviet administrators in the Voronezh elite. The only large city and industrial center of the region is Voronezh itself dominated by the enterprises of the Military-Industrial Complex (MIC).

12 See note 3 of Chapter 2.

13 =Communist.

14 In the Soviet Union the Military-Industrial Complex was the best funded group of enterprises; in the 1990s, because of the decomposition of the State and its military programs, and because of the economic crisis, the funding ceased, and the MIC workers became strong supporters of the communists.

15 Short for *Komsomolskaya Pravda*

16 Yekaterinburg was called Sverdlovsk between 1924 and 1991 after a Soviet leader; later it got its original name back, but the area surrounding it, of which it is the principal town, has kept the name Sverdlovsk region. A similar situation applies to St. Petersburg and Leningrad region, although in this case the region is a separate subject of the Federation without any principal town.

11 The story of *Peterburg – 5 Kanal*

1 The description of the St. Petersburg media landscape is based on several sources: a collection of articles in *Sreda* (1998), No. 6; Licenses of the Federal service of the Russian Federation on broadcasting for St. Petersburg and its region, catalogues of broadcasting TV companies, of TV producing companies of St. Petersburg, and of print media of the North-West of Russia, registered by the North-West regional board of the State committee on press by late 1998; and, finally, interviews and informal talks with journalists dating to the same period.

2 Since attaining the status of "subject of Federation" in 1993, St. Petersburg and Moscow were separated from the respectively named regions surrounding them; surrounding St. Petersburg, furthermore, kept the name that the city had borne in 1924–91: Leningrad; since then it has the strange impression of being attached to a non-existent town. Unlike other subjects of the Federation, Moscow and Leningrad regions do not have principal towns, and their administrations are located in the respective cities. The latter, though, do not have principal towns either, and the post of the governor in them coincides with that of the mayor. Therefore, the St. Petersburg mayor was renamed governor in 1996, while the Moscow head kept the old title.

3 See note 3 of Chapter 2.

4 *Red Arrow* is the name of the famous express-train running between Moscow and St. Petersburg.

12 The story of *NTV*

1 In saying this, Dorenko was opposing himself to the bald, stout, short and relatively old Luzhkov.

2 *Gazprom-Media* is a daughter company of *Gazprom* responsible for its media business.

13 Change in the coverage of the Chechen wars

1 For an earlier version of this chapter, see Koltsova 2000a.

2 Radio *Liberty* cannot be accused of inaccurate reporting; on the contrary, it often gave facts that could not be found in Russian media.

3 Wahhabism, with its attachment to Shariat, is not typical of the local Muslim tradition, and has been actively imported to Chechnya after the collapse of the Soviet Union.

4 Major players of the "Caspian oil" game are represented by: the USA as the most powerful player, Russia as the owner of the only functioning pipeline; and all neighboring countries: Azerbaijan, Georgia, Turkey, Iran, Turkmenistan and some others. The Caucasus mountains form a narrow neck separating the inland Caspian Sea (east Caucasus) from the Black sea (west Caucasus); the latter is connected to the Mediterranean by the Bosphorus Strait belonging to Turkey. There are several potential ways by which Caspian oil may be transported to the West. The first way goes southwards through Iran to the Persian gulf – given the attitude of the USA to this country, this is not an option for the US administration. Another way is through Turkmenistan, Afghanistan and Pakistan to the Arabian sea – given the ongoing instability in this region, this seems unrealistic. All other ways are through the Caucasus. One, through Azerbaijan and Georgia, is dependent, on the one hand, on Turkey's will to let oil tankers through the Bosphorus, and on the other, on Russia's pressures on the two countries – in particular, through its military presence in Georgia. The Azerbaijan-Turkey route has the strong support of the USA, but is much more expensive than the existing way through Russia. The latter until recently included a pipeline through the Caspian republic of Dagestan, Chechnya and several Russian oblasts, and tanker transportation through the Black Sea. Despite its cheapness, it is not free from shortcomings, such as the limited capacity of the Novorossiysk port and of the Bosphorus and, again, dependence on Turkey.

5 Beslan (pop. 30,000) is a town in the republic of Northern Ossetia, the only Christian region in the Caucasus. September 1 is a big holiday in Russia when all schoolchildren (many of them with their parents) line-up in their school yards to celebrate the beginning of the new academic year. On September 1, 2004 a group of terrorists, supposedly of different nationalities, attacked such a gathering at School Number 1 in Beslan and rounded up about one thousand children and adults into the school gymnasium. There they were kept for three days without food, nearly without water and with very few possibilities to use toilet. Because of the extreme heat in the gymnasium most children took off all their clothes, except underwear. The causes of the spontaneous attack on the building on the third day are still unclear. On the one hand, the experience of past terrorist acts suggests that the authorities do not see any other way of handling such crises except attack. On the other hand, the mess during the operation and its taking place in the day time might bear out the truthfulness of the official version about the spontaneous character of the attack. According to this version, the attack began after an explosion inside the gym that blew a hole in the wall and prompted children to run away, with the terrorists immediately

opening fire at their backs. Some analysts claim that the explosion might have been made by the military themselves in order to put responsibility for the start of the attack on the terrorists, and in order to give at least some hostages a chance to run away. During the operation, more than 300 people perished, most of them children.

Bibliography

"Chechenskiye khroniki 1998": "Чеченские хроники 1998" (1998), available at: www.vif2.ru/static/645/78129.html (accessed 7 November 2004).

"Chechenskiye khroniki 1998/1999": "Чеченские хроники 1998/1999" (1999), available at: www.vif2.ru/static/645/78139.html (accessed 7 November 2004).

"Gde nachinayetsya monopoliya?": "Где начинается монополия?" (1999), материалы круглого стола Центра «Право и СМИ», *Среда*, 2. Available at: www.internews.ru/ sreda/8/25.html (accessed 1 November 2004).

"Osnovnyye piar-kampanii v tsentralnykh rossiiskikh SMI za aprel.": "Основные пиар-кампании в центральных российских СМИ за апрель. Подготовлено группой ПР и ПК *Lobbynet*", *Стрингер* 13.06.2001. Available at: www.stringer-news.ru/Publication.mhtml?PubID=905&Menu=&Part=0 (accessed 5 October 2004).

"Separatizm, islam, neft": "Сепаратизм, ислам, нефть", 25.01.2000. Available at: www.vif2.ru/static/645/78127.html (accessed 7 November 2004) .

Abubakarov, T. (1998): Абубакаров, Т.(1998) *Режим Джохара Дудаева. Правда и вымысел.* Москва: б.и. Available at: www.vif2.ru/static/645/78099.html (accessed 7 November 2004).

Agafonov, A. (2000): Агафонов, А. (2000) "Победил телевизор", *Среда*, 2. Available at: www.internews.ru/sreda/19/32.html (accessed 1 December 2004).

Altheide, D. L. and Snow, R. P. (1979) *Media logic*, Beverly Hills, CA: London: Sage.

Androunas, E. (1993) *Soviet Media in Transition. Structural and Economic Alternatives*, Westport, Connecticut, London: Praeger.

Ang, I. (1994) "The realm of uncertainty: the global village and capitalist postmodernity", in D. Crowley and D. Mitchell (eds) *Communication Theory Today*, Cambridge: Polity Press: 193–213.

Avdeev, V. and Simonov, A. (1997): Авдеев, В., Симонов, А. (ред.) (1997) *Журналист в поисках информации*, Москва: Права человека.

Avdeev, V., Simonova, M. and Simonov, A. (1998): Авдеев, В., Симонова, М., Симонов, А. (ред) (1998) *Ежегодник Фонда защиты гласности (отчет за 1997 год)*, Москва: Права человека.

Baroody, J. R. (1998) *Media Access and the Military: The Case of the Gulf War*, Lanham: University Press of America.

Becker, J. (2004) "Lessons from Russia: A neo-authoritarian media system", *European Journal of Communication*, Vol. 19(2): 139–63.

Belin, L. (1996) "Private media come full circle", *Transition*, 18: 62–4.

—— (1997) "Politicization and Self-Censorship in the Russian Media", paper at the national conference of the AAASS, Seattle, Washington. Available at: www.rferl.org/nca/special/rumedia4/index.html (accessed 8 October 1999).

Blinova, O. (2000): Блинова, О. (2000) *Медиа-империи России*, Москва: СПИК-
-Центр.

Bonnel, V. and Freidin, G. (1995) "Televorot. The role of television coverage in Russia's August 1991 coup", in N. Condee (ed.) *Soviet Hierogliphics: Visual Culture in Late Twentieth-Century Russia*, Bloomington and Indianapolis: Indiana University Press; London: BFI Publishing: 22–51.

Broadcasting after Communism (1995). Special issue of *Javnost – The Public*, Vol 2(3).

Bystritsky, A. (1994): Быстрицкий, А. (1994) "Сказки Венского леса", *Известия* 11.03.1994: 9.

Certeau, M. de (1984) *The Practice of Everyday Life*, Berkeley, Los Angeles, London: University of California Press.

Chigishev, Yu. (1998): Чигишев, Ю. (1998) "Достоинства красноярской прессы", *Среда*, 4–5. Available at: www.internews.ru/sreda/4-5/3.html (accessed 1 December 2004).

Collon, M. (2002): Коллон, М. (2002) Нефть, PR, война: глобальный контроль над ресурсами планеты, Москва: Крымский Мост-9Д, Форум.

Couldry, N. (2000) "Media organizations and non-media people", in J. Curran (ed.) *Media Organizations in Society*, London: Arnold: 273–87.

Curry, J. and Dassin, J. (eds) (1982) *Press Control around the World*, New York: Praeger.

Davis, H., Hammond, P. and Nizamova, L. (1998) "Changing identities and practices in post-Soviet journalism: The case of Tatarstan", *European Journal of Communication*, 3(1): 77–97.

Delyagin, M. (1999): Делягин, М. (1999) "Экономика Чеченского террора", *Коммерсант-Деньги*, 15.09.1999: 7.

Dimmick, J. and Coit, P. (1982) "Levels of analysis in mass media decision-making", *Communication Research*, 9(1): 3–32.

Dmitrieva, O. (2004): Дмитриева, О. (2004) "Хроника терактов в России"/, *СтранаRu* 06.09.2004. Available at: terror.strana.ru/stories/04/09/06/3533/ 225893.html (accessed 24 November 2004).

Dmitrova, Yu. (1999): Дмитрова, Ю. (1999) "Киселев или Доренко. Цена рейтинга-3", *Среда*, 9: Available at: www.internews.ru/sreda/15/19.html (accessed 1 December 2004).

Dolgopyatova, T. (1998): Долгопятова, Т. (рук. авт. коллектива) (1998) *Неформальный сектор в Российской экономике*, Москва: Институт стратегического анализа и развития предпринимательства.

Dorenko, S. (1998): Доренко, С. (1998) "Доренко в школе Познера. Стенограмма учебного занятия в школе телевизионного мастерства под руководством Владимира Познера", *Среда*, 2–3: 10–12.

Dorsheva, N. (2000): Доршева, Н. (2000) "Как чеченцы стали террористами"/, *Право знать: история, теория, практика*, No 1–2, январь–февраль 2000. Available at: www.ksdi.ru/right/2000_37_38(1_2)/dorocheva_37_38.html (accessed 23 November 2004).

Downing J. (1988). "Trouble in the backyard: Soviet media reporting on the Afghanistan conflict", *Journal of Communication* 38(2): 5–32.

—— (1996) *Internationalizing Media Theory. Transition, Power, Culture*, London, Thousand Oaks, New Delhi: Sage.

Dragin, I. (2002): Драгин, И. (2002) "Анализ открытых источников. Подробности 'кухни'", *Русский журнал*, 19.02.2002. Available at: www.russ.ru/ politics/20020219-dra.html (accessed 1 December 2004).

Dubin, B. (2001): Дубин, Б. (2001) "От инициативных групп к анонимным медиа: массовые коммуникации в российском общества конца ХХ века", *Pro et Contra*, Vol. 6(2): 3–32.

Dunkerley, W. (2003): Данкерли У. (2003) "Роль СМИ в экономическом развитии России", *Отечественные записки* 4(13). Перевод Г.Дашевского. Available at: www.strana-oz.ru/?numid=13&article=586#t*3t* (accessed 4 September 2004).

Dzyaloshinsky, I. (1997): Дзялошинский, И. (1997) "Нужен ли россиянам прямой доступ к информации?"/, Авдеев, В., Симонов, А. (ред) *Журналист в поисках информации*, Москва: Права человека: 6–18.

Elliot, P. (1983) "Media organizations and occupations", in J. Curran and M. Gurevitch (eds) *Mass Media and Society*, London.

Ellis, F. (1999) *From Glasnost to the Internet: Russia's New Infosphere*, New York: St. Martin's Press.

Ericson, R., Baranek, P. and Chan, J. (1989) *Negotiating Control: A Study of News Sources*, Toronto: University of Toronto Press.

Fedorov, V. (2001): Федоров, В. (2001) "Шаг влево, шаг вправо … Или пресса на войне", *Военная библиотека Федорова*, 23.02.2001. Available at: www.warlib.ru/ index.php?id=000017 (accessed 23 November 2004).

Fedotov, M. (1997): Федотов, М. (1997) "Российский маятник: от цензуры к свободе и обратно", Е. Кандыбина, А.Симонов (ред.) *Законы и практика средств массовой информации в Европе, Америке и Австралии*. Москва: Права человека: 185–223.

Firsov, V. (1969): Фирсов, Б. (1969) "Ваше мнение о телевидении", предварительный отчет об исследовании аудитории Ленинградского телевидения. Москва: Комитет по РиТВ при совете Министров СССР.

—— (1971): Фирсов, Б. (1971), *Телевидение глазами социолога*, Москва: Искусство.

Fomin, A. (2000): Фомин, А. (2000) "Рынок компромата", *Стрингер* 01.06.2000. Available at: Part 1: www.stringernews.ru/Publication.mhtml?PubID= 1183&Menu=&Part=0>; Part 2: www.stringer-news.ru/Publication.mhtml? PubID=1184&Menu=&Part=0 (accessed 14 September 2004).

Fossato, F. (1998) "Russian media empires in decline. How Russia's financial crisis hurts the media – an analysis", Radio Free Europe/Radio Liberty, 16.10.1998. Available at: www.rferl.org/specials/russia/media4/analysis.asp (accessed 5 November 2004).

—— (1999) "Russia: media face dire financial straits", Radio Free Europe/Radio Liberty, 06.01.1999. Available at: www.rferl.org/features/1999/01/F.RU. 990106133610.asp (accessed 5 Noveber 2004).

Fossato, F. and Kachkayeva, A. (1997) "Russian media empires", Radio Free Europe/Radio Liberty, 26.09.1997. Available at: www.rferl.org/specials/russia/ media/ (accessed 5 November 2004).

—— (1998) "Russian media empires IV", Radio Free Europe/Radio Liberty, 20.05.1998. Available at: www.rferl.org/specials/russia/media4/ (accessed 5 November 2004).

—— (1999) "Russian media empires V", Radio Free Europe/Radio Liberty, August 1999. Available at: www.rferl.org/specials/russia/media5/ (accessed 5 November 2004).

—— (2000) "Russian media empires VI", Radio Free Europe/Radio Liberty, September 2000. Available at: www.rferl.org/specials/russia/media6/ (accessed 5 November 2004).

Foucault, M. (1977) *Discipline and Punish: The Birth of the Prison*, trans. A. Sheridan, London: Penguin.

—— (1996): Фуко, М. (1996) *Воля к истине*, Москва Магистериум, Касталь.

—— (1999): Фуко, М. (1999) *Надзирать и наказывать: Рождение тюрьмы*, Москва: Ad Marginem.

Fox, E. (1997) *Latin American Broadcasting. From Tango to Telenovela*, Luton, UK: University of Luton Press.

Gelman, V. (2000): Гельман, В. (2000) "Трансформации и режимы. Неопределенность и ее последствия", В.Гельман, С.Рыженков, М. Бри (ред.) *Россия регионов: трансфоормация политических режимов*, Москва: Весь мир: 16–60.

Gerbner, G. (1969) "Institutional pressures on mass communicators", in P. Halmos (ed.) *The Sociology of Mass Media Communicators*, Keele: University of Keele: 205–48.

Glaser, B. G. and Strauss, A. L. (1967) *The Discovery of Grounded Theory: Strategies for Qualitative Research*, Chicago: Aldine.

Glasgow University Media Group (1976) *Bad News*, London: Routledge and Kegan Paul.

Gleizer, M. (1989): Глейзер, М. (1989) *Радио и телевидение в СССР (1917–1986)*, Москва: Искусство.

Golding, P. and Murdock, G. (1991) "Culture, communication and political economy", in J. Curran and M. Gurevitch (eds) *Mass Media and Society*, London etc.: Edward Arnold: 15–31.

Goryaeva, T. (2000): Горяева, Т. (2000) *Политический контроль советского радиовещания в 1920–1930- х годах. Документальная история*, Москва: РОССПЭН.

Gotova, N. (2000): Готова, Н. (2000) Темная лошадка, *Компания* 21.08.2000. Available at: www.ko.ru/document.asp?d_no=2015 (accessed 29 November 2004).

Grossberg, L., Wartella, E. and Whitney, D. (1998) *Mediamaking: Mass Media in a Popular Culture*, Thousand Oaks, London, New Dehli: Sage.

Grozny, D. (1998): Грозный, Д. (1998) "Местный привкус пирога", *Среда*, 6: 16–18.

Grushin, B. and Onikov, L. (1980): Грушин, Б., Оников, Л. (ред.) (1980) *Массовая информация в советском промышленном городе*, Москва: Политиздат.

Hall, S. (1977) "Culture, the media, and the ideological effect", in J. Curran *et al.* (eds) *Culture, Media, Language*, London: Edward Arnold: 315–48.

Hallin, D. (1986) *The "Uncensored War": The Media and Vietnam*, New York: Oxford University Press.

Hallin, D. and Papathanossoupulos, S. (2002) "Political clientelism and the media: Southern Europe and Latin America in comparative perspective", *Media, Culture, and Society*, 24(2): 175–95.

Herman, E. and Chomsky, N. (1988) *Manufacturing Consent: The Political Economy of the Mass Media*, New York, Toronto: Random House.

Hopkins, M. (1970) *Mass Media in the Soviet Union*, New York: Pegasus.

Jakubowicz, K. (1995) "Lovebirds? The media, the state and politics in Central and Eastern Europe", *Javnost – The Public*, 2(1): 51–69.

—— (1996) "Civil Society and public service broadcasting in Central and Eastern Europe", *Javnost – The Public,* 3(2): 51–69.

Kachkayeva, A. (2001): Качкаева, А. (2001) "Десять лет пост-советских СМИ", доклад на ежегодной конференции факультета журналистики МГУ, 22.01.2001.

Kandybina, Ye. and Simonov, A. (1999) Кандыбина, Е., Симонов, А. (ред.) (1999) *Законы и практика средств массовой информации в странах СНГ и Балтии. Фонд Защиты Гласности,* Москва: Галерия.

Karl, T. L. and Schmitter, P. (1991) "Models of transition in Latin America, Southern and Eastern Europe", *International Social Science Journal*, 43(128): 269–84.

Khatuyev, A. (1998): Хатуев, А. (1998) "Чечня: цензура рынка и шариата", *Независимая газета* 3.11.1998. Available at: clcr.h10.ru/russian/arhiv/chechnja/cenzura_rynka.htm (accessed 18 November 2004).

Khokhlov, A. (1998): Хохлов, А. (1998) "Криминальная журналистика", лекция на летней школе факультета журналистики СПбГУ 05.07.1998.

Kogan-Yasny, V. (1999): Коган-Ясный, В.В. (1999) "Политический аспект отношений Федеральных органов власти Российской Федерации с Чеченской республикой в 1990–1994 годах", переработанная статья из книги: Коган-Ясный В.В. *Чеченские перекрестья: Статьи, очерки, документы*, Москва, 1995. Available at: www.vif2.ru/static/640/77711.html (accessed 7 November 2004).

Koltsova, O. (1999): Кольцова, О. (1999) "Производство новостей: скрытые механизмы контроля", *Журнал социологии и социальной антропологии*, 3: 87–104. Available at: www.soc.pu.ru:8101/publications/jssa/1999/3/5kolz.html (accessed 16 September 2004).

—— (2000a) "Change in the coverage of the Chechen wars: reasons and consequences", *Javnost – The Public*, 7(4): 39–54.

—— (2000b): Кольцова, О. (2000) "Разорванная коммуникация: прагматическая концепция языка и профессиональные практики журналистов", Ю. Качанов, А. Бикбов (ред.) *Пространство и время в современной социологической теории*, Москва: Институт социологии РАН: 79–102.

—— (2001a) "News production in contemporary Russia: practices of power", *European Journal of Communication,* 16(3): 315–35.

—— (2001b): Кольцова, О. (2001) "Кто и как влияет на производство новостей в современной России", *Pro et Contra*, T. 6(2): 80–106 . Available at: www.carnegie.ru/ru/pubs/procontra/55944.htm (accessed 1 November 2004).

—— (2001c): Кольцова, О. (2001) "Производство новостей: типы влияний на работу журналистов", В.Воронков, О.Паченков, Е.Чикадзе (ред.) *Невидимые грани журналистов*, Труды ЦНСИ, вып. 9: Санкт-Петербург: 109–23. Available at: www.indepsocres.spb.ru/sbornik9/9_kolts.htm (accessed 1 November 2004).

Koneva, Ye. (1998): Конева, Е. (1998) "Цена рейтинга", *Среда*, 4–5: 17–23.

Konstantinov, A. (1998): Константинов, А. (1998) "Политическое расследование в Российских СМИ", лекция на летней школе факультета журналистики СПбГУ, 01.07.1998.

Kornilov, S. and Rzhevsky, M. (2003): Корнилов, С., Ржевский, М. (2003) "Почем глас народа?", *Вслух о …* 02.09.2003. Available at: www.vslux.ru/article.phtml?id=1570 (accessed 5 October 2004).

Kostikov, V. (1997): Костиков, В. (1997) *Роман с президентом*, Москва: Вагриус.

Kuper, A. and Kuper, J. (1999) *The Social Science Encyclopedia*, London and New York: Routledge.

Lange, Y. (1997) *Media in the CIS. A Study of the Political, Legislative and Socio-economic Framework. The European Institute of Media.* Brussels: European Commission.

Lemberg, K. (2000): Лемберг, К. (2000) Пресса и криминал в Екатеринбурге, *Среда*, 3. Available at: www.internews.ru/sreda/20/23.html (accessed 1 December 2004).

Lenin, V. (1979): Ленин, В. (1979) "С чего начать?", *Полное собрание сочинений*. 5-е изд. Т. 5. Москва: Издательство политической литературы.

—— (1975): Ленин, В. (1975) "Партийная организация и партийная литература", *Сборник произведений В.И.Ленина для учащихся средних школ и средних учебных заведений*. 3-е изд. Москва: Издательство политической литературы.

Liberman, S. (1999a): Либерман, С. (1999) "Вторая Чеченская", *Среда*, 10: 9–14.

—— (1999b): Либерман, С. (1999) "Вторая Чеченская. Акт следующий", *Среда*, 11: 13–16.

Lilin, V. (1998): Лилин, В. (1998) "Первая информационная", *Среда*, 2–3: 49–53.

Makarov, R. (1998): Макаров, Р. (1998) "Как заставили замолчать радио 'Титан'", А. Симонов (ред.) *Зоны бесконфликтности (Положение СМИ и свобода слова в некоторых "благополучных" субъектах Российской Федерации)*. Москва: Права человека: 49– 55.

Malkin, Ye. and Suchkov, Ye. (2000): Малкин Е., Сучков Е. (2000) *Основы избирательных технологий*, Москва: Русская панорама.

Manaev, O. (1995) "Rethinking the social role of the media in a society in transition", *Canadian Journal of Communication*, 20: 45–65.

Mancini, P. (1993) "Between trust and suspicion: how political journalists solve the dilemma", *European Journal of Communication*, 8: 33–51.

Manheim, J. B. (1998) "The news shapers: strategic communication as third force in newsmaking", in D. Graber, D. McQuail, and P. Norris (eds), *The Politics of News: the News of Politics*, Washington, DC: Congressional Quarterly Press: 94–109.

Markelova, Ye. (1999): Маркелова, Е. (1999) "Областной молот и городская наковальня", *Среда*, 1. Available at: www.internews.ru/sreda/7/22.html (accessed 1 December 2004).

Martín-Barbero, J. (1993) *Communication, Culture and Hegemony: From Media to Mediations*, London, Newbury Park, New Delhi: Sage.

McNair, B. (1996) "Television in post-Soviet Russia: from monolith to mafia", *Media, Culture and Society,* Vol. 18: 489–99.

—— (2000) "Power, profit, corruption, and lies: The Russian media in the 1990s", in J. Curran and M.-J. Park (eds) *De-Westernizing Media Studies*, London and New York: Routledge: 79-94.

McNulty, M. (1999) "Media ethnicization and the international response to war and genocide in Rwanda", in T. Allen and J. Seaton (eds) *The Media of Conflict: War Reporting and Representation of Ethnic Violence*, New York: Zed Books.

Mickiewicz, E. (1988) *Split Signals: Television and Politics in the Soviet Union*, New York, Oxford: Oxford University Press.

—— (1997) *Changing Channels: Television and the Struggle for Power in Russia*, New York, Oxford: Oxford University Press.

Molotch, H. L. and Lester M. J. (1974) "News as purposive behavior", *American Sociological Review*, 39: 101–12.

Mozolin, A. (2003): Мозолин, А. (2003) "Обзор медиарынка Екатеринбурга", неопубликованная рукопись, Екатеринбург.

Mukhin, A. (2000): Мухин, А. (2000) *Информационная война в России*, Москва: Гном и Д.

Munck, G. and Leff, C. (1997) "Modes of transition and democratization. South America and Eastern Europe in comparative perspective", *Comparative Politics*. Vol. 29(3): 343–62.

Murray, J. (1994) *The Russian Press from Brezhnev to Yeltsin: Behind the Paper Curtain*, Vermont: Edward Edgar.

Myalo, K. (2002): Мяло, К. (2002) *Россия и последние войны XX века (1989–2000). К истории падения сверхдержавы*, Москва: Вече.

Nechitaylo, A. (1999): Нечитайло, А. (1999) "Кто будет начальником Кузбасса?", *Новая газета* 25.10.1999: 3.

Nivat, A. (1998) "His Master's voice. Russian journalists feel the grip of the media moguls", *Transitions*, June 1998: 42–7.

—— (2000) *Chienne de guerre*, Paris: Fayard.

Ovsepian, R. (1999): Овсепян, Р. (1999) *История новейшей отечественной журналистики (1917–1990-е годы)*, Москва: Издательство Московского Университета.

Paletz, D. (ed.) (1987) *Political Communication Research: Approaches, Studies, Assessments*, Norwood: Alex Publishing Corp.

Panfilov, O. (compiler), Simonov, A. (ed.) (1995): Панфилов, О. (сост.), Симонов, А. (ред.) (1995) *Журналисты на Чеченской войне. Факты, документы, свидетельства. Ноябрь 1994 – декабрь 1995*, Москва: Права человека.

—— (1997): Панфилов, О. (сост.), Симонов, А. (ред.) (1997) *Пресса на территории России: конфликты и правонарушения* 1996, Москва: Права человека.

—— (1999): Панфилов, О. (сост.), Симонов, А. (ред.) (1999) *Информационная война в Чечне: факты, документы, свидетельства, ноябрь 1994 – сентябрь 1996*. Available at: www.internews.ru/books/infowar (accessed 1 November 2004).

Panfilov, O. (2004): Панфилов, О. (2004) *История Андрея Бабицкого*, Москва: Права человека, 2004.

Pankin, A. (1999): Панкин, А. (1999) "Пресса: проблемы выживания и ангажированности", М.Дзялошинская, И.Крестникова (ред.) Роль прессы в формировании гражданского общества в России. Москва: Институт гуманитарных коммуникаций:163–170.

Pekurny, R. (1982) "Coping with television production", in J. S. Ettema and D. C. Whitney (eds) *Individuals in Mass Media Organizations*, Beverly Hills: Sage: 131–43.

Petrov, N. and Tyukov, N. (1998): Петров, Н., Титков, А., Глубоцкий, А. (1998) "Вологодская область", М.Макфол, Н.Петров (ред.) *Политический альманах России 1997. Том 2. Социально-политические портреты регионов*, Москва: Московский Центр Карнеги. Available at: www.carnegie.ru/ru/pubs/books/volume/218810kalmyk.pdf (accessed July 15, 2004).

Petrov, N. and Zapekly, (1998): Петров, Н., Титков, А., Запеклый, А. (1998) Петров, Н., Титков, А., Запеклый, А. (1998) "Таймырский (Долгано-Ненецкий) автономный округ", М. Макфол, Н. Петров (ред.) *Политический альманах*

России 1997. Том 2. Социально-политические портреты регионов, Москва: Московский Центр Карнеги. Available at: www.carnegie.ru/ru/pubs/books/volume/220526krasyar.pdf (accessed July 15, 2004).

Petrov, N., Titkov, A. and Glubotsky, A. (1998): Петров, Н., Тюков, Н. (1998) "Республика Калмыкия", М. Макфол, Н. Петров (ред.) *Политический альманах Политический альманах России 1997. Том 2. Социально-политические портреты регионов*, Москва: Московский Цснтр Карнеги. Available at: www.carnegie.ru/ru/pubs/books/volume/221637vologda.pdf (accessed July 15, 2004).

Petrov, N., Titkov, A. and Mukhin, A. (1998): Петров, Н., Титков., А., Мухин, А. (1998) "Свердловская область", М. Макфол, Н. Петров (ред.) *Политический альманах России 1997. Том 2. Социально-политические портреты регионов*, Москва: Московский Центр Карнеги. Available at: www.carnegie.ru/ru/pubs/books volume/224768sverdlov.pdf (accessed July 15, 2004).

Petrov, N., Titkov, A. and Zapekly, A. (1998): Петров, Н., Запеклый, А. (1998) "Красноярский край", М. Макфол, Н. Петров (ред.) *Политический альманах России 1997. Том 2. Социально-политические портреты регионов*, Москва: Московский Центр Карнеги. Available at: www.carnegie.ru/ru/pubs/books/volume/226384taimyr.pdf (accessed July 15, 2004).

Petrovskaya, I. (1998): Петровская, И. (1998) " 'Время' БАБ", *Известия*, 21.11.1998: 4.

Philp, M. (1996) "Power", in A. Kuper and J. Kuper (eds) *Social Science Encyclopedia*, London and New York: Routledge: 657–61.

Pironkova, O. (2000): Пиронкова, О. (2000) " 'Живые новости', или о времени и пространстве в телевизионном эфире", *Социологические исследования*, No 8: 65–74.

Politkovskaya, A. (2004): Политковская, А. (2004 *Анна Политковская о войне в Чечне. Архив статей 1999– 2004*. Available at: www.hro.org/war/anna/ (accessed 23 November 2004).

Punanov, G. and Loginov, A. (2000): Пунанов, Г., Логинов, А. (2000) "Главный редактор попался на взятке. Репортеры 'Известий' проводят свое расследование", *Известия* 15.02.2000: 6.

Rantanen, T. (2002) *The Global and the National: Media and Communications in Post-Communist Russia*, Lanham, Boulder, New York, Oxford: Rowman & Littlefield Publishers.

Rantanen, T. and Vartanova, E. (1995) "News Agencies in Post-Communist Russia: From Monopoly to State Dominance", *European Journal of Communication*, 10(2): 207–20.

Rapoport, A. (1999): Рапопорт, А. (1999) "Страсти по Якову Лондону", *Среда*, 6–7. Available at: www.internews.ru/sreda/12-13/6.html (accessed 1 December 2004).

—— (2000): Рапопорт, А. (2000) "Страсти по Якову Лондону 2", *Среда*, 8–9. Available at: www.internews.ru/sreda/24/15.html (accessed 1 December 2004).

Richmond, S. (1997) "'The eye of the state': An interview with Soviet chief Censor Vladimir Solodin", *The Russian Review* 56: 581–90.

Rikhter, A. (1998): Рихтер, А. (ред.) (1998) *Журналистика и война. Освещение российскими СМИ военных действий в Чечне*, Москва: Центр права и средств массовой информации.

Roxburgh, A. (1987) *Pravda: Inside the Soviet News Machine*, London: Victor Gollanez.

Rykovtseva, Ye. (1998): Рыковцева, Е. (1998) "Яма: Почему ВГТРК бессмысленно проверять", *Среда*, 2–3: 13–17.

Schlesinger, P. (1987) *Putting "Reality" Together: BBC News*, London: Routledge, 2nd edition.

Schudson, M. (1991) "The sociology of news production revisited", in J. Curran and M. Gurevitch (eds) *Mass Media and Society*, London, New York, Melbourne, Auckland: Edward Arnold.

Shmarov, A. and Polunin, Yu. (2000): Шмаров, А., Полунин, Ю. (2000) "Все влиятельные люди России", *Эксперт*, 38: 50–68.

Shoemaker, P. and Reese, S. (1996) *Mediating the Message: Theories of Influences on Mass Media Content*, New York: Longman, 2nd edition.

Siebert, F., Schramm, W. and Peterson, T. (1998): Сиберт, Ф., Шрамм, У., Петерсон, Т. (1998) *Четыре теории прессы*, Москва: Вагриус.

Simonov, A. (1998): Симонов, А. (ред.) (1998) *Зоны бесконфликтности (Положение СМИ и свобода слова в некоторых 'благополучных' субъектах Российской Федерации*, Москва: Права человека.

—— (1999): Симонов, А. (ред.) (1999) *Ежегодник Фонда Защиты Гласности. Итоги 1998 года*, Москва: Галерия.

—— (2001): Симонов, А. (ред.) (2001) *Гласность-2000: Доклад, комментарии, очерки.* Москва: Галерия.

Simonov, A. and Gorbanevsky, M. (2000): Симонов, А., Горбаневский, М. (ред.) (2000) *Ежегодник Фонда Защиты Гласности. Итоги 1999 года*, Москва: Галерия.

Smaele, H. de (1999) "The applicability of western media models on the Russian media system", *European Journal of Communication*, 14(2): 173–89.

Sosnovskaya, A. (2000): Сосновская, А. (2000) *Трансформация журналистских практик и самоидентификация журналистов (сравнительный анализ на материале России и Швеции)*, диссертация на соискание степени кандидата филологических наук, Санкт-Петербург: Санкт-Петербургский государственный университет.

Sparks, C. (1995) "Introduction: The emerging media systems of post-communism", *Javnost – The Public*, 2(3): 7–17.

Sparks, C., with Anna Reading (1998) *Communism, Capitalism and the Mass Media*, London, Thousand Oaks, New Dehli: Sage.

Splichal, S. (1994) *Media Beyond Socialism: Theory and Practice in East-Central Europe*, Boulder, San Francisco, Oxford: Westview Press.

Suyetnov, A. (1992): Суетнов, А. (1992) *Каталог нетрадиционных изданий* (1985–1991) 2-е изд., дополненное, Москва: Центр образовательных программ института новых технологий образования.

Svarovsky, F. (2002): Сваровский, Ф. (2002) "Информационные войны, или Как специалисты по PR покупают СМИ", *Ведомости* 28.01.2002. Available at: www.vedomosti.ru/newspaper/article.shtml?2002/01/28/40373 (accessed 5 October 2004).

The Media after Communism (1994) Special issue of *Media, Culture and Society*, Vol. 16(2). Ed. by C. Sparks.

Titkov, A. and Zapekly, A. (1998): Титков, А., Запеклый, А. (1998) "Республика Башкортостан", М. Макфол, Н. Петров (ред.) *Политический альманах России 1997. Том 2. Социально-политические портреты регионов*, Москва: Московский

Центр Карнеги. Available at: www.carnegie.ru/ru/pubs/books/volume/ 218305bashkir.pdf (accessed July 15, 2004).

Titkov, A. and Tyukov, N. (1998): Титков, А., Тюков, Н. (1998) "Чеченская республика Ичкерия", 'М. Макфол, Н. Петров (ред.) *Политический альманах России 1997. Том 2. Социально-политические портреты регионов*, Москва: Московский Центр Карнеги. Available at: www.carnegie.ru/ru/pubs/books/ volume/220021chechn.pdf (accessed July 15, 2004).

Trakhtenberg, A. (2004): Трахтенберг, А. "Екатеринбургские СМИ". E-mail (14 июля 2004).

Tuchman, G. (1978) *Making News: A Study in the Construction of Reality*, New York: Free Press.

Tunstall, J. and Palmer, M. (1991) *Media Moguls*, London: Routledge.

Turow, J. (1992) *Media Systems in Society*, New York and London: Longman.

Urban, M. (1993) "The Russian free press in transition to a post-communist society", *The Journal of Communist Studies*, 9(2): 20–40.

Varshavchik, S. (1998): Варшавчик, С. (1998) "Высокий профессионал с государственным лицом", *Общая газета* 17–23.12.1998: 13.

—— (2000a): Варшавчик, С. (2000) "Государственное регулирование по-русски", 11.05.2000. Available at: www.deadline.ru/varsh/000511.asp. (accessed 5 November 2004).

—— (2000b): Варшавчик, С. (2000) "Добродеев пошел в авгиевы конюшни ВГТРК", 01.02.2000. Available at: www/deadline.ru/varsh/var000201.asp. (accessed 5 November 2004).

—— (2000c): Варшавчик, С. (2000) "Рэкетир Лесин и пакт Кох–Гусинский", 22.09.2000. Available at: www.deadline.ru/articles/clumns/varshav/default. asp?22092000. (accessed 5 November 2004).

—— (2001): Варшавчик, С. (2001) Архив статей за 1999–2001 годы. Available at: www.deadline.ru/default.asp?wci=Author&a_no=18 (accessed 5 November 2004).

Volkov, V. (1998) "Limits to propaganda: Soviet power and the peasant reader in the 1920s", in J. Raven (ed.). *Non-Commercial Publishing in Comparative Perspective*, Massachusets: University of Massachusets Press.

—— (1999) "Violent entrepreneurship in post-communist Russia", *Europe-Asian Studies,* Vol. 51(5): 741–54.

—— (2002) *Violent Entrepreneurs: The Use of Force in the Making of Russian Capitalism*, Ithaca: Cornell University Press.

Weber, M. (1968) *Economy and Society: An Outline of Interpretative Sociology*. Vol. 1. New York: Bedminster Press.

Weber, M. (1990): Вебер, М. (1990) "Политика как призвание и профессия", М. Вебер. *Избранные произведения*, Москва: Прогресс.

Winseck, D. (1992) "Gulf war in the global village: *CNN*, democracy and the information age", in J. Wasco and V. Mosco (eds) *Democratic Communications in the Information Age*, Toronto: Garamond Press; Norwood, N.J.: Ablex.

Wolfe, T. (1997) "Imagining journalism: politics, government and the person in the press in the Soviet Union and Russia, 1953-1993", PhD thesis, Detroit: University of Michigan.

Yakovenko, I. (2000): Яковенко, И. (ред.) (2000) *Общественная экспертиза: анатомия свободы слова*, Москва: б.и.

—— (2001): Яковенко, И. (2001) Доклад на научно-практической конференции

"Журналистика в 2000 году: реалии и прогнозы развития", Москва: факультет журналистики МГУ.

Yefremova, V. and Ratinov, A. (2000): Ефремова, В., Ратинов, А. (2000) "Результаты мониторинга нарушений, связанных с деятельностью средств массовой информации в Российской Федерации за 1999 год", аналитический доклад ФЗГ (сокращенный вариант). Available at: www.gdf.ru/old/monitoring/index.html (accessed 7 November 2004).

Yevgenieva, O. (1999): Евгеньева, О. (1999) "Нефтяной лоббизм и информагентства", *Среда*, 11: 31–4.

Yuskevits, S. (2000) "The role of the journalist in transition", Paper at VI ICCEES Congress, Tampere.

Zadorin, I. (2000): Задорин, И. (ред.) (2000) *СМИ и политика в России: Социологический анализ роли СМИ в избирательных кампаниях*, Москва: Socio-Logos.

Zakharov, A. and Krivosheyev, A. (2001): Захаров, А., Кривошеев, А. (2001) "Секретные материалы общего пользования", *Итоги* 25.06.2001: 12. Available at: www.itogi.ru/paper2001.nsf/Article/Itogi_2001_06_25_12_3217.html (accessed September 14 2004)

Zassoursky, I. (1999): Засурский, И. (1999) Масс медиа второй республики. Москва: Издательство Московского университета.

—— (2000) "Politics and media in Russia in the nineties", Paper at the VI ICCEES Congress, Tampere.

Zassoursky, Y. (1999) "Open society and access to information: to what degree Russian media contribute to the openness of society", in Y. Zassoursky and E. Vartanova (eds) *Media, Communications and the Open Society*, Moscow: Faculty of journalism/IKAR: 30–1.

Zassoursky, Y., Kolesnik, S. and Svitich., L. (1997): Засурский., Я, Колесник, С., Свитич, Л., Ширяева, А. (1997) "Журналисты о правах и свободах личности и СМИ (российско-американское исследование)", *Вестник Московского университета* Vol. 10(3): 20–36, (5): 14–43.

Zassoursky, Y. and Vartanova, E. (eds) (1998) *Changing Media and Communications*, Moscow: Faculty of Journalism/IKAR.

—— (eds) (1999) *Media, Communications and the Open Society*, Moscow: Faculty of Journalism/IKAR.

Zhao, Y. (2000) "From commercialization to conglomeration: The transformation of the Chinese press within the orbit of the party state", *Journal of Communication*, 50(2): 3–26.

Zinchuk, Yu. (1998): Зинчук, Ю. (1998) "Журналисты в горячих точках", лекция на летней школе факультета журналистики СПбГУ 07.07.1998.

Documents and other sources

Normative acts

Law of the Union of Soviet Socialist Republics "On press and other mass media": Закон Союза Советских Социалистических Республик "О печати и других средствах массовой информации", 12.06.1990.

Law of the Russian Federation "On mass media": Закон Российской Федерации "О средствах массовой информации", 27.12.1991.

Law of the Russian Federation "On state secrets": Закон Российской Федерации "О государственной тайне", 21.07.1993.

Law of the Russian Federation "On advertising": Закон Российской Федерации "О рекламе", 18.07.1995.

Decree of the President of the Russian Federation No 2255 "On improving state regulation in the sphere of mass communication": Указ Президента Российской Федерации No. 2255 "О совершенствовании государственного управления в сфере массовой информации", 22.12.1993.

Edict of the government of the Russian Federation No 1359 "On licensing of broadcasting of TV and radio communications ..." and "Regulation on licensing of broadcasting ...": Постановление правительства Российской Федерации No. 1359 "О лицензировании телевизионного вещания, радиовещания и деятельности по связи в области телевизионного и радиовещания в Российской Федерации", 07.12.1994, и "Положение о лицензировании телевизионного вещания и радиовещания в Российской Федерации", утвержденное указанным постановлением правительства.

Regulation "On Federal tender committee on broadcasting": Положение "О Федеральной конкурсной комиссии по телерадиовещанию", приложение 1 к приказу Министерства Российской Федерации по делам печати, телерадиовещания и средств массовых коммуникаций No. 9, 28.09.1999.

"Rules of accreditation of mass media representatives at the department of the assistant of the President of the Russian Federation S. V. Yasterjembsky" and "Order of organization of visits by and work with journalists accredited at the department of the assistant of the President of the Russian Federation S. V. Yasterjembsky, in the Chechen republic", January 2000: "Правила аккредитации представителей средств массовой информации при аппарате помощника Президента Российской Федерации С.В.Ястржембского" и "Порядок организации посещения и работы с журналистами, аккредитованными при Аппарате помощника Президента Российской Федерации С.В. Ястржембского, Чеченкой республики", январь 2000.

Other official documents

Licenses of the Federal service of RF on broadcasting for St. Petersburg and its region, studied in November 1998.

Catalogue of broadcasting TV companies of St. Petersburg registered by the North-West regional board of the State committee on press. November 1998.

Scenarios of news stories of St. Petersburg affiliate of one national TV company covering July 1998–January 1999.

Attachment 6 to agreement about transfer and purchase of shares between *Gazprom-Media* Ltd and Gussinsky, V. A. 20.07.2000.

Field notes

Field notes 1: observation at newspaper editorial office, January–June 1997, 40,000 words.

Field notes 2: observation in TV newsrooms, November 1998–December 1999, 30,000 words.

Collection of newspaper articles on the story of *Peterburg–5 Kanal*, 38 articles, 1994–9.

Collection of pieces on the *Media-MOST* case from the Internet: thirty-two journalistic articles and interviews and eighty news agency reports.

Index